From Words to Worlds

THE JOHNS HOPKINS SERIES IN
CONSTITUTIONAL THOUGHT

Sanford Levinson and Jeffrey K. Tulis,

Series Editors

From Words to Worlds

EXPLORING CONSTITUTIONAL FUNCTIONALITY

Beau Breslin

The Johns Hopkins University Press

Baltimore

2 4 6 8 9 7 5 3 1

The Johns Hopkins University Press
2715 North Charles Street
Baltimore, Maryland 21218-4363
www.press.jhu.edu

Library of Congress Cataloging-in-Publication Data

Breslin, Beau, 1966–
From words to worlds : exploring constitutional functionality / Beau Breslin.
    p. cm. — (The Johns Hopkins series in constitutional thought)
Includes bibliographical references and index.
ISBN-13: 978-0-8018-9051-2 (hardcover : alk. paper)
ISBN-10: 0-8018-9051-9 (hardcover : alk. paper)
1. Constitutional law—Philosophy. 2. Political science. I. Title.
K3165.B743 2008
342.001—dc22   2008010641

A catalog record for this book is available from the British Library.

Special discounts are available for bulk purchases of this book. For more information,
please contact Special Sales at 410-516-6936 or specialsales@press.jhu.edu.

The Johns Hopkins University Press uses environmentally friendly book materials,
including recycled text paper that is composed of at least 30 percent post-consumer waste,
whenever possible. All of our book papers are acid-free, and our jackets and covers are
printed on paper with recycled content.

To my mother and father

Every word [of the Constitution] decides a question between liberty and power.

—JAMES MADISON, 1792

CONTENTS

One of the notable highlights of the walking tour of Montpelier, James Madison's stately home nestled in the foothills of Virginia's Blue Ridge Mountains, occurs when one enters a small room on the second floor. It is here, we are told, that the principal architect of the American Constitution prepared for the Philadelphia Convention. Surrounded by books, newspapers, letters of correspondence, pamphlets, and other writings, Madison imagined a vision for government in that room, a vision of political order that would eventually form the core of the "Virginia Plan" and later, the United States Constitution. The story goes that the diminutive Virginia statesman sat, mostly alone, and pored over treatises of political theory, works of history, and descriptions of early democratic government. He put quill to parchment in that room and sketched out a plan. If you believe in the ubiquitous influence of the American Constitution, that room occupies an important place in the history and development of the modern world.

The image of Madison conceiving of a plan for order is stirring. He believed the process of bringing a world to life out of the power of words required a solitary period, followed by a collective dialogue in which his ideas would be tested. Much of the work that went into the final draft was undertaken alone; yet all the exploration, contemplation, and energy that characterize those months and years of intense reflection would have been fruitless without the help of Madison's many colleagues and critics. Letters from friends sustained him; conversations before and during the Philadelphia convention influenced him; and eventually the draft of the Constitution that was signed on September 17, 1787, which can be traced directly back to Madison's original vision, represented a collective expression of open dialogue and intense debate.

Even though the stakes are decidedly lower (are there any?) and the product is far less majestic, the process of writing this book mirrors Madison's approach to constitutional construction. The crafting of this book was, most of the time, a solitary exercise. And yet the pages that follow are the product of wonderfully stimulating collective conversations about the nature of constitutions and constitutional thought. The wisdom of several participants in that conversation—of George Thomas, Justin Crowe, Douglas Edlin, Ken I. Kersch, Wayne Moore, Gary Jacobsohn, Will Harris, and Austin Sarat—is, I hope, reflected in the pages that follow. Correspondence and dialogue with them has helped in so many ways to sharpen my arguments and energize my curiosity. A special thanks goes also to two of the most prominent members of that ongoing exchange: Sanford Levinson and Jeffrey Tulis, the editors of the Johns Hopkins Series in Constitutional Thought. In addition, I have benefited from the collective conversations and infinite generosity of many colleagues at Skidmore College. Thanks is extended in particular to Ron Seyb, Kate Graney, Steve Hoffmann, Bob Turner, Aldo Vacs, Natalie Taylor, Flagg Taylor, Roy Ginsberg, Dan Nathan, Chris McGill, Allie Taylor, Barbara McDonough, David Karp, Grace Burton, John Howley, Paula Newberg, and Muriel Poston. They too have helped me take my original ideas and transform them into reasonable arguments. Finally, Henry Tom, executive editor at the Johns Hopkins University Press, deserves my gratitude. As always, he was a model of professionalism and grace throughout the entire process.

My most important muse is my family. My parents, Jud and Wendy, and my in-laws, Jim and Mary Starke, represent the very best of a generation that acutely understood the importance of constitutions. My siblings and their spouses—Ned, Lindsey, Dave, Kristen, Matt, Jamie, Larry, Tina, and Jimmy—also deserve my profound gratitude. But in many ways this book was written with the next generation in mind. My daughter, Molly, and her cousins, Jane, Ben, Kimberley, Jemma, and Lucas, must now carry on the constitutional dialogue. It is a tall but essential task. Lastly, everything is insignificant in my life—and that certainly includes the contemplation of constitutional ideals and collective dialogues about political order—compared to my love for my wife, Martha. Even when I am alone in thought, because of her my life is never solitary.

From Words to Worlds

Introduction

❈ ❈ ❈

Constitutions matter. That simple statement—that constitutions *really* matter—hardly seems surprising until one honestly reflects on the state of constitutionalism around the world. To put it mildly, constitutional regimes are at different stages of development and are having differing degrees of success with their fundamental law. Some, like Canada and Iraq, are governed by basic texts that were drafted or influenced by imperialist forces. Others, like the countries of Eastern Europe, have engineered constitutional charters that not only reflect a heritage largely unfamiliar to those in the West but also attempt to combine what may be incompatible political and economic impulses. Still others, such as Israel, have chosen to forego the modern practice of relying on a *written* constitution and have instead opted for the interpretive flexibility that accompanies an *un*written text.[1] Finally, countries, such as South Africa, which have insisted that their modern constitutional documents would be the panacea for a longstanding history of ethnic or regional conflict, are now realizing that it takes more than a constitutional charter to bind a citizenry.

Even in the United States, the polity that arguably redefined the entire concept of constitutionalism more than two centuries ago, the position of the constitutional text in public life is at best curious. Recent surveys indicate that the public's perception of the Constitution is that it remains an important document; but those same surveys also reveal a disturbing ignorance as to the specifics of the text itself.[2] Americans think the Constitution is important, but they can't tell us what it says. To add to its puzzling place in the public eye, consider also its comparative position alongside the Declaration of Independence as one of America's two cornerstone public documents. The lofty principles espoused in the Declaration seem to reverberate more easily with the American temperament, while the complex and sometimes dry language of the Constitution seem somehow less memorable. It is revealing that citizens of the United States are eager to celebrate the moment in which the colonies declared their independence from England—July 4—but few are eager to celebrate September 17—the day the newly drafted constitution was presented to the public for ratification—as the anniversary of the birth of a new nation.[3] Almost everywhere we look, it seems, constitutions have become surprisingly marginalized.

Added to this implicit marginalization of the constitutional text is the argument, shared by practitioners and laymen alike, that constitutions cannot be all that important if they are so often circumscribed by political leaders at times of crisis. The suggestion seems to be that, when push comes to shove, a constitution—mere words on a page—is no real barrier to the authority of self-interested and desperate officials or that the survival instincts of individuals in power will always prevail over even the most authoritative constitutional provisions. Examples abound, from the isolated instances when political leaders ignore specific clauses of the text to the tyrants in Third World countries who see the constitutional document as an unnecessary obstacle in their quest for power.[4]

Finally, a good many scholars have added to the debate surrounding the importance of the constitutional text by examining constitutional politics from a variety of perspectives. Yet aside from the emergence of exciting new studies in comparative constitutionalism—studies, it is important to note, that often recognize the primacy of the constitutional document—and a fresh spate of volumes that describe how constitutions help to design good democratic polities,[5] surprisingly few in recent years have explicitly acknowledged the importance *of the text itself*. Even some of the most respected constitutional scholars have fallen prey to the notion that constitutional texts enjoy only secondary importance. Many contemporary public law scholars either ignore the proposition that the documents themselves matter or, what is even more likely, inadvertently disavow it. Take the current political science and legal literature for example. Despite a slight resurgence of interest in the subject, for almost five decades now the academy has insisted that constitutional engineering, as well as the study of constitutions more generally, can be a fruitless endeavor. The idea that constitutions can regulate human behavior is, in the words of one constitutional theorist, "preposterous."[6] One of the foremost legal scholars of the last half-century—Joseph Raz—is even less sanguine about the enterprise: "A powerful case can be made to the effect that a substantive theory of constitutions and of constitutionalism has limited application. Its application is to some countries and to some constitutions only."[7]

Even when scholars hover close to the topic of constitutional theory, they often miss the forest for the trees; indeed, there is an imbalance in the constitutional literature in favor of discussions about all things judicial—judicial power, judicial interpretation, judicial independence, and so on. When not interested in the behavior of judicial bodies or the attitudes of judicial actors, entists in particular have focused their energies primarily on the of constitutional interpretation and judicial review.[8] They inevita courts as the center of constitutional inquiry.[9] Occasionally—and, I might add, with increasing frequency—distinguished scholars will broaden the scope of inquiry by considering the impact of other institutions, particularly the executive and legislative branches, on the interpretive project.[10] Scholars of American political development and "New Historical Institutionalism," for example, explicitly or implicitly call for a reduced role for the judiciary in the interpretation of the Constitution—an interesting proposition to be sure. And yet they too are still interested in exploring questions of constitutional *interpretation* and not specifically questions related directly to the theory underlying the *need for constitutions*. Like so many others, they apparently view the constitutional document through the prism of institutional politics.[11]

The reality for most legal and political scholars is that institutions are influenced by, and contribute to, the meaning of the constitutional text. The text derives its meaning from the branches responsible for interpreting its many clauses and principles. I certainly think that is a fair assessment of modern constitutional politics and one that should not (and cannot) be discredited. And yet such a pronouncement immediately implies the marginalization of the constitution itself. If we focus on what institutions say about the constitution as the primary (exclusive?) means to provide textual definition, we invariably neglect the principle that a constitution exists independently of the institutions it creates.[12] The constitution is out there. We can see it and touch it in most cases. It exists prior to the formation of the government and is the mechanism responsible for creating those governmental bodies that will eventually give it definition. How, then, does a constitution somehow become less relevant once institutions are charged with the duty of providing meaning to its terms?

This book aims to redirect our attention back to constitutions themselves, back to the documents themselves. The claim that "constitutions matter" includes the recognition that what makes them matter are the institutions, culture, traditions, and so on that give life to a polity; but the texts matter too, both for symbolic and practical reasons. My hope is that this project will be situated within a broader debate about constitutional politics much like the "New Criticism" movement in literary theory was situated within a broader conversation about the indeterminacy of a literary text. In that discussion, prominent scholars and artists wrestled with such weighty issues as what counts as part of a narrative, and is the literary text itself definitive or are other factors—the context in which a novel is written, the background of the author, the personal values of the reader, and so on—part of the text. Among the most important consequences of that debate was a reinvigoration of the importance of the text as text. Many (perhaps even most) ultimately rejected the idea that the text in isolation was definitive, that a work of literature could be read and understood absent the contextual realities that influence author and reader. But the emergence of the debate managed to accomplish something very important: it redirected attention back to the text itself. People were forced to confront the text as an independent entity, and even though many rejected its utter isolation, the confrontation was certainly worthwhile. In this work I too reject the idea of the constitutional text as definitive, but I also refuse to endorse the idea that such texts are irrelevant.

Put another way, my primary aim is quite simple: to acknowledge the importance of texts as instruments to order political societies, as documents that use words to create worlds. In the same way that impressive scholarship has advanced our understanding of the "legal" constitution (from Ronald Dworkin and others) and the "political" constitution (from Keith Whittington and others), I hope to advance the discussion by focusing on the "textual" constitution. To do that successfully—to remind people of the importance of constitutions—requires that we take texts seriously as political documents and that we explore their many subtle features. That is not to say that this project represents a return to the "legal formalism" of the late nineteenth century, an approach to understanding law that was based on the principle that buried beneath poorly crafted statutes, judicial opinions, and constitutions were discoverable truths. It will bear repeating throughout the book that constitutions around the world are distinct, and rightly so; the environment in which a constitution emerges will profoundly influence its character and composition. But there are some similarities both in the aims and in the functions of many of the world's constitutions. There are, to put it differently, important features that characterize most contemporary constitutions. This book tries to illuminate those features.

The Importance of Constitutional Texts

Why are constitutional texts worth studying? In large part, constitutions are profoundly important because they help to form collective public identities; they help to shape a country's public character. They are models for a political world that go well beyond describing the architectonic features of a polity's government institutions. The very best ones have a spirit, a transcendent quality that encourages public veneration. The worst ones become symbols of a faltering and

disordered community. Their primary value probably cannot easily be quanti-
fied; indeed, they imagine and then help to realize a shared collective existence.
In short, when they are successful they bring to life a political world primarily
through the mechanism of a single text drafted with a unique and fundamental
status.

South Africa's recent experience with constitutional change provides a vivid
illustration of the value of a constitution to a nation's collective identity. There
should be little doubt that the process of adoption, which included widespread
deliberation, consensus building, and conciliation, was essential to the future
success of the polity's post-apartheid order; but it was the instrument itself—the
constitution itself—that literally brought to life a distinct political community.
Nelson Mandela's words on the eve of South Africa's constitutional ratification
are illuminating: "And so it has come to pass," he said, "that South Africa today
undergoes her rebirth, cleansed of a horrible past, matured from a tentative beginning, and reaching out to the future with confidence."[13] Later in the speech he
describes the adoption of a new constitutional charter as placing all South Africans on a "new road" with an altogether different "soul." For Mandela, the document represents a "rebirth," a "cleansing," in that a new and different political
community based on the principles of equality, liberty, democracy, and dignity
was born. It marks a tangible historic transition from an old regime to a new one,
and accompanying that transition is the plan, laid out in the specific clauses and
provisions of the constitutional text, for realizing the imagined political community. As Mandela implies, a constitution's greatest impact lies in its ability to
envision a distinct political community.

Part of what makes constitutional texts so important is that much of the world
has embraced them as unique compositions. Often the constitutional document
itself is an important tangible symbol of collective identity, but even when a constitution is absent, the *idea* of constitutions as devices to control arbitrary and
capricious authority is powerful and comforting. As is evidenced by Mandela's
comments, constitutional documents enjoy a certain reputation, a credibility
rarely matched by any other political or nonpolitical treatise. If we are to believe
Mandela, they enjoy the power to give birth to a nation. As such, they are fundamentally different than religious texts, statutory laws, policy proposals, narratives, and other written (and even unwritten) documents. Their purpose is
distinct from these writings, partially because they come with certain expectations that other documents do not enjoy. A narrative or story will not ordinarily
organize an entire political community around certain defined principles and
goals. A religious tract might do that in some sense, but even so, most religious

documents enjoy a different reputation and a narrower purpose in the post-Enlightenment age. Indeed, in some sense constitutions have replaced religious doctrines as the principal organizing instrument of a particular society. Leaders now look to constitutions to announce their country's legitimacy on the international stage. A typical regime will have only one constitution, with most political communities considering their historical development as beginning from a single constitutional founding. Citizens often revere their constitutional text. James Madison, in fact, insisted that one of the ingredients for a successful constitution was a healthy veneration of the text by succeeding generations of citizens.[14]

It might be useful to recall the words of Alexander Hamilton, who, writing as Publius, underscored the importance of general constitutional deliberation by claiming, "The subject speaks its own importance, comprehending in its consequences nothing less than the existence of the Union."[15] Of course, Americans are not currently in a state of fundamental constitutional change, but a number of regimes around the world are in the precise position the United States was in more than two centuries ago. Their constitutional texts are new and untested. The institutions of their polities have not yet had an opportunity to comment on the many complex clauses of their governing charters. Constitutional foundings in South Africa, Greece, Switzerland, Turkey, Croatia, New Zealand, and many more are not even a generation old.

For those regimes in particular, and for all constitutional regimes in general, the constitutional text rightfully remains at the forefront of political debate. Unclouded by institutional interpretations, these states are still grappling with the most basic issues of constitutional government: What can our constitution do? What *should* it do? Some of the answers to these questions were uncovered during the writing and ratification stages, but rarely do constitutional engineers consider all of the broad theoretical purposes of a constitutional document. The heart of this project, therefore, is a discussion of the various functions performed by constitutions. If constitutions matter, we ought to stop and consider what it is they do, or rather, what it is they are *supposed* to do. This book represents one attempt to understand the various functions of the modern constitutionalist text.

Organized in chronological sequence, beginning with a description of the inevitable destruction of an old regime that accompanies a new constitutional founding and ending with a constitution's most visible function—its mandate to limit the potentially abusive power of government—this book explores the most critical design features of constitutions. Envisioning the development of a constitution and its polity over time, roughly the first half of the book explores those functions that are most visible, or at least most contested, around the founding: the constitution's transformative role, its aspirational quality, and its design features. In large part the aim of the modern constitutional founder is to wrestle with the questions that animate the first half of the book: Why does a polity need a new constitutional vision? What vision for a political future should a polity embrace? What political design gives a polity the best opportunity to realize that vision?[16]

The second half of the book then turns to the components of a constitution that come into focus a bit more after the founding moment has passed: its role as manager of political conflict, its ability to ensure recognition of different constituencies, and its capacity to both empower and limit the polity's political institutions. The entire project rests on a simple assumption: that constitutionalist texts, while differing dramatically in the degree to which they successfully manage politics, do not differ widely in their functional purpose. I will argue that those fully operative (or at least reasonably operative) constitutional charters that subscribe to the basic principles of constitutionalism all have similar features, even if those features translate into very different political practices. The documents aim to achieve similar goals, and for that reason it is important that we keep the texts—and not just the institutional interpretation of those texts—in our sights. This is particularly true as we witness the birth of new constitutional regimes around the world.

In the modern era, constitutions perform at least seven different functions. This book is an attempt to explain each.[17] After a general overview of constitutions and constitutionalism in chapter 1, chapter 2 explores the process of *constitutional transformation*, defined here as the power of the constitution to help destroy an old polity and create a new one. Chapter 3, on *constitutional aspiration*, examines the role of constitutions in imagining a more perfect political community. Often articulated in preambles and rights guarantees, a country's aspirations for its collective future find a home within the constitutional draft. Chapter 4 then examines one of the more generally understood features of the modern constitutional experiment: the role of the text to structure or *design* a polity's institutions in a specific, self-conscious way. After that, chapter 5 turns to the issue of *constitutional conflict*. Frequently, the aim of most constitutions is to manage (although not eliminate) certain institutional conflict. In so doing, a constitution will inevitably create conflict as well. Chapter 6 then explores the recent trend to see constitutions as providing important avenues for minority groups to find meaningful *recognition* in the political dialogue. Chapter 7, on *constitutional empowerment*, considers the role of the text in empowering institutions of government to make decisions in the name of their constituents. (This power, incidentally, is critical to the legitimacy of public policies and initiatives that emerge from institutions such as legislatures, executives, etc.). Chapter 8 returns to a theme introduced in chapter 1, the theme of *constitutional limits*, in which I examine the essential function of a constitution to limit the power of the sovereign, or, more accurately, the power of practical reflections of the sovereign within the institutions of government.[18]

My goal is not to comment on how successfully modern constitutionalist documents achieve or realize their various constitutional functions; again, I am interested in what they *aim* to do, not how well they do it. An analysis of the comparative success of various constitutional polities is the responsibility of scholars far more gifted than I.[19] My focus instead is on broader *theoretical* questions, ones that can stand apart from studies (both empirical and theoretical) of the nature of constitutional law and yet encompass those inquiries: What are constitutions? What are their purposes? What do they aim to accomplish? Why do framers construct them in the first place? To answer these and other questions, I will examine the most obvious design features of the modern constitutionalist text as well as some of the less recognized functions of those documents. In the end, my hope is that the chapters of this book, taken together, will present a portrait of the modern constitutional instrument. My wish, in other words, is that this book may give the reader a small glimpse into why polities around the world so often look to constitutions to perform critically important tasks ranging from collective identity formation to preventing the rise of potentially abusive political power. Assuming that I am successful at that primary objective, I will then conclude by returning briefly to a discussion of why constitutions matter, focusing this time on the increasing importance of constitutions in an unstable and violent world.

What Is Meant by a Constitutional Text?

Before turning to the task at hand, it is important to define a bit more clearly the scope of this project. A more complete definition of *constitution* will follow in the subsequent chapters, but for now it is necessary to confront some of the broader theoretical definitions. By constitutional text, I mean to limit the inquiry to those formal (though sometimes unwritten) instruments whose primary purpose is to order a political society. I am principally interested in the collections of words and phrases found in a country's fundamental law that, when taken as a whole, attempt to usher in a distinct public life. I certainly recognize that the constitutional document only tells part of the story and that a comprehensive understanding of any contemporary polity requires going far beyond the constitution's words and phrases, but the collections of words themselves are important and worthy of sustained attention. This book is a theoretical exploration of the functions of certain modern constitutional texts, not of the events that gave rise to these texts or the institutions charged with maintaining these texts. Those are important inquiries, to be sure; they are not part of this inquiry, however.

I would like to think that this book stands alongside (not in opposition to) some of the most interesting scholarship on constitutional theory that has surfaced in the past few years. For example, it has become fashionable of late to view constitutions as something more than just words on a particular document. That is, a group of important political and constitutional theorists have suggested that a simple reading of the words in the text represents a tragically narrow view of constitutions.[20] They argue that constitutions are more than just simple documents that we can see and read. Rather, they are dynamic institutions that ebb and flow with changes in the political and social climate. The actual constitutional documents, in other words, represent just the tip of the iceberg; the real meaning of constitutional texts can be found only by looking at how they have been influenced and shaped by the many political forces of a polity.

John Finn, for example, recently explored the question "What is the Constitution?"[21] His conclusions are indicative of the trend to see constitutional texts as something far greater than simply a collection of clauses and phrases on parchment paper. About the American constitution, he writes that there are "two principal constructions," a "Juridic," or legal construction, and a "Civic," or political construction. The Juridic, he writes,

> regards the Constitution primarily as a legal document, "as the supreme law of the land." It emphasizes legality and how law trumps (or transforms) politics. Insofar as the Constitution is law it is not—or it is more than—politics or policy. It "defines the rules of the game, not winners and losers; . . . it shapes the contours of politics, not the content." The Civic Constitution emphasizes not the legal character, but rather the political character of the basic charter, its status not as supreme law but as political creed. It envisions a political order in which constitutional questions, although partly questions of law, are fundamentally and first questions about politics, about the broad principles and normative commitments that comprise our commitment to shared community.[22]

Finn's objective is to articulate a conception—a definition—of American constitutionalism that acknowledges these two, sometimes competing, understandings of the constitutional experiment.

In both theory and practice, I think Finn and the others are onto something here. There *are* competing conceptions of constitutional polities (especially in the United States) that must be recognized. The constitution of a country *does* include more than just the text. Still, if we are to admit that reality, we also must be prepared to admit to the marginalization of the text itself. Once we see constitutional documents as more than text, as made up of institutional interpretations or societal movements—or, in the case of John Finn, as legal and political conceptions—we tend to relegate the documents themselves to the side. The text is seemingly replaced by the broader and admittedly more subtle understanding of a constitutional "project" or "enterprise." Make no mistake, I am not suggesting that any analysis of constitutionalism that comprehends the text as more than just the tangible parchment is misguided. I too will suggest exactly the same thing, especially in the chapters on constitutional transformation and constitutional aspiration. Similarly, I am not arguing that the institutions responsible for interpreting the text are themselves somehow unimportant. On the contrary, these attempts to understand the constitution through the lens of institutional interpretations, or as reflecting some type of interplay between the various organizations and constituencies of the polity, seem not only sophisticated but also quite compelling. And yet, despite their sophistication and accuracy, there may be something lost when the actual text is no longer the primary instrument that occupies our attention. For me it is somewhat unsettling to insist that the text itself is secondary to the constellation of political bodies that it helped to create in the first place. It is, after all, the words of the text that help to create the complex worlds in which we live.

At the outset, it is probably important to admit to a few other particulars of this book. As I mentioned above, my objective is not to comment on the success of individual constitutions in achieving the goals set out in the document. This project is a work of constitutional theory; it examines the abstract notion of constitutional functionality: what constitutions aim to do, regardless of the degree to which they successfully do it. Very good books have been published on "workable" or "unworkable" constitutions around the world (Gary Jacobsohn's work on Israel and India comes to mind,[23] as does Akhil Amar's on the U.S. Constitution and its amendments[24]), but no book that relies heavily on the texts themselves explores the more general functions of the constitutional form. I try to do that by looking at the words of the text. My data is the texts themselves. Drawing a distinction between constitutional *texts* and constitutional *practice* may not satisfy all, but it is the essence of constitutional theory. Put simply, I recognize that the question of how constitutions function on the ground is different than what they say. Nonetheless, this book draws general conclusions about constitutions, not by seeing if they actually accomplish what they set out to do (which is important, but would result in a far different book), but by exploring the promises they make in the words of the document. Again, if we believe that constitutions matter, then we must believe that the words matter too.

As such, this book aspires to provide a broad and general outline of the component features of a large percentage of constitutions around the world. What it does not aim to do is draw conclusions about *all* constitutions. It is perhaps most important to note that I examine only a portion of the constitutions of the world. I am specifically interested in a defined subset of constitutional charters—described in the first chapter—that adhere to the principle of constitutionalism and that are more or less respected by those in positions of power. As will become clear, not all constitutions can claim to be both constitutionalist and authoritative. Luckily, however, many can. This project is centered exclusively on several texts within this broad category.

Within that category, I draw heavily from four charters that are representative of the type of constitutional texts so often replicated around the world. The U.S. Constitution obviously belongs in this group, for countries have borrowed from its design and language practically since it was introduced two centuries ago. In addition, I look to the constitutions of Canada, South Africa, and, less frequently, the constitutions of Eastern Europe, for helpful illustrations. I chose these texts carefully; they reflect the type of questions, struggles, processes, and language that are commonly seen in modern constitutional foundings. Eastern European constitutions are instructive because, as early models of post-Communist charters, they have tried to incorporate complicated economic and political realities into a single written form. Canada's constitution, amended so dramatically in 1982, is a prime example of a constitutional document that tries to account for significant cultural and linguistic differences in its population. South Africa's constitution neatly illustrates the type of fundamental law—heavily detailed, lengthy, and primarily concerned with rights—that emerges from a political society rife with economic, ethnic, and racial tension. Of course, not all of the illustrations will come from these four texts, but they provide anchors to the broader theoretical discussions that follow.

The study is not, therefore, a work of comparative constitutionalism, at least not in any traditional sense. My intention is not to suggest that certain constitutions are better or worse at realizing the functions set out below or that one constitution represents the paradigm example of a text devoted to a particular constitutional function. A discussion of that magnitude would require intellectual gifts that I do not possess—at a minimum an understanding of particular languages, cultures, economics, and histories. At first glance, I may be accused of ignoring Akhil Amar's important caution: that understanding constitutional texts "without context" is mostly an empty enterprise.[25] The context I have chosen to use is one that considers the universe of constitutional texts in an attempt to announce some conclusions about these important documents. To say something general about constitutionalist constitutions requires that we look beyond America's immediate borders to the charters of other nation-states. It requires that we examine primarily the words of the constitutional texts, knowing that those words are important for the purpose of describing constitutional functionality but that they do not tell us the whole story.

There is surely a comparative quality to this work. One thread in this study is the notion that the currently popular style of constitutional texts is the product of an evolutionary trend in political order. Constitutional instruments, in other words, have developed over the last several centuries. For example, they are typically far longer and more detailed than they used to be. Their preambles often reflect idiosyncratic tales of oppression and tyranny, whereas in the past they rarely did so. They are also designed in ways that reveal a keen distrust of framers and politicians alike. Perhaps this last quality is not unique to contemporary constitutions, but I will attempt to show that the level of distrust among subjects and leaders is more acute now than at any other time in modern constitutional history. The comparisons that animate this study are therefore vertical rather than horizontal, historical rather than national. In other words, I will draw comparisons of constitutions through time, being careful not to make an explicitly normative claim about whether they are somehow better at the present than they used to be. They are different now, to be sure, and my instincts tell me they might in fact be less effective in organizing and regulating political communities. But these are just my instincts, nothing more.

I also cannot claim that every modern constitutionalist text performs all seven constitutional functions all of the time. Most are committed to the constitutional functions outlined in the chapters that follow. Even so, to imply that all carry out each of the seven functions is misleading. Some texts are at different stages of development, while others will likely never embrace specific functions. The constitutional function defined in chapter 6 (the one discussing constitutional recognition) is a case in point. Not all constitutions in the modern era have become declarations of the principle that marginalized groups should find meaningful political recognition in the fundamental law. Not all constitutions, in other words, can claim to protect, much less identify, specific subcommunities within the polity. More and more have done so in recent years, including Canada (in terms of the French-speaking population) and South Africa (in terms of specific ethnic and regional groups), but it would be wrong to assert that all have.

Similarly, it is necessary to point out that a definition of what qualifies as a constitution does not depend on the presence of all of these functions. Much of the first chapter is devoted to constructing a comprehensive definition of the term "constitution," so it is unnecessary at this point to go into great detail about the topic. Suffice it to say that constitutions take a multitude of forms—some are written, some are unwritten, some are constitutionalist, some are non-constitutionalist, some are liberal, some are communitarian—and that the presence or absence of the functions described in this book does not turn a constitution into something unconstitutional or turn an ordinary law into a constitutional provision. Again, it is useful to draw on the recent trend of modern constitutions to function as powerful voices for historically marginalized groups as an illustration. The original 1867 Constitution did not recognize French culture as an integral part of Canadian constitutional law, and thus Canadians, prompted by threats of secession, sought a radical transformation of their constitutional document in the late 1970s and early 1980s. The result was the 1982 Canadian Charter of Rights and Freedoms, a comprehensive set of amendments to the original nineteenth-century text. With the 1982 Charter, the Canadian constitution became a much more liberal, tolerant, and inclusive text, but it did not turn the original uninspired document into a full-fledged constitution. The 1867 Constitution already qualified for that title.

In the end, what I can claim is that these limitations in no way derail the overall scope of the project. Those who study constitutions—or even institutional interpretations of constitutional texts—will, I hope, recognize that the majority of the world's charters subscribe to most, if not all, of the various functions examined in the chapters below. Certain constitutions *do*, in fact, aim to limit the power of the sovereign; they *do* design political institutions in particular ways; and they *do* set out aspirational goals for the polity. These important texts *are* written in part to regulate political conflict; they *do* construct a new vision of political life; and they *do* seek to empower the institutions of the polity to act on behalf of the sovereign. The fact that not all of them perform all of these functions at every point in a polity's history does not alter the reality that constitutional texts serve important purposes, that they endeavor to realize certain critical objectives, and that they are worthy of our focused attention. My simple task in this book is to elucidate that essential truth.

CHAPTER ONE

Constitutional Order

An exploration of constitutional functionality logically begins with an understanding of constitutions. Almost every regime around the world boasts a constitution. From the most tolerant to the most oppressive, polities are consistently able to point to some form of constitutional documentation as their own. It is true that not all political regimes adhere to the principle of constitutionalism, the idea that political power is both created and controlled; but few societies in the modern era have deliberately spurned the practice of crafting and adopting a constitutional charter.

And yet we know that not all constitutions are alike. A quick glance at the constitutions currently governing the roughly 260 nations of the world reveals that they appear to be quite distinct. Texts are structured differently; they protect a variety of diverse priorities and constituencies; they articulate an assortment of aspirations; they aim to promote a range of political goals; and, perhaps most importantly, they derive from very different political and social realities. Some even remain unwritten. In light of this widespread diversity, it is appropriate to begin to comprehend the range of constitutional functions by sketching a few basic definitions. More specifically, we ought to identify the difference between constitutions, as fundamental legal documents, and the principle of constitutionalism.

The push during the summer of 2005 to draft a new constitution for Iraq highlights some of the confusion that inevitably plagues discussions involving terms like *constitutionalism* and *order*. Iraq has a new constitutional document. The text includes provisions for free and fair elections, governmental checks and balances, and accommodation of the religious pluralism that so obviously defines the nation. The problem, it seems, is that for many casual observers the existence of a constitutional text is sufficient to turn Iraq, with a recent tradition of totalitarian rule, into a liberal-democratic regime—the text, in short, is the remedy for decades of authoritarian control. The reality, however, cannot be farther from the perception. A constitution alone is not enough to turn any regime, let alone one that has no experience in democratic rule, into a model of political justice. More is required, and once we introduce additional principles and concepts, the waters begin to get muddy. A constitution is easy to imagine. What is difficult to imagine are the components needed to make the document workable.

For some time now, the definitional lines separating the concepts of *constitution* and *constitutionalism* have become blurred. Perhaps due to the sudden increase in constitution-making in the latter half of the twentieth century, what was once a relatively simplistic understanding of constitutional government—one that was based entirely on the existence of a constitutional text—has taken on greater nuance. Presently, a definition of constitutional government that merely acknowledges some constitutional document no longer suffices. Some regimes boast constitutional texts, but we would not call them constitutionalist. Others are constitutionalist in principle but have decided, for whatever reason, to do without a written charter. A few regimes, in fact, embrace neither concept: they do not own a constitutional text, nor do they subscribe to the principles of constitutionalism.

On this broad point, Graham Walker notes, "Every polity, insofar as it is a polity, has a constitution, but not every polity practices constitutionalism."[1] Similarly, Giovanni Sartori claimed that "[e]very state [has] a constitution but only *some* states [are] constitutional."[2] Constitutions are public "texts" that organize and empower a political regime; they pattern the political institutions in a specific way, and they constitute (or create) a citizenry. They may be written or unwritten, but at their most basic level they identify political authority and authorize it to make particular decisions on behalf of the common good. Moreover, they organize the polity for certain clearly defined aims or goals; effective constitutions, that is, help to cultivate imagined political communities. Albert Blaustein and Jay Sigler understand this concept with unique clarity. They contend that modern constitutional documents represent a dramatic shift in the way political power is ordered. Prior to the introduction of the written constitutional text, political authority was based on the sovereign's mostly conceptual, and thus intangible, political ideology. After the birth of written charters, Blaustein and Sigler insist, constitutions were able to "reduce the abstractions of a political ideology [by placing it] into a concrete reality."[3] That is, these documents were aimed at textualizing what was mostly a shifting and elusive conception—the specific priorities of the sovereign. The result was the birth of modern constitutionalism.[4]

Constitutions

What qualifies as a constitution has changed dramatically over time. Some might describe constitutions in just one way—as documents whose main purpose is to organize, regulate, and govern political territories. Yet *constitution* refers to order, regardless of whether that order is formally recorded or documented. In fact, prior to the introduction of the modern constitutional charter in the eighteenth century, what might accurately be defined as constitutional looked quite a bit different than what we presently recognize. Constitutions typically consisted of a combination of formal and informal institutions. Pre-Enlightenment constitutions consisted of all or some of the following descriptive features and informal conventions: (1) a description of the polity's political organization; (2) a series of customary beliefs that acted as a means of informal social control; and (3) a set of longstanding traditions that helped to maintain some semblance of political order. In all, constitutions were a compilation of formal but often unconnected texts and informal and largely unwritten conventions.

Each of these components of a premodern constitution served a few basic purposes. The organization of a polity's political divisions, for example, characteristically implicated questions related to sovereignty: Where does the locus of power lie? Which departments (monarch, parliament, etc.) control the governing process? The interplay between a kingdom's specific political institutions might not be formally recorded, since they were often maintained through force and/or tradition, but they were almost always evident, at least to those embedded within them. These relationships, in other words, were not likely to be formally recognized in a written document, but more often than not the monarchy, the parliament, and the subjects of the regime were cognizant of their roles in relation to one another.

Customs and traditions, those informal institutions that also comprised early constitutions, were by contrast far less transparent. These institutions sought to regulate the actions of the sovereign by appealing to longstanding religious and secular beliefs. The thinking was that perhaps the sovereign king would be limited in the sweep of his potentially coercive power if he were regularly reminded of the intimate relationship he maintained with God. God's force, coupled with a monarch's conviction that he ruled at the mercy of a higher power, suggested that tyrannical behavior would be curtailed. The problem was that the idea was often more compelling than the reality. Success in controlling the actions of the king through internally derived mechanisms like religious teachings and historical customs was all too rare. In fact, monarchical leaders regularly justified abusive measures in the name, not in spite of, God. The principle that the king is law, rather than that the law is king, often prevailed.

Classical constitutions were thus unique reflections of a particular time and place. In Hegel's words, "A constitution is not just something manufactured; it is the work of centuries, it is the Idea, the consciousness of rationality so far as that consciousness is developed in a particular nation."[5] In one sense there were actual "texts" that served constitutional functions prior to the Enlightenment: the Iroquois Constitution is considered by many to be a species of modern fundamental law. Certain famous written agreements between sovereign and subject—documents such as the Magna Carta in 1215, the British Declaration of Rights in 1689, and the early American social compacts—also qualify as constitutions. Even so, it is more likely that any restrictions on the authority of the monarch came not from parchment barriers but from internal laws and parochial beliefs. Bolingbroke put it best in 1733: "By constitution we mean, whenever we speak with propriety and exactness, that assemblage of laws, institutions and customs, derived from certain fixed principles of reason, directed to certain fixed objects of public good, that compose the general system, according to which the community hath agreed to be governed."[6]

As it did in so many other ways, the Enlightenment challenged the basic assumptions of the classical style of constitutions. In fact, the most successful constitutional forms that emerged during and after the Enlightenment looked far different than those that preceded man's journey into rationalism. Whereas constitutions were vague, undocumented, and primarily lodged in the mind of the sovereign prior to the late eighteenth century, they were transformed by the spirit of the Enlightenment into altogether different things. To put it simply, constitutional framers, after the mid-eighteenth century, aimed to achieve a certain degree of political transparency and objectivity through the constitutional instrument. In most cases these constitutions were also written. They were laid out for the world to see; subjects of the sovereign now had a tangible record—a written document—that articulated and fixed the scope of governmental power.

State constitutions in the former British colonies of eastern North America, followed eventually by the general U.S. Constitution, led the way in establishing a new paradigm of constitutional government. A formal written text that both created and empowered governmental institutions, that identified political authority and yet simultaneously curtailed it, and that emerged not from force but from deliberation and discourse, was at the time a radically new idea. Both the Articles of Confederation and later the U.S. Constitution represented a thorough departure from the classical version of constitutions where the scope and depth of political power were mostly intangible. Two of the most influential American framers, John Jay and Alexander Hamilton, said it best. Jay wrote that Americans were "the first people whom heaven has favoured with an opportunity of deliberating on and choosing forms of government under which they should live."[7] Similarly, Hamilton declared in the first *Federalist*, "It has been frequently remarked that it seems to have been reserved to the people of this country, by their conduct and example, to decide the important question, whether societies of men are really capable or not of establishing good government from reflection and choice, or whether they are forever destined to depend for their political constitutions on accident and force."[8]

The shift in the design of constitutions could not have occurred if the founding generation in America had not embraced the core principles of the Enlightenment. Figures like James Madison, Benjamin Franklin, Gouverneur Morris, James Wilson, and others were profoundly influenced by the political writings of the major Enlightenment philosophers, especially such thinkers as Montesquieu, Locke, and Blackstone. They borrowed liberally from the earlier writers' specific ideas about proper governmental systems, but perhaps more importantly, they bought into the broader Enlightenment themes of the period such as popular rule, consent of the governed, equality, liberty, and constitutionalism. The American Founders were committed to an idea that humans were in some sense free of the influence of a higher religious authority. As such, the principles of the Enlightenment inspired the fledgling nation to seek independence and to abandon the old rules that dampened their colonial experience. The first generation of Americans sought to carve out a new world that was not subject simply to the often-inflexible rules of religious faith. Indeed, the American Revolution was as much a revolt against the tyranny of ignorance and superstition as it was a revolution against the British Crown.

An important component of the rejection of the dominance of religion during the Enlightenment was the belief that man was responsible for his own destiny. Logic further dictated that communities of men—political societies, in other words—could control their own collective destinies so long as the institutions of government were properly designed. That, of course, accounted for a dramatic shift in the definition of sovereignty in the late eighteenth century. Rather than lodging primary decision-making power in the institutions of government, as prior regimes had done, the American Revolution marked a turning point in the very nature of political power.[9] The people were now sovereign. They could now decide what design of government they preferred. Political authority was relocated from the few to the many, and as long as the republican framework held up, it would forever be situated in the collective peoples of the United States.

But more significantly, the American Founders also believed that reason through deliberation could ensure a political future that was both energized and stable. Enduring political regimes, in other words, could be achieved through careful planning and rational thought; designing political systems to maximize stability and freedom, the Founders thought, was mostly a *scientific* endeavor. That philosophy helps explain the widespread use of conventions as instruments to both create and ratify constitutional texts. A convention is a deliberative body summoned together for a common purpose. Any constitutional convention resembling the one in Philadelphia in 1787 serves multiple purposes: it provides individuals from different backgrounds the chance to participate in the crafting of a shared future. In a liberal-democratic regime, it empowers the product—the constitution itself—with a higher degree of legitimacy than if the text was the creation of a single individual. And, finally, a constitutional convention—a body meeting for a fixed moment in time, with a single purpose, and that will sunset after the process of drafting is complete—helps to differentiate the ordinary from the fundamental, the regular or common law from the primary or supreme law.[10] This exact principle was repeated frequently during the Massachusetts Constitutional Convention of 1779; it was often noted that the body charged with creating the fundamental law could not be the same body that enacts ordinary law.

Yet their greatest virtue is that constitutional and ratifying conventions of the sort that gave rise to the American polity rest entirely on the principle of faith—not faith in some deity, but faith in the ability of humans to design their own political lives and create their own political communities. It is perhaps illuminating that, according to Madison's notes, not once during the long summer of 1787 did the delegates to the constitutional convention formally resolve to seek the wisdom of God. In Franklin's words, "The Convention, except three or four persons, thought prayers unnecessary."[11]

Beginning in the eighteenth century, therefore, constitutions took on a new appearance. In addition to their now tangible or written quality, these modern constitutions were very public documents. They were shared by a population that, at least in a limited sense, experienced a sense of ownership in the documents themselves. Most were born out of tyranny, and thus constitutions created by representatives and ratified by citizens were viewed as evolutionary. To many, they represented a significant advance in the theory of just political systems.[12] The idea of formal, written texts to control man's coercive instincts had been embraced; the question remained whether the Enlightenment experiment with constitutional government would be successful. The answer to that question would come only if modern political states were to embrace the principle of constitutionalism.

Constitutionalism

The principle of constitutionalism is of course distinct from the constitutional text itself. The principle derives from a *subset* of modern constitutions whose architecture clearly places primacy on the very specific themes of *limited* and *restrained* government, or rather, on the idea that "basic rights and arrangements [should] be beyond the reach of ordinary politics."[13] In Charles McIlwain's words, "Constitutionalism has one essential quality: it is a legal limitation on government; it is the antithesis of arbitrary rule; its opposite is despotic government, the government of will instead of law."[14] Daniel P. Franklin and Michael J. Baun further note that constitutionalist government can be defined as government by rules. "Every society," they write, "must make decisions concerning the distribution of scarce resources, and those decisions must be enforced. This being the case, the constitutional regime of a state requires not only the enumeration of rules of public behavior but the establishment of an institutional structure for the implementation of that law. Thus, the concept of constitutionalism rests on two pillars, a theory of justice and process."[15] Jon Elster offers a similar definition: "[Constitutionalism] is a state of mind—an expectation and a norm—in which politics must be conducted in accordance with standing rules and conventions, written or unwritten, that cannot be easily changed."[16]

The principle of constitutionalism is actually quite complex, and a more complete definition will emerge in chapter 8. For now, a basic sketch is all that is necessary. In part, constitutionalism is the rule of law applied to constitutional charters: a regime that adheres to the dictates of constitutionalism is a polity that endeavors to divorce fundamental substantive and procedural decisions about the good from the human impulse to think self-interestedly. Broadly understood, constitutionalism refers to the principle that ideas and words can act as a safeguard against the inevitable tendency of political leaders to place power over the right. One should not equate a constitutionalist text with a "workable" text or even with a Western style of constitutional charter. There are plenty of examples of constitutions that purport to protect individuals from the potentially abusive powers of political leaders but that are filled with empty promises. Again, the distinction between constitutional *texts* and constitutional *practice* is important to keep in mind.

Perhaps no one has captured the essence of constitutionalism quite as completely as Thomas Paine. Writing in the late eighteenth century, Paine described with profound subtlety the requirements of constitutionalist government. He was not satisfied to rest on the notion that good government was simply limited government. Instead, he identified what is necessary for a government like that in the newly constituted United States to qualify as legitimate. To begin, he noted that a constitution must exist independent of the government it creates.[17] It must, in other words, be "antecedent" to the actual political institutions charged with the responsibility of crafting ordinary law. Secondly, there must be an acknowledgement that the constitution is a reflection of the will of the sovereign people. It should capture a particular belief, idea, or ethos. Thirdly, Paine insisted that as part of its reflective quality, there must also be a general admission that the constitutional text is supreme. That is, when juxtaposed against ordinary acts of the legislature, the constitutional text is paramount. The overall thrust of his general theory of constitutionalism can be observed in the following quote: "A constitution is not the act of a government, but of a people constituting a government, a government without a constitution is power without right. A constitution is a thing *antecedent* to a government; and a government is only the creature of a constitution."[18]

Thomas Paine understood that the definition of constitutionalism included two basic components. The first was the idea that constitutions create power. Their purpose is to identify those institutions that will carry on the ordinary and sometimes mundane business of running a complex political society; thus the need for a clear separation between the constitution, as fundamental law, and the legislature, as purveyors of ordinary law. The second component of constitutionalism is the requirement that polities identify specific mechanisms that will successfully limit the power of the sovereign. Techniques to limit governmental power through constitutional force can take many forms, including separation of powers, federalism, checks and balances, and the most popular tool, the list of safeguards and protections more commonly recognized as the bill of rights. Yet regardless of whatever form(s) it may take, the principle of constitutionalism insists that mechanisms are grounded within the constitution itself that successfully offset the possibility of unfettered and capricious rule.

The U.S. Constitution provides a ready example. Most obviously, the American constitution embraces the notion of limited or constrained power by virtue of its being a constitution of enumerated powers. Paraphrasing Hamilton in *Federalist* 84, the Constitution itself acts as a buffer against tyrannical rule because "government cannot claim more power than it is constitutionally granted."[19]

Yet even within the American text there are a number of additional safeguards that inhibit the abuse of power. Political authority, for one, is distributed among three coequal branches and two distinct governmental levels. That power is further diffused through the process of checks and balances or shared political authority. Finally, as a concession to the Anti-Federalists, the Bill of Rights was added to further provide insurance against the concentration of federal political power.

The American case is obviously not the only illustration. Take America's neighbor to the north. The 1982 Canadian Charter of Rights and Freedoms is a unique experiment in the potential power of constitutionalism. Through political negotiation, Canada was able to craft a constitutional document that not only supports traditional freedoms such as that of free expression but also protects freedoms that may be unique to countries with deep-seated cultural differences. Canada's constitution, in other words, takes seriously the Montesquieuan notion that successful political regimes must be aware of their own particular features. For example, by virtue of chapter 23 of the Charter, encroachment on the right of French-speaking Canadians to educate their children in their native tongue violates the constitution. Similarly, the Charter goes so far as to stipulate: "Everyone has the right to use English or French in any debates and other proceedings of the legislature of New Brunswick." The point is that Canadians are using the power of the constitutional text to constrain the English-speaking majority from trampling on the rights of minority linguistic communities. The principle of constitutionalism is aimed squarely at the protection of Canadian linguistic pluralism; its power is being expended to promote the principle of tolerance.

To those in the West, the model of constitutional government is one in which citizens, who presumably have been granted some voice in the political process, agree to certain rules that regulate their conduct and, more critically, the conduct of their elected (and certain unelected) officials. This model—the liberal-democratic model of constitutional government—relies on the principle that legitimate government is (and should be) restrained by the rule of law. The main purpose of a constitutional text, many modern Westerners would admit, is to constrain the inevitable tendency of political leaders to extend, and even abuse, their power. From Locke to Publius to contemporary draftsmen around the world, controlling the passions and appetites of government leaders for increased power has been the primary ambition of the liberal-democratic constitutional text.

Nonconstitutionalism

Now contrast that vision of restrained political power through constitutional mechanisms with its opposite—nonconstitutionalism. To be sure, liberal-democratic polities—constitutionalist polities—are not the only examples of constitutional government. Nathan J. Brown has noted that the Arab experience with constitutional texts seems to counter the experience of most Western regimes.[20] Arab countries have constitutional texts; some even resemble those in the West. However, Brown is quick to point out that constitutional charters in Arab nations are often used to *empower* leaders rather than limiting or constraining them: "[Arab] Constitutions have generally been written to augment political authority; liberal constitutionalism (aimed at restraining political authority) has generally been at most a secondary goal."[21] Similarly, H. W. O. Okoth-Ogendo has concluded that some polities, particularly those located in central and northern Africa, do not view constitutions as mechanisms to promote limited and stable government. Instead, these texts often have a much simpler and pragmatic purpose: they serve to declare the regime a sovereign state within the international community. They are, in the words of Ivo Duchacek, a nation's "birth certificate."[22] Okoth-Ogendo insists that many African constitutions perform other functions beyond a simple announcement of sovereignty, but securing liberal-democratic institutions and controlling the potential for abuse of power are typically not among them.[23]

Again, a liberal-democratic constitution would resemble the one animating the U.S. political system. This constitutional text is constitutional*ist* precisely because its various sections are designed to define and subsequently restrain the power of the government. Furthermore, by every measure the U.S. Constitution is authoritative—the institutions of government mostly obey the broad contours of its wording. Consider the example of Kenya as a contrasting illustration. Recently, the Kenyan constitution has been altered to "reflect the full complement of powers already being exercised by the police under penal and public security legislations."[24] It was amended in the 1980s, not to provide greater freedom for the citizens or to further restrain the power of the Kenyan leadership, but rather to enhance the authority of the state. Such a constitution would not be considered constitutionalist because of its lack of concern for limiting the power of government, yet no one can suggest that those in power carelessly refuse to observe the text's principal provisions either. The text was carefully amended precisely because the Kenyan polity is committed to some form of constitutional government. Differing in function and ambition from liberal-democratic texts, the Kenyan constitution is therefore both authoritative and *non*constitutionalist.

The absence of constitutionalist principles does not necessarily make a consti-tution any less of a constitution; it just makes it different. A number of factors can help explain the lack of constitutionalist traditions in those countries that still possess constitutional texts. Most involve economic inequalities, political abuses, and/or social constraints. Certain Latin American countries, for example, sup-port a distinctive style of capitalism and free market economics that often im-pedes the prioritization of constitutionalism.[25] Societies where farmers are not always free and industrial production is often inefficient are typically societies where the principle of constitutionalism has not yet found root. Put differently, the vast inequalities in wealth and opportunity will often hinder any revolution in favor of greater constitutionalism. On this point Atilio Boron remarks, "Latin American capitalism [has] produced, as a result of the secular decay of the old order, a host of extremely unequal societies in which the spirit of constitutional-ism and democracy could hardly survive."[26]

These same Latin American countries must also contend with a legacy of po-litical rule where authority is mainly concentrated in order to protect the inter-ests of the elite few. A sense of conservatism thus pervades powerful segments of Latin American society. The conservative outlook shared by most in power is of course antithetical to a constitutionalist posture in which the principle of limited or constrained government is viewed as paramount. Leaders, in other words, se-cretly ask: why seek radical transformation of the political society when the few individuals who have the capacity for successful revolution are the one's most benefiting from the status quo?

Similarly, political authority in certain countries is of such a nature that any potential transition to constitutionalist or limited government would require ini-tial, but equally dramatic, political changes. Countries with socialist traditions, for instance, must make the difficult transition from autocracy to democracy before they can even hope to tackle the issue of constitutional legitimacy. Those regimes that seek simply to transplant constitutional systems (like that found in the United States) onto their soil often find that what works well in one environ-ment does not always work well in another. It will be interesting to see over the next few decades whether the imposition of constitutionalist charters in parts of the world that are not accustomed to that particular style of fundamental law will be successful. What happens, in other words, when superpowers in the West seek to transplant a constitutionalist text on a nonconstitutionalist culture? It's a dif-ficult endeavor. The current situation in Iraq is just one case in point.

There are, of course, other illustrations. Consider the example of the Philip-pines. The 1935 Filipino Constitution was almost an exact replica of the American text. And yet conditions in the Philippines were not conducive to a constitutional regime based largely on the principles of shared powers and restrained government. The feudal system in the Philippines, combined with the country's economic dependency on the United States and its centralized political power, doomed the transplant to failure. The 1935 constitutional text was eventually replaced in 1987, but even that document suffers because it supports political principles that do not yet have a foothold in the region. Perhaps Montesquieu was correct: the difficulties in transplanting legal and constitutional systems from one arena to the next are both real and significant.[27]

Overall, the greatest hurdle for countries struggling with the idea of constitutionalism is a lack of faith on the part of citizens. In drafting the American text two centuries ago, James Madison wrote that a document espousing the fundamental law was necessary precisely because human nature is so corruptible.[28] Constitutionalists like Madison were by nature pessimists; they sought to design political institutions (including the constitution) that would successfully forestall the concentration and subsequent abuse of political power. Contemporary framers are no different. They regularly remind us that the primary benefit of an authoritative text is the restraint it places on political authority. To be sure, a degree of reverence encircles a constitutional text in places that value principles such as democracy, equality, and the rule of law; and that reverence is part of what gives the constitutional document its principal force. Still, respect does not come immediately, and even when it is present, it is often very fragile. Support for a constitutionalist regime can erode quickly. Thus the great irony in framing a constitutionalist system is that the mission of a constitutional founder is to embrace a view that humans cannot be trusted to control political power but that constitutions can.

Sham versus Fully Operative Texts

Scholars have tried to make sense of the variety of constitutions throughout the world by assigning various terms to their particular idiosyncrasies. Nathan J. Brown, for example, refers to the type of constitutions governing regimes in Africa and the Middle East as "nonconstitutionalist" in that they may serve the primary purpose of identifying political authority and organizing governmental institutions, but they do not in any way limit governmental power. Nonconstitutionalist constitutions, he insists, are authoritative in the truest sense of the word; their provisions are reliable, and the governmental institutions that enforce them rarely violate their terms.[29] The same can be said for constitutionalist texts like those found primarily in liberal-democratic regimes. Where liberal-democratic and nonconstitutionalist constitutions differ is in their capacity to control potentially abusive political authority; we should not confuse the fact that, insofar as political officials are unlikely to ignore nonconstitutionalist texts, they share with their constitutionalist cousins a degree of authority. Like the most enduring constitutionalist models of the West, nonconstitutionalist constitutions also carry a certain influence or power. The difference between constitutionalist and nonconstitutionalist constitutions is not that one is respected and the other is ignored, but that one (the constitutionalist example) regulates or restrains political power and the other (nonconstitutionalist) does not.

It may be useful at this point to resurrect Walter Murphy's theory that constitutions actually fall along a "spectrum of authority."[30] At one end are what he calls "shams," constitutions that are mostly ignored or violated by those in power. Murphy notes that the "principal function of a sham constitutional text is to deceive." Its provisions are meant to disguise the location of the real power within the state, which often can be found in a single tyrannical or authoritarian leader. Giovanni Sartori referred to these texts as "façade constitutions," while Herbert J. Spiro's preferred term was "paper" constitutions, and Karl Loewenstein's was "fictive" constitutions. Finn correctly posits that the distance between "sham" or "fictive" constitutions and ones that are authoritative can often be calculated by considering the distance between "political aspirations" and "reality."[31] The constitutions of the Soviet Union under Stalin or the People's Republic of China under Mao, all agree, are paradigmatic examples of "sham" or "fictive" constitutional texts. There was quite a divide between the promises of those texts and the reality of the nations' politics.

At the other end of the spectrum are those constitutional texts that Murphy describes as "fully operative." These are the texts that enjoy significant authority (although Murphy insists that no constitution enjoys "complete" authority) and are mostly successful at both binding a citizenry and (in the case of most constitutional*ist* texts) regulating the power of government.[32] These constitutional designs are ones in which the promises articulated in the document represent the political reality of that particular nation-state. Pledges of rights protections or divisions of power, or, on the other side, concentrations of power in the hands of an autocratic leader, would render the text fully operative if those pledges were manifest in the state's political practices. Accordingly, many of these constitutions would be described as constitutionalist, but not all. The U.S. Constitution is an appropriate example of the former; Arab constitutions are examples of the latter.

Constitutions therefore actually operate along two intersecting axes: constitutionalist versus nonconstitutionalist, and "sham" versus "fully operative." A constitutional text can purport to be constitutionalist insofar as it includes all the traditional mechanisms that limit the power of the sovereign. But that constitution can still be considered a sham. The governing charter of the former Soviet Union was just such a text. It included provisions for the protection of individual rights, and yet those provisions were mostly violated by Communist Party elites.[33] Similarly, a constitution can be nonconstitutionalist in that it augments rather than constrains the authority of the sovereign, but that same constitution may be fully operative insofar as it remains reasonably authoritative. Brown argues that Arab constitutions fall into this category: "The Saudi basic law, to give one example, is largely followed [and yet] no reader would take it to aim at establishing a constitutionalist democracy."[34]

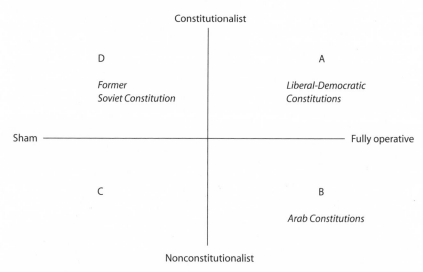

The simple diagram above provides a graphic illustration of the varieties of constitutional texts. Those constitutions that seek to limit the power of the sovereign and whose specific provisions are mostly respected or obeyed by those in political office fall somewhere in quadrant A. Those nonconstitutionalist texts whose aim is *not* to restrain the power of the government but instead to enhance it can be found in either quadrant B or C. Of course, there is a significant difference between quadrants B and C: quadrant B is reserved for those constitutions that are fully or reasonably operative but that do not portend to regulate or limit the will of the regime's political leadership. Brown indicates that Arab constitutions fall into this quadrant. Quadrant C, on the other hand, includes those texts that are neither authoritative nor constitutionalist; they are nonconstitutionalist shams. It is reasonable to assume that quadrant C cannot logically host any examples. Recognizing that in the post-Enlightenment era, a regime that shuns the principal features of a constitutionalist text will in some sense be condemned for its lack of commitment to individual rights, equality, and/or due process, few countries (if any) would go through the trouble of constructing a constitutional text that rejects constitutionalist maxims (and thereby empowers political leaders rather than limiting their authority) and would then decide that the best course of action is to ignore its own already unpopular constitutional text. That is, it seems doubtful that there are constitutional framers who believe it is wise to design a nonconstitutionalist political order, only to then see their design disregarded by political officials in favor of the opposite: justice and limited government. As far as I know there have not been any benevolent dictators for quite some time.

Finally, quadrant D hosts those constitutional texts that promise to abide by certain constitutionalist maxims but are then ignored by those in positions of authority. Sadly, this scenario occurs with frequency in every corner of the globe. The most famous example is the former Soviet Constitution, which included grand claims of individual freedom and justice but which was largely overlooked by Communist Party elites. Other texts that belong in Quadrant D can be found in polities ranging from Africa to Asia, to Central America, and so on; indeed, dictatorial or tyrannical regimes are the typical political systems that abandon constitutional promises of limited government. Similarly, military coups often result in an identical situation, where the new leadership has to "suspend" those constitutionalist safeguards that may have been enforced in the past (yet obviously not with enough frequency to deter the ambitions of an oppositional force) but that now must be sacrificed in the name of "maintaining public order." The example of Nicaragua comes to mind.

The example of the military coup presents an interesting possibility: that some constitutions can be located in different quadrants at different times in their evolution. Constitutions, in short, can start out in one quadrant yet can, through a series of events or circumstances, shift fairly easily into another. In fact, history recounts numerous examples of political leaders temporarily ignoring the dictates of a constitutional text because they believed that doing so would ultimately benefit themselves or the polity. And these illustrations are not just limited to self-interested dictators. Abraham Lincoln's suspension of the writ of habeas corpus during the American Civil War comes to mind as an instance where political authority was expended to temporarily marginalize a constitutional text whose primary role is to ensure that such an event never happens. We may insist that Lincoln's decision was correct, especially in light of the circumstances surrounding it. Even so, those instances cannot be labeled differently. Once an individual or group that enjoys political power deceives the public by ignoring or suspending the constitutional text, the text—even just for that temporary period—becomes some variation of a sham. So long as the polity's governmental institutions disregard the constitution, in other words, the message of its articles and clauses is rendered mostly meaningless.

Conclusion

The majority of constitutions around the world can be located within the quadrant that combines both constitutionalist principles and reasonably or fully operative authoritativeness. For that reason, the focus of this book will be entirely on those constitutions that purport to be constitutionalist and authoritative. It will not examine those instances in which a constitutional regime does not subscribe to the doctrine of constitutionalism, nor will it focus on constitutions that are deemed shams. Yet this book is not limited only to narrow categories. It is not, for example, focused solely on liberal-democratic constitutions, although the principle of constitutionalism is often confused with both liberal ideology and the practice of democracy. There are, in fact, examples of nonliberal constitutions that contain certain constitutionalist ideals. There are also examples of nondemocratic constitutions that support modern constitutionalist maxims. This work will therefore try to outline the features of all varieties of constitutionalist and authoritative texts. Its central questions will be: Might there be something that all fully operative constitutionalist constitutions—whether they derive from Western or Eastern polities, or whether they govern liberal or illiberal, democratic or nondemocratic regimes—share in common? Is there a thread that runs through all constitutionalist and authoritative charters? The answers, I believe, can be found by examining constitutional functionality.

CHAPTER TWO

Constitutional Transformation

It seems logical that any discussion of constitutional functionality should properly start at the chronological beginning, with the exploration of the inevitable transition and rebirth that accompanies constitutional foundings.[1] Indeed, constitutional foundings are curious and complicated moments.[2] For some polities the founding moment as well as the statesmen and stateswomen who participate in it are viewed with deep respect and reverence. For others, especially those states whose foundings occurred more gradually over a period of time, calls to celebrate political rebirth may not be quite as visible.[3] Constitutional foundings can also vary widely, depending on the circumstances that gave rise to the need for reform. They can be more administrative and less deliberative; they can occur because a political regime is in crisis or because a new source of power has emerged; they can even come about completely by accident.

Yet no matter how they occur, all constitutional foundings share a few critical features—first among them is the power of transformation. One function of modern constitutional texts is to transform political communities. Regimes today are born out of the literal or figurative ashes of previous political communities; they emerge from, and are influenced by, the institutions and structures of prior political worlds. In the modern era, that is, all nations were at one time or another fundamentally different political societies. Here again, the question of *how* a regime alters its collective identity through the process of constitutional transformation depends on the specifics of a polity's particular historical narrative: no two transformations are exactly alike. Indeed, some have undergone dramatic reform, while others have witnessed far more subtle conversions. Some acknowledge a feudal past, while others admit to a former colonial existence. Still others boast neither a colonial nor a feudal tradition but recognize that regime change has occurred as a result of such forces as industrial development, military coups, revolutions, post-Enlightenment rationalism, and so on.

The point is that all nation-states can look to some moment in their histories and see a different political world, one that no longer exists. Something sparked a transformation from a previous political world to a new and different one. Even regime change that seeks only to recover a previous vision of politics or that maintains a preexisting constitutional text with dramatically altered values and rules (such as in the case of the American Constitution after the Civil War) has to admit to some structure—some constitutional vision—that is no longer present. The concept of regime change, if it means anything, requires that there be some difference between the envisioned political structure and the unworkable one currently ordering the polity. There must be some transformation, for to replace the current constitutional system with an identical constitutional system is not to undergo regime change at all. It is telling that more and more often the practice of drafting constitutional documents has come to represent the particular moment of transformation.

The reality of regime change—of constitutional transformation—holds important lessons for the study of constitutional functionality. In other words, we can learn much about what a constitution is supposed to do by looking at the moment in which it is made. That moment (or moments) reveals not only the priorities of the new order but also the broad contours of what the political community should look like. Insofar as most contemporary political societies look to constitutional texts as the primary mechanism to announce and organize a collective existence, it can be said that constitutional foundings now serve a dual theoretical role. The initial role they play is most certainly negative: the adoption of a new constitutional charter represents the *destruction* of an existing political design. It represents the end of the past political world. The second and equally important role is more positive: constitutional foundings also represent the *birth* of a new community, the reformation of an altogether different political structure. Not always well-designed or even good in the moral sense of the term, a new political society emerges from a constitutional founding. Recall the words of Nelson Mandela, who understood the dual nature of constitutional foundings. He insisted that the founding moment represented a break from the past and a simultaneous "rebirth" for all citizens of South Africa. He further understood that what is most intriguing about this duality is that, rather than existing in tension, the destructive and renewal qualities of constitutional foundings operate together to bring about tangible constitutional transformation.

Constitutional Destruction

To begin, let us consider a constitutional founding's mostly negative role. New constitutions emerge out of the destruction of old and dysfunctional political orders. They are largely reactions to the faults and miscalculations of past political leaders. In the words of K. C. Wheare, constitutions emerge "because people wish to make a fresh start . . . to begin again."[4] Carl Friedrich described the emergence of constitutional texts as "flow[ing] from the negative distaste for a dismal past."[5] Peter Russell's claim is even more startling: "No liberal democratic state has accomplished comprehensive constitutional change outside the context of some cataclysmic situation such as revolution, world war, the withdrawal of empire, civil war, or the threat of imminent breakup."[6] Jon Elster, who notes that the "link between crisis and constitution-making is quite robust,"[7] further insists that the great paradox of founding moments is that "the task of constitution-making generally emerges in conditions that are likely to work against good constitution-making. Being written for the indefinite future, constitutions ought to be adopted in maximally calm and undisturbed conditions."[8]

Some of the most famous documents in the history of humankind—including the premodern Magna Carta and British Declaration of Rights—materialized primarily from a shared belief that the sovereign had been overly abusive and that a new mechanism was needed to keep the monarch from continuing his abusive tendencies. That new mechanism was a written compact—a contract or constitution—signed by the parties involved and aimed at the regulation of previously unfettered power.[9] In a very real sense, then, these constitution-like texts were a direct consequence of the previous events that gave rise to the call for new and different power arrangements. The ultimate contractual agreement between sovereign and subject—where each makes distinct promises of restraint and limitation of authority—thus represents a departure from a past political structure. The relationship between the king and certain citizens of the polity, in short, was fundamentally altered by a shared agreement, an agreement that, in the modern vernacular, resembles a constitutional text.

Accordingly, the process of altering existing political arrangements through constitutional fiat represents a destructive act.[10] Insofar as a new constitutional regime has replaced an old one, the political relationships that governed the institutions of the prior regime have been destroyed. And the dynamic of destruction is not just limited to pre-Enlightenment political relationships like the one between King John of England and his barons in the thirteenth century. Exchanging a modern constitutional structure that created and maintained autocratic rule with one that favors liberal democracy (or vice versa) represents a similarly significant political transformation, one that is most likely a consequence of the failure of the previous polity's specific design. Likewise, a constitutional transition that abandons a loose confederation of territorial units (as in the case of the Articles of Confederation) and adopts a structure that embraces more concentrated national power (as manifest in the U.S. Constitution) represents a destructive act.

Constitutional transformation thus comes in a variety of ways: it can be relatively sudden, as in the case of Lesotho, a tiny country in southern Africa that has weathered almost continual change during a mostly violent postcolonial existence; or it can be deliberate, as in the case of the 1996 constitutional renovation in Lesotho's surrounding neighbor, the Republic of South Africa. It can also reflect the values and principles of political regimes that are not necessarily close to home. To be sure, a large percentage of new constitutions adopted over the past half-century have been either borrowed or transplanted from texts in other parts of the world.

The actual drafting of a constitutional text often represents the polity's literal break from a preceding political order. Fresh constitutions are symbolic of a new era, of a new and distinct attempt to cultivate a different political community. Robert W. Gordon has written that constitutional transformation is one "general approach that liberal societies have adopted to undo historical injustice."[11] It seems clear that the series of constitutional charters adopted in France in the last two centuries—over a dozen in all—attest to this point. Each text not only represents a particular vision and structure for the people of France—one that, in each case, simultaneously builds on a past political idea and yet abandons or discards it—but in important ways they each mark an historical transition to a new constitutional vision and political structure for French politics. Regime change and thus constitutional change, in short, doesn't just arise from nowhere; it emerges from, and ultimately contributes to, the destruction of the community's earlier political order.

Constitutional framers are by nature interpreters. They construct foundational documents meant to organize and define particular political spaces; their role therefore is perhaps unsurpassed in importance. Yet they are a decidedly reactive lot. They create constitutional documents largely by reacting to—or interpreting—the events of the past, by considering what did not work in the prior political design and trying to anticipate what might work with a different constitutional structure. About framers, Duchacek wrote, "Constitutions offer a shorthand record of both their memories and their hopes."[12] Like judges, they are regularly reviewing precedent (in this case, constitutional texts) for insight into the formula that will provide a stable and secure state. Like historians, they seek to learn those lessons from the failures and successes of past political regimes.[13] Still, as a distinct type of interpreter, constitutional founders are inevitably quite cruel. As Robert Cover put it, "When interpreters have finished their work, they frequently leave behind victims whose lives have been torn apart by [the] organized, social practices of violence."[14] This statement is all too true. Anti-Federalists, among others, were the victims of America's constitutional transformation in the late eighteenth century,[15] while Communist Party elites were the victims of constitutional reform in Eastern Europe insofar as they were forced to relinquish some of their considerable authority. Indeed, the current holders of power are always the primary sufferers when constitutions are replaced.

The dynamic of constitutional destruction is also captured when we consider that most foundings typically occur at distinct moments in time. The events that might give rise to a constitutional founding will no doubt vary, but often we can identify a roughly fixed period that marks the emergence of a new constitutional regime. In the United States, we might agree that the constitutional founding took place in the late eighteenth century. More precisely, we might narrow that founding period to the time that began with the opening of the constitutional convention on May 25, 1787, and concluded with the ratification of the original text by New Hampshire, the ninth state to ratify, on June 21, 1788. Surely some will disagree with the dates, and in some sense every critique about the "period" surrounding the founding is justified (after all, foundings don't always represent fixed moments insofar as the act of amending the text represents a rebirth of sorts).[16] Yet a literal interpretation of constitutional founding—limited as it were to the time in which the text was drafted, debated, and ratified—comprehends a beginning and an end to the process.

More important, though, is the question of *why* it is important to identify the specific historical moment for a constitutional founding. Because foundings represent fixed moments in time, they symbolize a specific and usually identifiable political and/or cultural transformation. They are historical markers; they denote change. We regularly refer to different periods in a nation's history by which constitutional document is authoritative at that particular moment. Some constitutional transitions have a greater global impact than others, and some are realized only after the text has been in place for a long time; but all constitutional foundings represent some kind of replacement. Again, the conversion from an old regime, with presumably a different constitutional text, to a new political order can be dramatic, as in the case of those polities that witnessed revolutionary founding moments. Or it can be less dramatic, as illustrated by constitutional foundings that don't necessarily accompany acts involving force. History demonstrates, in other words, that certain constitutional transitions, like those that occurred in the twentieth century as a direct result of the events surrounding World War I and II, emerged in response to bloodshed and warfare. Others, like those in the United States in 1787 or Canada in 1982 were less obviously so. Still, regardless of how they came about, the birth of a new constitutional regime signifies a break from the past, a transformation of the old into something new. For that reason it is useful to see constitutional foundings as occurring more or less at precise moments in a nation's history.

Often a newly formed constitution will reflect procedural changes (going from a centralized system of government to a decentralized system, for example), but just as often the change in constitutions marks a dramatic shift in the *substantive* priorities of a polity. In many Eastern European countries, the abandonment of socialist-inspired constitutions and the embrace of more liberal and capitalist texts provide a perfect illustration of dramatic and substantive constitutional change. Drafting constitutions to capture the goal of more open, liberal, democratic, and capitalist societies characterized Eastern European constitutional reform movements of the early 1990s. Parallel illustrations can be found in both Canada and South Africa. In South Africa, the newly ratified constitution signaled a fundamental shift in the priorities of the (newly empowered) sovereign people. Equality and, to a slightly lesser extent, liberty, became the dominant constitutional principles in a state that had, for half a century, zealously spurned any effort to advance universal civil liberties or remedy racial and ethnic imbalances. The institutions of government were altered as a consequence of a new South African constitution, but more striking were the profound modifications to the substantive priorities of the democratic peoples. Chapter 1 of South Africa's now decade-old constitution is illustrative. It identifies the country's "Founding Provisions." Not surprisingly, the very first of these relates a commitment to "human dignity, the achievement of equality and the advancement of human rights and freedoms."[17] The legacy of apartheid is thus reflected in the new constitutional charter, and the result is not only a dramatically different procedural order but also a new substantive perspective. It appears as if the old principles of distrust, inequality, and hatred are replaced, at least in writing, by a new and powerful belief in reconciliation, freedom, and hope. The new constitutional document is an important component in that transformation.

The painstakingly deliberative process that distinguished constitutional foundings in countries such as South Africa, Poland, and Canada further demonstrates the point that the political climate in these countries is somehow different after the adoption of a new constitutional charter. Again, the ratification of South Africa's constitution finally shattered the formal political apparatus that supported the practice of apartheid. It did not completely alter race relations or class stratification—some might even argue that it further aggravated them—but it did signal the destruction of an old regime and the birth of a new one. Consider once again Nelson Mandela's words on the eve of South Africa's constitutional ratification. "And so it has come to pass," he said, "that South Africa today undergoes her rebirth, cleansed of a horrible past, matured from a tentative beginning, and reaching out to the future with confidence."[18] Later in the speech he describes the new constitutional draft as placing all South Africans on a "new road" with an altogether different "soul." It seems reasonable to conclude that the notion of political identity is captured in his understanding of a new political "soul." His concluding remarks give further credence to the argument that the founding moment represents a sharp departure from a prior world, as he pledges not only to achieve a shared future but also never to repeat the mistakes of the past. He concludes, "Our pledge is: never and never again shall the laws of the land rend our people apart or legalize their oppression and repression. Together, we shall march, hand in hand, to a brighter future."[19]

At one level, then, all constitutional transitions are inherently damaging. A constitutional transformation, assuming the text is not a sham, destroys an old way of life, and the act of destroying is inevitably a violent act. Here I am *not* referring to the type of violence that often precedes a constitutional founding moment, the type of physical violence that is the central component of most rebellions or revolutions, the type, in short, that Walter Benjamin famously described as "predatory violence."[20] Instead, I am referring to the metaphorical violence that marks a paradigmatic shift in political identity. To put it simply: new constitutional orders destroy—or do violence to—old constitutional orders at the precise moment of constitutional adoption. Law, as Benjamin, Cover, and other scholars have noted, is a violent institution. When the American framers met in Philadelphia during the summer of 1787 to revise the Articles of Confederation, they understood that the consequence of their deliberations would be a distinct political society, not just a different configuration of political institutions. The fact that they decided to discard the Articles of Confederation and start anew with a novel constitutional charter simply resulted in a more dramatically different vision for the country. Both the original plan to revise the Articles and the eventual decision to abandon them, in other words, did not change the fact that either text, if ratified, would have generated a new political world. Both plans did violence to the existing polity.

The same can be said for all constitutional foundings. The founding moments in places like Israel, Ghana, and modern Germany are characterized by fairly dramatic shifts not only in the structure of government, but also in the political lives of the countries' inhabitants. Institutions of government changed (or were created) in these countries when new constitutions were adopted, and thus the relationship of the citizens to each other and to their political agencies was altered. That is not to say that everyone was affected by the changes or even that most citizens supported them. It is to suggest that constitutional foundings create new political worlds on the ashes of destroyed ones. Even though it is perhaps only marginally recognizable in many geographical regions of these countries or the changes themselves are not felt for a long time, a new polity was born out of these constitutional transformations.

Constitutional Creation

There is, of course, much more to the notion of constitutional founding than its destructive power. Alongside the destructive tendencies of constitutional foundings, the process of constitutional *formation* represents another, equally important component of this unique transformation. Indeed, along with the inevitable destruction of an old polity comes the next step: the *creation* of a new political community, with a new conception of citizenship and a revised governmental design. Constitutions, that is, are quite unique in that they perform a critical creative function as well. More than perhaps any other single institution in a new political regime, constitutional texts contribute to a different vision for the polity, a new direction for the people of that particular political community. They reflect the wishes of a new (and not always just) sovereign. They typically identify a polity's substantive priorities, and they aim to set the polity on a renewed course. Constitutions are, in Friedrich's words, "symbolic expressions of the unifying forces in a community and they are supposed to strengthen them further."[21] Often a new constitutional text will be introduced with fanfare, celebrations will ensue, and even in some cases a new flag or national symbol or emblem will accompany the moment. These are all symbolic of the polity's new direction, its new vision.

The specific definition of constitution may be helpful here. To constitute is to make up, to form, to take disparate parts and shape them into a more or less coherent whole. The word itself implies transformation, the fashioning of a single identity from noticeably distinct parts or constituencies. When a constitution is born, the hope (in most fully operative and constitutionalist regimes) is that the text will unite similar or dissimilar peoples and give everyone a common foundation on which to live. Joav Peled referred to the power of some forms of constitutional government as establishing a type of citizenship whereby individuals enjoy the sense that they are contributing to the common good, that they are partners in deciding the collective destiny of the political community.[22] A constitutional founding, therefore, represents the original transformative moment, the commencement (it is hoped) of a polity's unified, and unifying journey.[23]

The most obvious definition of the term "founding" suggests that something was, at least until recently, lost or misplaced. Yet there is another definition of the concept that seems even more consonant with the idea of constitutional order. A founding is a "beginning," a "renaissance," an "origin" of sorts, a "birth." Hassen Ebrahim notes that a "constitution represents a discovery of nationhood because it reflects the soul of the nation."[24] It is the realization that something is adrift or astray and that specific action can set it on a noticeably different path. In the arena of constitutional politics, what was adrift, and what requires discovery, is a country's political identity—its collective character—as manifest not only in what Mandela and Ebrahim referred to as the country's "soul" but also in the precise design of the governmental institutions themselves. When a constitutional document no longer captures the particular identity of a political regime, the time has come for renewal, for finding a new collective identity. Jefferson, of course, thought that such a time came every generation. Other founders, from Madison to Mandela, were less sanguine about frequent constitutional conventions, but even they would admit that once a constitutional text is so out of step with the political ideals of a nation it is time for a constitutional correction. Madison, after all, was one of the more vocal proponents of scrapping the Articles of Confederation—a constitutional text less than a decade old—and replacing it with an original constitutional design.

Notable scholars have wrestled with the principle of constitutional transition. In referring to the United States, Akhil Reed Amar put it best: "The Constitution, after all, was not just a text, but an act—a doing, a constitut*ing*. In the Preamble's performative utterance, 'We the people . . . *do*' alter the old and ordain and establish the new."[25] Amar's point is to suggest that there is something transformative about the adoption of a new constitutional text. The event, or act, itself transforms, and thus creates, a citizenry.

On this point, Walter Murphy is additionally insightful:

> The goal of a constitutional text must . . . be not simply to structure a government, but to construct a political system, one that can guide the formation of a larger constitution, a "way of life" that is conducive to constitutional democracy. If constitu-

tional democracy is to flourish, its ideals must reach beyond formal governmental arrangements and help configure, though not necessarily in the same way or to the same extent, most aspects of its people's lives.[26]

Referring to the constitutional foundings in Eastern Europe, Murphy equates the transition from one constitutional people to the next with a certain degree of complexity: "It is one thing to master academic political science or legislative drafting; it is quite another to convert an entire population into a people who have internalized a new set of attitudes about relations towards government, the state, society, and themselves as citizens, who not only possess rights but are responsible for their own conditions."[27] Frequently, ordinary citizens are not directly involved in the task of constitution making. Even so, they are affected by changes in institutional design and a polity's substantive priorities. Murphy refers to that impact as the act of constitutional "conversion." It is, in short, the act of constitutional "transformation," where an entire people are transformed by the adoption of a new fundamental law.

No matter what one may call it, few would argue that for the past two hundred years constitutional foundings have occurred all over the world, many of which have been successful in constituting a new polity. The transition from the ineffective Articles of Confederation to the newly drafted Constitution of the United States marked not only a change in the design of governance (altering the old) but also a conscious act of rebirth (establishing the new). Similarly, the crafting of new constitutional orders in the former Soviet bloc was (and is) memorable precisely because they were (and are) characterized by more than just a simple institutional shift in authority. New constitutional charters in Eastern Europe resemble old ones in the West. In fact, constitutional framers in these countries anticipated new systems of government, and a noticeably different conception of citizenship has emerged from many of these constitutional foundings. Just one indicator is the increased engagement and participation in civic life of many Eastern Europeans over the past decade.[28] A people do not simply continue unaffected once a new constitutional document is founded or ratified. They are changed by the event just as much as the institutions of government are changed.

Jurispathic and Jurisgenerative Constitutions

To this point, the discussion of constitutional transformation has focused on foundings as single, isolated events. The broad claim has been that one function of modern constitutions is that they both destroy old regimes and create new ones.

Their founding typically represents fixed moments in time, and the documents themselves aspire to reflect some shared consensus about a renewed political order. Although deliberate on my part—as I've noted, any examination of constitutional functionality must begin with the founding moment—such a claim remains underdeveloped. It does not account for the complexity or subtlety of what emerges out of a constitutional transformation. It does not provide a glimpse into the ongoing practice of constitutionalist politics and why those original acts of constitutional destruction and creation continue even after the "founding period." It does not consider those moments in a polity's life when a constitution is so dramatically reconceived as to resemble an entirely new document.

In the remainder of the chapter, therefore, we should consider the following questions: What is the relationship between the original constitutional founding, as a destructive and creative act, and the ongoing practice of politics? Does the violence stop once the immediate responsibility for writing and ratifying the text is completed? How exactly do the newly crafted priorities of a regime dovetail with and/or replace the priorities of the past? What happens when segments of the citizenry do not subscribe to the recently created constitutional vision? Many of the answers to these (and other) questions can be found in the related concepts of jurispathic and jurisgenerative constitutionalism.

Perhaps no scholar was more curious about the transformative power of law than was the late Robert Cover. In his classic foreword to the 1983 *Harvard Law Review*, "Nomos and Narrative," Cover analyzed the relationship between the imperial state and the many insular, or paideic, communities that inhabit the polity. Eschewing the traditional arguments about the supremacy of courts to interpret the law, he maintained that all communities, whether large or small, create their own worlds, their own narratives of legal meaning. Inhabitants of those communities construct stories, in other words, that not only represent their particular collective interpretation of the law but also place their paideic communities within the context of the larger imperial state. He called the process of creating legal narratives "jurisgenesis" and the act of creation "jurisgenerative."

Cover was particularly interested in the delicate balance that exists when the identity, or narrative, of an insular religious community is threatened by the authority of a secular regime. The State, after all, is entitled to its own legal narrative. What happens, he asked, when the way of life of the Old Order Amish in the United States conflicts with the will of state and federal authorities over such subjects as the proper education of children? The Amish represent a distinct, insular community within the larger polity, and they have created their own legal narrative, based entirely on their collective religious convictions, that forbids children from attending public school after they reach a certain age. The State, on the other hand, wants to see all children attend school. And therein lies the tension. Referring specifically to liberal-democratic polities, Cover defines this tension as "the problem of the multiplicity of meaning—the fact that never only one but always many worlds are created by the too fertile forces of jurisgenesis—that leads at once to the imperial virtues and the imperial mode of world maintenance."[29]

In describing scenarios in which differing normative worlds collide, it is clear that Cover was troubled by the capacity of the State to monopolize legal meaning. Insofar as the relationship between political regimes and insular communities is one of unbalanced power, the likelihood that a community like the Amish can perpetuate and maintain its particularistic *nomos* is dubious. Cover argued that it will inevitably succumb to the power of the State, and its narrative will be altered as a result: "Law is a force, like gravity, through which our worlds exercise an influence upon one another, a force that affects the courses of these worlds through normative space."[30] He insisted that this is precisely what happened when Bob Jones University, an evangelical institution of higher learning located in the American South, was forced to alter its policy of refusing to admit unmarried African Americans (and prohibiting interracial dating) in order to avoid losing its tax-exempt status. The state's authority overwhelmed the Christian college and, sadly for Cover, the normative world created by the "citizens" of Bob Jones University was affected.

The Supreme Court was at the center of this clash.[31] Institutions like courts regularly impose their interpretation of law onto paideic communities, but Cover insisted that there is more to it than that: the political institutions of the State seek not only to force their will onto insular communities but also to maintain their coercive power. The process of coercion and maintenance, therefore, is a violent act. "Judges," he writes, "are people of violence."[32] "Because of the violence they command, judges characteristically do not create law, but kill it. Theirs is the jurispathic office. Confronting the luxuriant growth of a hundred legal traditions [or narratives], they assert that *this one* is law and destroy or try to destroy the rest."[33] Every interpretation of the law that somehow interferes with the way an insular community conducts its collective existence, therefore, is an example of state-imposed violence. When Cover references the death of the law, he refers specifically to the destruction of the normative world that is created within sub-polities by their capacity to write their own particular narratives. Rarely is the paideic community able to combat the power of the State, thus permitting Cover to remark that judges often become agents of official violence. Cover argued that "[u]ltimately, it is the state's capacity to tolerate or destroy [the] self-contained *nomos* that dictates the relation of the [paideic] community to its political host."[34]

Cover's analysis of the relationship between violence and the law also applies equally well when we think about fundamental law, about the relationship between new constitutional foundings and the past political identities that are always replaced at the moment of adoption or ratification. To put it plainly, if judges are violent people, then so are founders. Like the judge who alters or even destroys the narrative of the insular community when he refuses to adopt an alternate—or even contrasting—interpretation of the law, the founder does violence both to the regime's past identity (its past narrative) and to those who may still subscribe to it. To borrow from Cover's famous concluding phrase, constitutions "invite new worlds."[35] They create different "normative universes," and the consequence is that the national narrative begins anew. About the American Constitution, he wrote:

> Many of our necessarily uncanonical historical narratives treat the Constitution as foundational—a beginning—and generative of all that comes after. This is true even though the Constitution must compete with natural law, the Declaration of Independence, the Articles of Confederation, and the Revolution itself for primacy in the narrative tradition. Finally, the Constitution is a widespread, though not universally accepted basis for interpretations; it is a center about which many communities teach, learn, and tell stories.[36]

Cover makes two important points in this passage. First, he argues that many view the constitutional document, and thus the founding itself, as marking the beginning of a newly emerging national narrative. The Constitution becomes the plot of the new story while simultaneously replacing the former narrative. Secondly, he notes that by virtue of its central place in the national narrative, the Constitution also significantly informs the *ongoing* narratives of insular and imperial communities. This latest document, because of its foundational position as the fundamental law of the land—indeed, because of its importance as the primary source of political power and authority—will inevitably affect the stories that continue in smaller, more insular sub-polities. It can't be helped; in the world in which we live, very few paideic communities, Cover says, can hide from the reach of the nation's constitutional charter. The narrative force of the Constitution tugs both from above and below.

Perhaps unsuspectingly, the modern penchant to see the written constitutional text as an indispensable tool to announce a country's arrival on the international scene, or as the remedy for achieving a high degree of domestic legiti-macy, has contributed to the ongoing violence against sub-national enclaves. (It is probably appropriate to note that, at last count, close to three-fourths of all the nations of the world have adopted new constitutional texts in the past half-century). There is now a dominant national narrative that is primarily reflective of the interests and values of the country's constitutional framers—often a very small elite.[37] Such a narrative will inevitably alter the legal boundaries of every paideic community that resides within the larger polity. Recognizing this reality, Cover preferred a constitutional design that prioritizes the principle of toler-ance, or that at least permits paideic and imperial communities to coexist. But the prevalence of constitutions more generally as the ultimate source of political power renders the prospect of diminished violence to the traditions of distinct communities unlikely.

At this point it is important to admit the obvious: that a fresh constitutional identity is not meant to suggest that all members of the polity will subscribe to the replaced narrative, that there will be no losers, or that a new constitution will seamlessly reflect the values of a new citizenry—far from it. Different narratives will be born, many of which will arise in direct response to the latest identity of the State. Some narratives, in fact, may persist even after the institutions of the State have tried to destroy them. Certainly, some insular communities will remain mostly untouched by the constitutional transformation, but no paid-eic community will be completely unaffected. And dissent may emerge. In fact, Cover is careful to note that at some level the legal meaning that derives from an insular community, when juxtaposed against that emerging from the State, will always be tinged with hostility. When compared to the narrative of the State, a paideic community's story may be subtly different or it may be dramatically dif-ferent, but it will most certainly be different.

The success of a new constitutional regime depends on the level of commit-ment both the State and the various insular communities have to each other's jurisgenerative authority. That is, a fully operative and constitutionalist text will successfully constitute a population if, on the one hand, the State permits in-sular communities to create their own normative worlds, while, on the other, the paideic communities recognize and accept the right of the State to identify its own overarching *nomos*. There must, in short, be a shared level of commit-ment to the new constitutional narrative. That commitment does not have to be unconditional (consider the case of the Amish in the United States), nor does it have to occur only in liberal-democratic regimes (consider the communitarian example of Israel, where communities of non-Jews are afforded some jurisgenerative power).[38] Nonetheless, a successful constitutional experiment requires, at a minimum, that there be *some* recognition that each population enjoys the power to construct its own legal meaning.

In the end, a commitment to coexistence is a dominant characteristic of most liberal constitutional regimes, but it is not unique to them. To provide but one example, the German Basic Law has been described as a semi-liberal constitutional polity in that many traditionally liberal freedoms are balanced within the constitutional text by equally powerful communitarian principles.[39] And yet the German Basic Law also depends on the acceptance that some sub-polities will exist in relative opposition to the State's primary constitutional interpretation. Of course, such levels of commitment mean that the power of the State is always being tested. The constitution, that is, is always under scrutiny from those insular communities that seek to encourage constitutional destruction. Indeed, the prevention of constitutional revolution requires a somewhat delicate balance between paideic communities and imperial forces.

Cover understood constitutions. He insisted that a constitution will not only affect the citizenry at the moment of founding, creating a new collective identity for the entire polity, but it will continue to influence the various relationships those citizens cultivate within their insular communities and with the larger imperial regime. Thus the continuing influence of the constitutional document on the lives of its citizens mirrors the impact of the original founding moment: an enduring constitution—even one that spans a long period—will most likely be destructive, as in the case of the inescapable conflict surrounding differences in legal meaning or narrative.

Cover's intellectual relationship with constitutions, therefore, is most curious; and yet I think it is the troubled relationship he explores that most accurately reflects the dual nature of the constitutional enterprise. On the one hand, the late scholar was intensely disturbed by the power of constitutional texts. "Revolutionary constitutional understandings are commonly staked in blood," he wrote. "In them, the violence of the law takes its most blatant form."[40] And yet it is equally clear that he admired the positive force of liberal constitutionalism. He was quick to admit that constitutions were inherently creative, especially in their capacity to "generate" distinct paideic and imperial narratives.

In the end, then, Cover knew that violence has multiple meanings in the context of constitutional transformation. Throughout history leaders have resorted to violence, typically in the form of warfare, both to demonstrate a degree of power and, in the more extreme cases, to topple a neighboring regime. But the violence doesn't end there. It continues as long as constitutions (and those institutions that give meaning to the text) occupy a position that encourages the systematic disregard of competing narratives. Violence thus has regularly been used in a variety of ways as a tool to mark political change. The great irony of the first function of a constitutional text—and one that did not escape Robert Cover—is that these instruments are, in many ways, drafted precisely to deter the inevitable: among their many goals is one that aims to regulate the hubris of men, which history demonstrates has so often led to violence and destruction. Because they are written to provide future stability to a new polity, constitutional texts are meant to forestall the destructive capacity of potential constitutional transformations.

CHAPTER THREE

Constitutional Aspiration

☷ ☷ ☷

Robert Cover once remarked that constitutions are "the projection of an imagined future upon reality."[1] Like many contemporary constitutional theorists, he understood that the fundamental charter of a nation is far more nuanced than can be accurately captured by a definition centered predominantly on the text's procedural clauses or its architectural features. The document encapsulates much more than the simple calculation of political authority: which institutions of government will exercise which powers. It includes something less tangible, though no less important: a vision of the future for a specific and collective people.

Of course, Cover was not alone in his assessment of constitutions. Many scholars and jurists have joined him in embracing the idea that a constitutional document includes certain elements that are seemingly less noticeable to students of constitutional theory. Sanford Levinson and Thomas Grey correctly comprehend the subtlety of a constitutional text, referring separately to the American charter as "scripture."[2] So does Keith Whittington, who writes, "The written Constitution is not to be understood merely as a fundamental law structuring and limiting political powers but also as the sacred text of a community of moral and rational individuals. Such a sacred text is concerned with ideals as well as structures."[3] What these and other scholars share in common is the recognition that a constitutional text is not simply a momentary reflection of a particular time; nor is it a collection of dry and uninspiring procedural regulations. It has an enduring quality that is tied directly to the promises made within the text itself, promises that inform what we might call the "spirit" of the document.[4] Sometimes those promises are obvious, as in the case of the constitutional text that highlights its aspirations in sections such as "preambles," and "introductions." Sometimes the promises are less noticeable, especially when they are embedded within the often technical and mundane structure of the text itself. Some constitutions, like Canada's original 1867 draft, even define the polity's values through the comparative *absence* of aspirational statements. Modern constitutions, however, articulate some ambitions; they explicitly or implicitly outline the future goals of the polity, and in so doing, identify an aspirational vision for the polity itself. Indeed, the second function of the modern constitutionalist text is that it imagines a normative political society—a brighter political future—and then, if successful, it helps to bring about that envisioned community.

Defining Constitutional Aspiration

Before turning immediately to the intangible realm of theory, perhaps a simple definition is in order. What is meant by *constitutional aspiration*? To aspire is to seek to achieve something greater than what one presently has. While we typically think of aspirations as involving personal dreams and goals, institutions—like the text itself or the convention of constitutional designers charged with drafting or altering the text—can also aspire to something greater. Framers of constitutions around the world and over many generations have long believed that their mission is an inherently aspirational one: there is perhaps no greater reason to convene than to contemplate the appropriate constitutional design to help deliver a more promising future. More importantly, modern framers aspire to create a document that will instill confidence both at home and abroad in the institutions of the polity. Those framers have long insisted that a written constitutional text can help pave the way for a greater collective existence. Set out the rules prior to the birth of a new or reconstituted nation, and you maximize the possibility that ordered and stable political institutions will advance the particular ideals or values of that polity.

That is why in so many cases the constitutional text has a self-referential quality: these documents refer to themselves as the means to achieve a desired end. The U.S. Constitution is self-referential when it states in its preamble that "*in order* to form a more perfect union," we the people, "*do* ordain and establish *this* Constitution." Borrowing again from Akhil Amar's point about the active quality of the American draft: "The Constitution, after all, was not just a text, but an act—a doing, a constitut*ing*."[5] The same is true of the Polish constitution, whose preamble also embraces the principle that the constitutional text is an important means to achieve a brighter future. In fact, a shared belief that a constitutional document can be a vital part of a journey to a "more perfect" polity is a key component of any constitution-making and ratification process.

Gary Jacobsohn (to whom we are indebted for the phrase "constitutional aspiration") describes the progressive characteristics of all constitutional texts: "Common to the [constitution] is a conception, implicitly or explicitly incorporated in the document, of the kind of polity the constitution seeks to preserve and to become. This conception, or vision, will consist of a mix of attributes reflecting what is distinctive in the political culture as well as what are taken to be shared features of a universal culture of constitutionalism."[6] In an earlier treatment of the same subject, Jacobsohn uses the prism of Lincoln's disagreement with the Supreme Court decision in *Dred Scott v. Sandford* (1857) to comment on the scope of constitutional aspirations, insisting that the values embedded within the American constitutional text are both substantive and procedural. What is largely missing from contemporary scholarship, Jacobsohn further suggests, is an understanding that constitutional aspirations exist independent of institutions like the judiciary that give the text its primary meaning.[7] He concludes that modern constitutions, regardless of institutional attempts to interpret them, are "committed to the achievement of things seemingly beyond [their] immediate reach."[8]

In defining those qualities that give constitutions an aspirational dimension, Jacobsohn reminds us of two important considerations. First, he insists that all constitutions are imperfect. Because they set goals that are "beyond the [polity's] reach," constitutions unavoidably create gaps between the actual, or the present political reality, and the ideal, or the constitutional promise.[9] Second, he remarks that constitutional aspirations are in some sense particularist; they reflect the specific ideals and values of a distinctive political culture. Both considerations are essential to an understanding of constitutional aspiration. By definition, to aspire to something is to realize that one has not yet arrived, that one has yet to achieve the desired goal or state of perfection. Similarly, the particularist qualities embedded in each constitutional design force us to conclude that there may be a variety of ways to attain political progress. No two paths to political utopia are precisely alike. The aspirational statements of many constitutional charters may sound similar, and the use of the constitutional document to launch the journey may now be common, but the details of the attempt to realize a polity's primary aspirations will be influenced by very specific and altogether unique forces.

Scholars have occasionally borrowed the metaphor of the "promissory note," made famous by Martin Luther King's "I Have A Dream" speech, to further describe the aspirational qualities of a constitutional text.[10] The text is a promise to future generations. Keith Whittington, for example, describes the American text as a promissory note and then extrapolates on that one illustration to draw notable conclusions about the character of many constitutional charters.[11] There is a fundamental difference, he writes, between the essence of an unwritten text and that of a written document. The former permits—even encourages—the unconstrained development of aspirational principles throughout the life of the polity, whereas the latter—the written text—insists that the developing values or visions of a nation be made somehow consonant with "previously assumed fundamentals." In other words, a written constitution requires some awareness of its heritage and tradition; the polity's evolving aspirations will be deemed legitimate only if they account for the promises that were made at earlier moments in time.

The act of writing a constitution, therefore, commences a metaphorical dialogue between text and citizen (and future generations) about the pursuit of political perfection. Obvious questions that arise during this dialogue are: What will it take for this collective citizenry to reach a higher plane of political perfection? How might the polity achieve the ideal? What place do the values and aspirations of prior generations or founding principles have in this dialogue? Whittington calls the dialogue a "quest": "Once written, the constitutional text becomes a 'promise,' a promise by the people to their represented, and necessarily ideal, 'collective character.' Having committed itself to writing," Whittington continues, "the nation begins a quest to overcome itself, to become the perfect state represented in the text."[12]

Though Whittington and others are correct to insist that the *entire* constitutional document is a promissory note and that the constitutional text as a whole commences the polity's quest toward political perfection, there are locations within the standard charter where the expressed aspirations are more obvious. In particular, constitutional framers around the world now see preambles and bills of rights as logical places to make aspirational declarations and grand promises. This chapter is primarily an examination of these two forms.

Constitutional Preambles

It is interesting to note that although the word *preamble* dates back to the fourteenth century—where it literally meant "to walk before"—most early constitutions did not describe clauses at the beginning of the text identifying the reasons for adoption as "preambles." The early state constitutions of the American colonial period included introductory statements, but those statements were not self-consciously identified as preambles.[13] Neither was the famous introductory announcement in the U.S. Constitution called a preamble. It was not until well into the nineteenth century that constitutional framers began specifically and self-consciously referring to the introductory clauses as "preambles." Today, virtually every newly minted constitution includes a preamble, and only rarely do those documents actually omit the term from the general structure of the text itself.

Contemporary constitutional preambles are curious statements. Filled with exalted language and promises of a better tomorrow, these statements precede the more technical components of a constitutional design. They appear first, and thus they might arguably be considered the most important section of any modern constitutional text. After all, preambles are typically the portion of a traditional constitutional draft where the polity articulates its most important aims and objectives. It is the place, in other words, where constitutional framers proclaim their principal intentions, where they communicate their deepest aspirations for the newly created polity. Capturing the essential quality and importance of the text's introduction, a "Native of Virginia" wrote in 1788 that the preamble "is the Key of the Constitution."[14] Joseph Story echoed those sentiments almost a half-century later when he remarked, "It is an admitted maxim in the ordinary course of the administration of justice, that the preamble of a [constitution] is a key to open the mind of the makers, as to the mischiefs, which are to be remedied, and the objects, which are to be accomplished by the provisions of the [text]."[15]

The U.S. Constitution begins with the familiar phrase, "We the People," and continues by identifying the half-dozen or so goals that the Constitution promises to advance. Included in that list are vows to promote the principles of Liberty, Tranquility, and Justice, all in an effort to "form a more perfect Union." The aspirations acknowledged by the framers as most important include the obvious ones—freedom, the common defense, the general welfare, and so on—but they are certainly not the only ones. The announcement that the text derives from "the people of the United States" is, itself, an aspirational statement.[16] It signals a change in the nature of sovereignty as well as a shift in the organizational structure of the thirteen independent states. The locus of power, in other words, was transferred from the people of the several states to the people of the United States. At its most basic level, therefore, the simple statement that begins the Preamble represents a belief—a belief in a radically new design for governance. For that reason, it also represents a hope. What makes the statement so bold and yet so hopeful is that the framers enjoyed little assurance that the ratifying populace would accept such a transfer of authority.

More recently drafted constitutions have also used introductory language to convey a polity's aspirational goals. Eastern Europe represents the busiest recent laboratory in terms of setting constitutional aims. The Bulgarian constitution, for one, speaks of a "desire to express the will of the people of Bulgaria, by pledging loyalty to the universal human values of liberty, peace, humanism, equality, justice and tolerance; by elevating as the uppermost principle the rights, dignity and security of the individual, in awareness of our irrevocable duty to guard the national and state integrity of Bulgaria." The Polish and the Czech constitutions articulate similar themes, touching on both universal values and objectives that are quite specific to each individual polity. Each constitution's preamble tells a story of oppression, details the scope of liberty and equality, and embraces the idea of the text as an instrument to achieve meaningful political and social reform.

Consider the example of a single non-Western constitution, that of Cambodia. It is cited here because it so clearly illustrates those themes that are now common among contemporary constitutional documents. The Cambodian constitution uses its preamble to tell the story of the nation's decline over the past several decades and the constitution's importance in reversing that trend:

We, the people of Cambodia;

Accustomed to having been an outstanding civilization, a prosperous, large, flourishing and glorious nation, with high prestige radiating like a diamond;

Having declined grievously during the past two decades, having gone through suffering and destruction, and having been weakened terribly;

Having awakened and resolutely rallied and determined to unite for the consolidation of national unity, the preservation and defense of Cambodia's territory and precious sovereignty and the fine Angkor civilization, and the restoration of Cambodia into an "Island of Peace" based on multi-party liberal democratic responsibility for the nation's future destiny of moving toward perpetual progress, development, prosperity, and glory;

With this resolute will;

We inscribe the following as the Constitution of the Kingdom of Cambodia.

The preamble to the Cambodian constitution, like so many others, is intended to inspire, to identify constitutive bonds, and to provide a clear beacon for those who have been granted the authority to navigate the polity's political course. For that reason, it is indispensable.

And yet the actual legal influence of modern preambles is dubious. Preambles are rarely, if ever, used as authoritative legal doctrine. Courts around the world typically view them more as mission statements than as binding legal promises, and thus those who seek their aid in actual litigation are often disappointed. Sotirios Barber is correct, then, when he notes that "preambles are not applied to facts in ways that directly help settle lawsuits."[17] The U.S. Supreme Court has similarly suggested that preambles to state legislation—and, by implication, state constitutions—should be considered as expressing nothing more than a state's particular value preferences.[18] They are often broad declarations of general political goals and not specific clauses aimed at resolving specific political disputes. Precisely because of the preamble's comparative lack of enforcement power, a polity should have greater liberty there than in the rest of the constitutional text to proclaim unorthodox or controversial aims. If a political regime wishes to declare a stance on a particular issue, the Court seems to be saying, it is the preamble that provides the most powerful and effective vehicle.

Before we dismiss constitutional preambles as mere rhetoric, however, we ought to consider their effect on the interpretation of the entire document. If it is true that preambles reveal a polity's primary ends, then is it right, we may ask, to assume that political officials seek the guidance of these words in the practice of constitutional interpretation? Do courts use preambles and other aspirational statements as touchstones for the difficult task of deciphering vague constitutional clauses? Should they? Barber, Whittington, Jacobsohn, and others certainly think so. Barber writes that preambles should not be "excluded from a theory of constitutional meaning on [the] grounds that they are not laws."[19] Rather, they form a part of the constitutional whole and should be read as including important explanatory language. They inform the rest of the document insofar as they declare the polity's most important aspirations. Consequently, their impact extends far beyond the sometimes-lofty character of their words.

Preambles serve important civic lessons as well. The aspirational qualities of constitutions often begin with reference to the past. It seems unnecessary to repeat the primary thesis of the last chapter—that one of the principal functions of the modern constitution is that it destroys a previous polity and creates a new one—but it is important to recognize that the vision embedded within a new constitutional document is always closely tied to the events that prompted a constitutional change in the first place. In other words, the aspirations of a fresh constitutional design are inevitably informed by the faults and mistakes of the past. The French Constitution of 1791, which endorses the central tenets of the French Revolution, is one of the most striking examples. It begins,

> The representatives of the French people, organized in National Assembly, considering that ignorance, forgetfulness or contempt of the rights of man, are the sole causes of the public miseries and of the corruption of governments, have resolved to set forth in a solemn declaration the natural, inalienable, and sacred rights of

man, in order that this declaration, being present to all members of the social body, may unceasingly remind them of their rights and their duties.[20]

In this illustration, the constitutional document is meant not only to signal the abandonment of a regime best known for its abusive tendencies but also to act as a constant reminder of the specific vision embraced by the founding generation, a vision based on different conceptions of sovereignty, equality, and rights.

Common Themes

Over the past two centuries, many of the world's constitutional preambles have taken on a decidedly similar tone. That is, certain general themes now regularly appear in constitutional preambles, especially in those that accompany texts drafted and ratified in the last fifty years. To be sure, most constitutional preambles still embrace some form of what we might define as universal human values: freedom, liberty, equality, justice, and democracy. Many introductory statements also repeatedly reference God and/or the regime's particular religious heritage, a practice that began with premodern constitutional forms (the Magna Carta, for example) but that became quite standard in the late eighteenth and early nineteenth centuries.

Yet despite these broad parallels with preambles of the past, it is fair to conclude that current constitutional preambles look a good deal different than earlier ones. They have increasingly begun to include some reference, for instance, to the polity's dysfunctional or troubled past. In some cases, those references even rise to the level of narratives, describing in great detail the woes of the country's historical legacy. Contemporary preambles also mention the country's sense of nationalistic pride in overcoming those difficulties. Embedded in the sense of pride is a commitment to national identity that sometimes appears in isolation and sometimes is coupled with a vow to participate actively and responsibly in the community of nation-states. Relatedly, a number of preambles drafted recently also include a powerful statement of self-determination. The Estonian constitution, for instance, begins by declaring an "unwavering faith" and an "unswerving will to safeguard a state which is established on the inextinguishable right of the Estonian people to national self-determination." All three of these common themes are in a sense aspirational. Together, they denote a polity aiming to fulfill its highest ambitions.

Before exploring these specific similarities, it may be useful to draw at least one more general conclusion about the current state of modern constitutional preambles. Noteworthy when reviewing the present character of constitutional charters is that the development of preambles seems over time to mirror a similar development in the texts themselves: the preambles, like the drafts that follow, are far more detailed than they used to be. More scarce now are the preambles that rely exclusively on broad and expansive generalities, the ones that resemble the ideals expressed in the comparatively brief introduction to the U.S. Constitution. References to the values and aspirations of the polity, even if they echo earlier preambles, are spelled out in language far more specific, and far more elaborate, than the language used to craft preambles in the eighteenth and nineteenth centuries. Compare, for example, the preamble to the 1990 Mozambican constitution, with its multiple paragraphs and particularistic historical details, with the brevity and scope of the U.S. Constitution's preamble.[21] Many of the ideas are the same, but the wording of the Mozambican charter is more vivid. The preamble to that document reads:

> At zero hours on 25 June 1975, the Central Committee of the Mozambique Liberation Front (FRELIMO) solemnly proclaimed the total and complete independence of Mozambique and its establishment as the People's Republic of Mozambique.
>
> This was the culmination of a centuries long process of resistance to colonial rule. It was the unforgettable victory of the armed national liberation struggle, led by FRELIMO, which united, under the same ideals of freedom, unity, justice and progress, patriots from all levels of Mozambican society.
>
> The Constitution, as then proclaimed, recognized the determinant role of FRELIMO as the legitimate representative of the Mozambican people. Under its leadership, the process of the exercise of state power as an expression of the people's will was begun.
>
> The State that we created has made it possible for the Mozambican people to strengthen democracy and, for the first time in its history, to exercise political power and to organize and direct social and economic affairs at a national level.
>
> The experience of the operation of State institutions and the exercise of democracy by citizens has created the need for change and new definitions.
>
> After 15 years of independence, the Mozambican people, in the exercise of their inalienable right to sovereignty and determined to consolidate the nation's unity and to respect the dignity of all Mozambicans, adopts and proclaims this Constitution, which shall be the fundamental law for all political and social organization in the Republic of Mozambique.

The fundamental rights and freedoms enshrined in the Constitution are the
achievements of the Mozambican people's struggle to build a society of social
justice, where the equality of citizens and the rule of law are the pillars of
democracy.

We, the Mozambican people, determined to strengthen our country's political
order, in a spirit of responsibility and pluralism of opinion, have decided to
organize society in such a way that the will of the citizens shall be the most
important precept of our sovereignty.

The Mozambican preamble, like that of the United States, speaks of grand
ideals like justice, freedom, and peace, but it does so within a very particularistic
frame. It also articulates these values within the context of a detailed historical
narrative, even going so far as to embed the literal date of independence within
the constitutional document. Such is the way of many constitutional preambles—and many constitutional texts—drafted in the twentieth century.

The expansion of constitutional preambles is a symptom of a particular view
of contemporary constitutional engineering, one that sees the public text as a
considerable force in resisting the rise of tyranny, especially within a world where
many eyes are watching. This view might be characterized as a consequence of a
powerful belief in the principle of constitutionalism, combined with an equally
powerful recognition that oppression will be met with international condemnation. Contemporary framers appear to have more faith in the strength of the
constitutional text as a public pronouncement, but less faith in the good will
of government officials. The result is often a constitutional document that tries
to anticipate any potential for government abuse, one that is so detailed and
lengthy as to resemble a treatise rather than a charter. Fewer and fewer framers
are following the advice, espoused most famously by Chief Justice John Marshall in *McCulloch v. Maryland* (1819), that the nature of a constitution "requires
[only that] its great outlines should be marked, its important objects designated,
and the minor ingredients which compose those objects be deduced from the
nature of the objects themselves."[22] It seems that with constitutions, bigger is
now better.

The same is often true with preambles. Consider, for example, the South African constitution, which is (to put it mildly) lengthy. The constitutional charter
itself has fourteen chapters, 243 sections, and more than 1000 separate clauses.
The official reprint of the constitution, released by the South African government
immediately following the ratification of the text, is a full 187 pages in length. The
document's preamble, while perhaps not as lengthy, is similarly detailed, cover-

ing themes ranging from an ugly racial past to universal human rights, from the virtue of representative democracy to the need for collective healing. The South African constitution begins,

> We, the people of South Africa,
> Recognise the injustices of our past;
> Honour those who suffered for justice and freedom in our land;
> Respect those who have worked to build and develop our country; and
> Believe that South Africa belongs to all who live in it, united in our diversity.
> We therefore, through our freely elected representatives, adopt this Constitution
>   as the supreme law of the Republic so as to -
> Heal the divisions of the past and establish a society based on democratic values,
>   social justice and fundamental human rights;
> Lay the foundations for a democratic and open society in which government is
>   based on the will of the people and every citizen is equally protected by law;
> Improve the quality of life of all citizens and free the potential of each person; and
> Build a united and democratic South Africa able to take its rightful place as a
>   sovereign state in the family of nations.

Notably, the South African constitution and its preamble have been described as one of several paradigm examples created because of this "global faith" in the principle of constitutional limits. Heinz Klug refers to the pressure experienced by South African constitutional framers as they entered into deliberations for a new constitutional order.[23] That pressure, he notes, centered on the need to embrace "globalizing constitutionalism," or the practice of nation-states to use the mechanism of constitutional limitation not only to structure and organize the internal polity but also to gain a degree of international credibility. South African framers needed to announce to the world that what they were undertaking merited universal respect; they needed to convince the international community that the replacement of apartheid with a more inclusive political system would work. The drafting of a constitutional document represented an essential first step in that process. So was the message espoused in the constitution's introductory statement. The constitutional preamble, Klug says, is an important part of that overall legitimacy project: it articulates those standards to which the rest of the document endeavors to reach, including standards like democracy and justice that were largely missing from South Africa's past.

Reference to Historical Abuses

The South African constitution and its preamble effectively illustrate the recent trend among contemporary framers to favor specific details over sweeping generalities in the construction of constitutional clauses. The introduction to the South African constitution is also a good illustration of the related tendency of contemporary preambles to reflect the missteps of the past. In fact, many constitutions (especially in the developing world) espouse elaborate tales of woe, filled with vivid descriptions of oppression, inequity, political tyranny, scandal, corruption, ethnic, religious, and/or regional conflict. These narratives embedded within the constitutional text—and typically as part of the text's preamble—are often used to frame the drafters' vision for a new political order where none of the previous maltreatment will recur. They serve the dual purpose of justifying the need for a new constitutional text to mark an important transition away from the problems of the past and providing a glimmer of hope that a reconstituted polity will somehow lead to a better life. Once again, consider a non-Western and slightly extreme example. The former Congolese constitution, adopted in March 1992, identifies the dominant visionary principles of the regime and yet simultaneously places them within the context of a long history of political abuse.[24] The text begins with this preamble:

> Unity, Work, Progress, Justice, Dignity, Liberty, Peace, Prosperity, and Love for the Fatherland have been, since independence, notably under mono-partyism, hypothesized or retarded by totalitarianism, the confusion of authorities, nepotism, ethnocentrism, regionalism, social inequalities, and violations of fundamental rights and liberties. Intolerance and political violence have strongly grieved the country, maintained and accrued the hate and divisions between the different communities that constitute the Congolese nation. Consequently, We, the Congolese People, concerned to: create a new political order, a decentralized State where morality, law, liberty, pluralist democracy, equality, social justice, fraternity, and the general well-being reign…order and establish for the Congo the present Constitution.

Statements like this one found in Congo's 1992 charter are inherently optimistic. The message of these accounts seems to be that the constitutional text will cure all—or at least most—of the country's political ills. Other preambles echo these same sentiments. Perhaps the most famous recent example of a constitutional document that articulates a clear aspirational vision deriving from the tragedies of the regime's political past can be found in Poland's constitution. The preamble to the 1997 Polish constitution refers to the break with the former

Soviet Union as an important historical moment. It also references the country's long struggle for independence, its "thousand year heritage," the "best traditions" of previous Polish regimes, and the considerable "labors" of Poland's ancestors, as things worthy of constitutional mention. Most interesting, perhaps, is the preamble's implicit reference to the Holocaust. The framers deliberately included a declaration that the constitutional text is an important vehicle meant to "[bind] in community [the regime's] compatriots dispersed throughout the world." The entire preamble, in fact, is charged with emotion:

> Having regard for the existence and future of our Homeland, Which recovered, in 1989, the possibility of a sovereign and democratic determination of its fate,
> We, the Polish Nation - all citizens of the Republic,
> Both those who believe in God as the source of truth, justice, good and beauty,
> As well as those not sharing such faith but respecting those universal values as arising from other sources,
> Equal in rights and obligations towards the common good - Poland,
> Beholden to our ancestors for their labors, their struggle for independence achieved at great sacrifice, for our culture rooted in the Christian heritage of the Nation and in universal human values,
> Recalling the best traditions of the First and the Second Republic,
> Obliged to bequeath to future generations all that is valuable from our over one thousand years' heritage, Bound in community with our compatriots dispersed throughout the world,
> Aware of the need for cooperation with all countries for the good of the Human Family,
> Mindful of the bitter experiences of the times when fundamental freedoms and human rights were violated in our Homeland,
> Desiring to guarantee the rights of the citizens for all time, and to ensure diligence and efficiency in the work of public bodies,
> Recognizing our responsibility before God or our own consciences,
> Hereby establish this Constitution of the Republic of Poland as the basic law for the State, based on respect for freedom and justice, cooperation between the public powers, social dialogue as well as on the principle of aiding in the strengthening the powers of citizens and their communities.
> We call upon all those who will apply this Constitution for the good of the Third Republic to do so paying respect to the inherent dignity of the person, his or her right to freedom, the obligation of solidarity with others, and respect for these principles as the unshakeable foundation of the Republic of Poland.

Historical references are now commonly found within the expressions of contemporary constitutional preambles. The principle of constitutional aspiration, therefore, has taken on a decidedly particularistic flavor in recent years. Those universal values that often encompassed the entire introduction to constitutional texts of the eighteenth and nineteenth centuries—again, such values as freedom, liberty, justice, and equality—are still present, but now they are more likely framed within a historical narrative that aims to remind political leaders, citizens of the polity, and the world community of the various abuses that plague the regime's past. Contemporary constitutional framers apparently believe that the path to greater freedom or a higher sense of justice must begin with the process of constitutional cleansing. Thus the constitution becomes the country's symbol of optimism and renewal, what Nelson Mandela referred to as a country's "rebirth." Indeed, the promises of a brighter future are made more credible by referring to a dismal, or at least more difficult, past.

National Identity and International Responsibility

The use of constitutional preambles to announce a clean break from an oppressive tradition has also prompted powerful declarations of national identity.[25] Both the Cambodian and Mozambican preambles, above, separately reference their country's fierce sense of pride as one reason for the birth of their individual constitutional orders. In particular, the Cambodian constitution describes, with unusually emotive language, the decline and revival of a once "outstanding civilization," a civilization that, in the words of the framers, "radiates like a diamond." The source of pride captured in the words and phrases of the Cambodian constitution relates directly to that country's emergence from the grip of a brutal dictatorship. The document implies that the population's survival of more than two decades of the cruelest possible leadership is something for all to celebrate. It is also something to announce to the world. The scope of our tragedy, Cambodians claim, warrants inclusion in the regime's most important and most visible public document. It would not be enough simply to condemn the atrocities of the past through ordinary legislative decree or simple executive order. Placing the message in the fundamental law lends greater force and credibility to its meaning. The same intention can be discerned when viewing the Mozambican constitutional text.

The preamble to the 1946 French Constitution is stylistically similar. Although not specifically about independence or dictatorships, it speaks of the sense of dignity that country experienced by assisting allied forces in the victory over

German oppression. The preamble's introductory passage also articulates an important yet subtle message of moral exceptionalism: the constitutional text—the country's primary public document—celebrates tangible distinctions between French citizens and citizens of other countries. "In the morrow of the victory achieved by the free peoples over the regimes that had sought to enslave and degrade humanity," the translated preamble begins, "the people of France proclaim anew that each human being, without distinction of race, religion or creed, possesses sacred and inalienable rights." Tied to statements in the preamble regarding French military success, therefore, is an interesting effort to distinguish that country's moral compass from the misguided view of morality found in those countries that engaged in the evil of genocide. What is notable is that there appears to be an implicit attempt to disassociate the French perspective on the dignity and equality of all citizens from the morally unjustified policies pursued by political officials just across the border. We are distinct from our neighbors to the east, seems to be the point of the constitutional preamble.

Since World War II, a number of drafted constitutional texts, especially those in Eastern Europe, have included language that not only articulates the distinctiveness of the particular regime but also includes statements acknowledging the place of the polity within the international community of sovereign states. These preambles include important claims of national identity and pride, but they also concede the polity's responsibility to other countries. Consider the preamble to the 1992 Constitution for the Czech Republic:

> We, the citizens of the Czech Republic in Bohemia, Moravia, and Silesia, at the time of the renewal of an independent Czech state, being loyal to all good traditions of the ancient statehood of Czech Crown's Lands and the Czechoslovak State, resolved to build, protect and develop the Czech Republic in the spirit of the inviolable values of human dignity and freedom, as the home of equal and free citizens who are conscious of their duties towards others and their responsibility towards the whole, as a free and democratic state based on the respect for human rights and the principles of civic society, as part of the family of European and world democracies, resolved to jointly protect and develop the inherited natural and cultural, material and spiritual wealth, resolved to abide by all time-tried principles of a law-observing state, through our freely elected representatives, adopt this Constitution of the Czech Republic.

The Czech constitution admits to some role as part of "the family of European and world democracies." That particular section of the preamble is informed by previous passages that emphasize the country's commitment to human rights, civil society, democracy, and human dignity. Other constitutions have echoed those same connections. The preamble to the Constitution of Ireland is even more explicit in acknowledging a role for the country in the community of nations. It speaks of the duty to establish "concord with other nations." It further admits to the importance of individual freedom, social order, and national unity. The Polish preamble is another example. It underscores the state's interests in "cooperat[ing] with all countries for the good of the Human Family." The Slovakian constitution, adopted in 1992, is a fourth example. That document highlights the need for Slovakia to maintain "lasting peaceful cooperation with other democratic states."

A closer inspection of the events that gave rise to the recent constitutional transformations in Eastern and Central Europe seems to confirm commitments to both internal and external constituencies. Jon Elster insists that the constitution-making process in the region is a "gigantic natural experiment" because the polities of Eastern Europe are neither "too similar nor too different" to derail a comprehensive comparative analysis.[26] One similarity demonstrated in the language of several Eastern and Central European constitutional preambles (and one that Elster does not mention) involves the statements alluding to one's responsibility to the community of nations. There are likely two reasons for the common tone of these passages. First, it is probable that some commitment to international responsibility is derivative of the type of "global" pressure Klug identifies in the South African experiment.[27] There are models of constitutional documents that are hard to ignore, especially those from neighbors directly across the border. Once one Eastern European constitution was drafted that included reference to "the family of European and world democracies" (as the Czech constitution did early on), others saw it in their national interest to follow suit.[28] The second reason, while related to the first, is a bit more cynical. There is little doubt that the former Soviet states are all scrambling to establish greater economic, political, and cultural connections to Western European regimes. This attempt comes at the same time that these countries seek to sever (or at least weaken) whatever ties still remain with Russia. The thinking among constitutional framers is: What better way to announce the Europeanization of a newly independent state than to textualize it in the constitutional preamble? The force and credibility of the constitutional document, they insist, advances particular aspirational goals of the polity in ways that other political mechanisms simply cannot. Constitutionalizing one's obligation to others seemingly makes the commitment more credible.

Self-determination

A country's confessed duty to participate economically, politically, environmentally, and morally in the community of nations has also led directly to the incorporation of self-conscious expressions of sovereignty within a polity's public charter. More and more constitutional preambles, in other words, are including explicit statements of independent self-determination. Obviously, many of the former Soviet bloc countries were quick to embrace the principle of sovereign rule and self-determination in their constitutional preambles. A long history of foreign control will do that to a recently independent state.[29] The proclamation in the Estonian constitution, above, is perhaps the most forceful, but the general sentiment expressed in that document is widely shared within the region. Article III of the Slovene constitution notes that the country is "founded on the permanent and inalienable right of the Slovene nation to self-determination." The 1994 Constitution for the newly independent Republic of Belarus begins with an interesting statement, drawing not only on the issue of national sovereignty but broadly on all of the themes discussed in this chapter:

> We, the People of the Republic of Belarus, emanating from the responsibility for
>   the present and future of Belarus;
> recognizing ourselves as a subject, with full rights, of the world community and
>   confirming our adherence to values common to all mankind;
> founding ourselves on our inalienable right to self-determination;
> supported by the centuries-long history of development of Belarusian statehood;
> striving to assert the rights and freedoms of every citizen of the Republic of
>   Belarus;
> desiring to maintain civic harmony, stable foundations of democracy, and a state
>   based on the rule of law;
> hereby adopt this Constitution as the Basic Law of the Republic of Belarus.

There are, of course, similar examples of sovereignty claims in constitutional texts that order polities outside of Eastern Europe. The preamble to the 1992 Spanish constitution mirrors those in the former Soviet satellite states. It includes specific reference to the "exercise of [the country's] sovereignty," the standard protections of human rights, democratic principles, and justice; a commitment to fostering the different "cultures, traditions, languages, and institutions" of Spain; and the "strengthening of peaceful relations and effective cooperation among all the peoples of the earth." The third clause of the Turkish constitution's preamble, originally adopted in 1982 under military rule but later amended in 2001 to reflect the first stage of constitutional and political reforms, sounds similar: "The understanding of the absolute supremacy of the will of the nation and of the fact that sovereignty is vested fully and unconditionally in the Turkish nation and that no individual or body empowered to exercise this sovereignty in the name of the nation shall deviate from liberal democracy and the legal system instituted according to its requirements."

Claims of sovereignty within constitutional documents are not surprising when one considers how texts in the past half-century have become a regime's primary calling card. Scholars have remarked that one primary function of the constitutional text in the modern era is to announce publicly the existence of an independent nation.[30] It is a rite of passage of sorts for a political regime to proclaim its arrival on the international scene by endorsing a constitutional text. Declarations of sovereignty, therefore, do not have to be explicitly mentioned in the constitutional document for there to be some tangible recognition of self-determination. The simple existence of a drafted and ratified constitutional charter—marking a transformation from a prior political world to a new one—is often enough for a country to declare its sovereign statehood.

Positive Rights

The promise of positive rights (also known as "welfare rights") has entered the imagination of constitutional framers lately. These claims, which differ dramatically from the traditional view of rights guarantees as principally *limitations* on the power of government, belong to the broader discussion of constitutional aspiration because they represent a particular type of constitutional promise, another style of promissory note, if you will. Most are not subtle. A guarantee of universal healthcare or the assurance of future employment surely makes a powerful statement when it is lodged alongside guarantees of free speech and freedom of conscience within a constitution's list of individual rights. This is especially true when we consider the importance modern polities place on bills of rights—they are often viewed now as the nucleus of the modern constitutional instrument. These promises are not abstract in the way that expressions of a polity's commitment to principles like justice, equality, and freedom are. Either the polity delivers on its promise or it does not. And yet in some sense positive rights are no different than codifying the general aspirations of a political society in the constitution's preamble. They too represent promises made to present and future generations.

Over the past half-century, a number of constitutional charters have embraced the idea of positive rights.[31] These assertions of positive rights typically take many forms, but they inevitably revolve around certain standard topics. Article 25 of the Japanese constitution is a unique example. Its broad language asserts, "All people shall have the right to maintain the minimum standards of healthy and cultured living." More commonly found, though, are the more specific guarantees of access to healthcare, social security, housing, education, travel, employment, and environmental safety. A standard protection of economic rights, for example, might resemble the one found in the Argentine constitution. Chapter I, Section 14, clause 1 of that charter stipulates, "Labor in its several forms shall be protected by law, which shall ensure to workers: dignified and equitable working conditions; limited working hours; paid rest and vacations; fair remuneration; minimum vital and adjustable wage; equal pay for equal work; participation in the profits of enterprises, with control of production and collaboration in the management; protection against arbitrary dismissal; stability of the civil servant; free and democratic labor union organizations recognized by the mere registration in a special record."

The South African constitution's list of freedoms is remarkably aspirational. All rights guarantees in the South African text were drafted in the positive tense. From Chapter II, Article 19, which protects individuals exercising their "political choices," through Chapter II, Article 35, which protects individuals' due process rights, successive articles defend the right to citizenship, movement and residence, trade, occupation and profession, labor relations, the environment, property, housing, health care, food, water, social security, children, education, language and culture, cultural, religious and linguistic communities, access to information, just administrative action, and access to courts. Every single clause of every single article in the South African bill of rights is written in positive form.

Recognizing positive rights in a constitutional document begins with a subtle understanding of prose. There is a noticeable difference in the character of an individual right when it is framed by language encouraging the polity's institutions to *ensure* the substance of the right, as compared to the character of negative rights, which simply insists that the polity's institutions *not interfere* with the exercise of those freedoms. In other words, the language of positive rights is distinct from the language of negative rights in that the former is distinguished by an affirmative grant of freedom, while the latter is more accurately characterized by a limitation on the power of government.

The traditional understanding of rights is that their primary function is to remove certain choices from the often insensitive (and sometimes oppressive) will of majorities. In the words of Justice Robert Jackson, "The very purpose of a Bill of Rights was to withdraw certain subjects from the vicissitudes of political controversy, to place them beyond the reach of majorities and officials and to establish them as legal principles to be applied to the courts."[32] Historically, creating space for individual freedom by self-consciously constraining the power of political actors has been the favored mechanism for identifying rights. Positive rights, which take a fundamentally different approach to the creation of individual space, also help to constrain the power of political officials. And yet they do something more: they seemingly empower majorities (through their representatives in government) to actively secure specified freedoms. The nature of the tone of positive rights seems to mandate that these same political officials take affirmative steps to ensure that freedoms are not only protected but also distributed. If negative rights can be described as claims *against* the state, positive rights should be described as pledges *by* the state.

Take the right to free speech as an example. In Canada's constitution, that freedom, like all others, is expressed as a positive right. Article II, Section B of the Canadian Charter of Rights and Freedoms states, "Everyone has the following fundamental freedoms: freedom of thought, belief, opinion and expression, including freedom of the press and other media of communication." Ownership of the right is directed at the individual; each citizen, the clause admits, is entitled to a certain amount of space to disseminate reasonable or outlandish messages. The First Amendment to the U.S. Constitution, by contrast, speaks not of individual ownership of the right but of the government's inability to restrict the right to free speech. Accordingly, the same right of free speech is expressed as a negative freedom: "Congress shall make *no* law...abridging the freedom of speech." The space to express outlandish messages is still created, but it is done so by very different means. In other words, the right to free speech in each country amounts to roughly the same entitlement, but the manifestation of that right—of how that right is viewed by the public and enforced (or not enforced) by political institutions—is very different.

The problem arises when we consider how a polity intends to enforce those freedoms that it values so highly. Positive rights create very real expectations. That is not to say that negative rights don't create expectations, but the expectations surrounding negative rights are of a different sort. Constitutions that rely on positive rights, including the South African, Canadian, and Japanese exemplars, also include a section in the text that outlines the process of enforcement.[33] Inevitably, that process involves the country's judiciary. Because of these clauses, courts are then constitutionally charged with the responsibility of monitoring the success of government initiatives aimed at advancing the substance of the rights themselves. When a polity declares that every citizen has a right to adequate housing and then does not deliver on that promise, the onus falls to the judiciary to invent a solution that recognizes the constraints on political institutions and the need for a citizen body to have faith in the efficacy of its constitutional form. And that poses difficulties, especially if the courts do not have the power to enforce their own decisions.

In thinking about the Japanese constitution's pledge to "maintain standards of healthy and cultured living," Hiroyuki Hata remarks that the country's courts could adopt one of three approaches. The first, the "abstract rights theory," suggests that courts are empowered only to "declare" the government's inability to sustain a "healthy and cultured living" as a violation of the text. They can do no more than publicly shame the government; their powers do not extend beyond that simple assertion. Under the second approach, defined as the "concrete rights theory," courts are "legally obligated not only to declare the Diet's failure to guarantee the minimum standards of wholesome and cultured living unconstitutional, but also to force the Diet to legislate in order to achieve this goal." The third approach, which the author defines as the "programmatic declaration rights theory," does neither. Under that approach, individuals are barred from seeking judicial remedy when their expectations go unmet.[34]

If we assume that the three theories animating the debate over Article 25 of the Japanese constitution can be broadly applied to other political situations, the complexity of the entire discussion of positive rights comes more sharply into focus. The judicial response to the question of unmet expectations depends, of course, on the particulars of that regime's political, constitutional, and historical traditions. Some polities will recognize judicial bodies that are able to command specific legislative action.[35] Most will not. And yet even if *all* courts are empowered to direct legislatures to provide the necessary resources to meet the constitutional standards today, those standards will eventually rise, giving way to the need for future courts to reenter the debate over positive rights. There is a never-ending theoretical cycle with positive rights; once you think you have met certain expectations, you realize that new expectations have been imagined and that they are now out of your reach. That is, the existence of positive rights helps to perpetuate those constitutional "gaps" Jacobsohn identified between the "actual"—defined here as the political reality of impotent courts, limited resources, and so on—and the "ideal"—as expressed in the constitution's list of rights and liberties. In that sense the expectations created by the inclusion of positive rights in the country's fundamental law are tantamount to precisely the same type of aspirations we now find in most constitutional preambles.

Insofar as positive rights help imagine a polity where all citizens meet a minimum standard of living, they contribute to the aspirational quality of the constitutional document. Their existence in the text is a subtle reminder that the polity has not yet achieved a state of political perfection and that the nation has not yet ended its quest by successfully "overcoming itself."[36] Of course, this reality removes us completely from any debate over whether these rights are enforceable. To claim that an important function of a modern constitutional text is to articulate particular aspirations—to envision a polity that is superior to the one currently inhabited—does not depend on the capacity of the state to deliver on its promises. If our interest is simply to uncover the various functions of a constitutionalist constitution, it should not matter whether a political regime will eventually realize its goals. I think it is even fair to say that most will not.

If recent history is any indication, it seems that some constitutional framers, in fact, have very short memories. Despite witnessing the collapse of several political regimes because constitutional promises went largely unmet (including some Eastern European countries), these framers continue to view the constitutional document as the place where their most sacred values should be textualized. They fervently believe in the practice of embedding their most important aspirations in the country's primary public document, even as they worry that such a practice will trigger, once again, the call for their services. These framers seem to subscribe to a common conviction: that a modern constitution needs to nurture a sense of renewal—a sense of hope—and that the most effective means for doing so is to embrace the principle of constitutional aspiration.

Conclusion

In the end, the central purpose of a constitutional text is to bind a citizenry around certain collective values or principles. "To constitute means to make up, order, or form," Walter Murphy reminds us, and presumably that order should be animated or informed by a normative conception of the good.[37] A constitution is a polity's attempt to model or design a blueprint for political perfection; it is a roadmap of sorts that sketches a plan for achieving a "more perfect union." One of the central functions of a modern constitutional text, therefore, is to embrace certain clearly defined aspirations, to articulate the founders' view of an improved society, and to identify the architectural mechanisms to make it happen. Preambles often perform the task of isolating the polity's highest values, although by no means are they the only place where constitutional aims are mentioned. Somewhere within a modern constitutionalist text, in any case, we will find a proclamation of the polity's deepest and most commanding aspirations.

We thus end where we began, with the words and ideas of scholars such as Robert Cover and Gary Jacobsohn. Cover, we might recall, insists that constitutions are the "projection of an *imagined* future upon reality," while Jacobsohn contends that constitutions are "committed to the achievement of things seemingly *beyond* [their] immediate reach." Both, of course, are correct. Constitutional texts that subscribe to the principles of constitutionalism and that are defined as mostly authoritative by those in power inevitably imagine a polity that is beyond our current conception of reality. In some sense, then, the enterprise of constitution-making includes an engagement with fantasy; it is a political project that rests almost entirely on the belief that an appropriate constitutional design will help deliver a more promising collective future. But it is even more than that. The principle of constitutional aspiration goes to the heart of the continued use of texts as means to order political societies. Indeed, the idea that future generations are beholden to particular constitutional limits imposed by people of the past is perhaps made more palatable if those in the present recognize that they play an important part in an aspirational journey, for to actualize a "more perfect union" requires that the values articulated at the founding be advanced—and in many cases shaped—by every succeeding generation.[38] The constitutional text, as it is constructed to do, thus ties the past, the present, and the future to the promise of a better world.

CHAPTER FOUR

Constitutional Design

⌖ ⌖ ⌖

To this point most of our discussion has focused on a constitution's literal introduction (preamble) and chronological beginning (founding). We have explored the process of constitutional transformation and the practice of embedding specific aspirations within the constitutional text. It is not yet time to abandon completely our examination of constitutional beginnings, since the legacy of constitutional framers endures long after these statesmen and stateswomen have completed their original task. Yet it is appropriate to turn our attention now to what many consider the heart of the text—the articles and clauses that create and define the specific institutions of the polity. The aim of this chapter is to examine the third function of a modern constitutional instrument—designing the various political institutions of the community in a self-conscious way. The concept of constitutional design refers both to the process of situating the institutions of a polity in a specific and particular manner and to the general architectural nature of the modern constitutional instrument itself. More to the point, this chapter will explore how framers, and eventually ordinary citizens, order the institutions of the polity by creating, empowering, and limiting them within the constitutional form so as to achieve the polity's expressed objectives. The values and aspirations of a polity, in other words, will not easily be realized without the proper institutional design to help deliver them. It is in the constitution where that design is most clearly expressed.

Order Through Design

All constitutions purport to design the political apparatus of constituted communities: what form of government should be adopted and what arrangement of political institutions is necessary to adequately constitute an imagined community. It might be useful to recall that the definition of *constitution* includes the principle of self-conscious design: to constitute means "to order," to make up or to place the component parts into a clearly defined configuration. It might also be useful to add one important element to this simple definition: a constitution's design—its institutional configuration—will reflect a country's break with its past and its hopes for the future. That is an important theme throughout this chapter's discussion. There is, in other words, a direct and substantial connection between the design of political institutions, the polity's historical past, and the likelihood of the constitution's promoting (and delivering) those aspirational values imagined at the founding.

It would hardly be surprising, then, to learn that the majority of time spent in any constitutional convention is devoted to ordering the specifics of a political system, including identifying the particulars of the public institutions that will, once the constitution is ratified, enforce the rules and advance the aspirations laid out in the text. Framers are fixated on such questions as What should government institutions look like? and What role should they have (both independently and together) in the process of ordinary governance? The question of the proper political order is precisely what occupied the minds of James Madison, James Wilson, Gouverneur Morris, and all the other delegates to the American constitutional convention. Various general plans for ordering the institutions of the polity were proposed, including the Virginia Plan submitted by Madison and the New Jersey Plan introduced in response. Each, if endorsed, would have created a political structure distinct from the one ultimately adopted. Eventually, the delegates to the convention settled on a compromise plan, including portions introduced by representatives from Connecticut, which altered once more the overall arrangement of America's political institutions.

Those framers knew that a polity's long-term success in achieving its desired goals is based in large part on the type of political system endorsed through the constitutional document. A federalist system will doubtless produce different political processes and outcomes than a system based on the principal of unitary centralized power. That is because the institutions required to manage politics in the former structure will differ from those institutions needed to regulate the political scene under the latter system. Similarly, a system of government designed around the principle of countervailing power will produce vastly different political effects than would a system in which power resides in a single institution (say, an executive). So too would a system that favors a loose confederation, or a canton political structure, or a parliamentary system, and so on.

One of the principal functions of a constitution, therefore, is to organize or coordinate the institutions of the polity. The self-conscious distribution of political power to various derivative political offices is a complicated and often delicate endeavor. Walter Murphy, who clearly understands the design function of a constitution, writes: "At a minimum, an authoritative constitutional text must sketch the fundamental modes of legitimate governmental operations: who its officials are, how they are chosen, what their terms of office are, how authority is divided among them, what processes they must follow, and what rights, if any, are reserved to the citizens."[1] Echoing the reality of many recent constitutional transformations, Murphy further notes that constitutions design political institutions not randomly, but rather *for a particular purpose*. It is barely possible, he writes, "to conceive of a constitutional text as solely ordering offices . . . . Easier to imagine is a text that would attempt to arrange offices to carry out particular kinds of norms, perhaps those of democratic theory."[2]

Murphy is not the only constitutional thinker to recognize that a central purpose of constitutions is to devise a specific structure for government; history provides a number of additional examples. William Penn, writing as early as 1682, insisted that the chief task of a constitution is to fashion a frame of government that would minimize the evils of sin.[3] Seventy years later, Montesquieu spoke of institutions being arranged so as to produce moderation in government.[4] Thomas Jefferson understood that the health of a republic depended on the compatibility of society's priorities with the constitutional structure of government. When they were in sync, he argued, the polity would likely function efficiently. Yet when there was an incongruity between the particular interests of a people and their constitutional design, the polity would inevitably disintegrate. "Each generation," he wrote, "is as independent of the one preceding as that [one] was of all which had gone before. . . . It has then, like them, a right to choose for itself the form of government it believes most promotive of its own happiness."[5] Jefferson's solution to this problem was to convene a constitutional convention every generation—every nineteen years or so—to draft a new plan for government. He understood, like Montesquieu before him and the framers of modern constitutions after, that a country's fundamental law could not qualify as a constitution if it did not at least include a clear design for governance.

As an important part of the deliberative ordering of institutions, a modern constitution creates the conditions for the emergence of a distinct national identity. Through the process of ordering (or reordering) political institutions in a particular way, the text ushers in a new vision of politics, a new direction for the collective people of the polity. Murphy, Fleming, Barber, and Macedo capture the point most accurately when they refer to a constitution's simultaneously narrow and broad character. "In its narrowest sense" they write, "the term constitution connotes government organization and processes and, in it broadest sense, a people's way of life; a constitutional text refers to a document or set of documents that claims to describe as well as prescribe the political order."[6] The point is that constitutions are the reflections of the framers' self-conscious choices regarding institutional configuration. They are the architectural blueprints for the construction of distinct political societies. They set up an arrangement of political offices and institutions that will, in the eyes of the constitutional designers, maximize the possibility of achieving the polity's endorsed aspirations.

Two things thus emerge from the type of deliberations typically heard in constitutional conventions, each of which contributes to the creation of that new "way of life." First, a plan for a broad system of governance (say, a federal system with coordinate national branches) is needed. Once that plan is envisioned, the specific institutions required to manage that broad system must be constructed. In America, the Constitution creates a federal republic where power is shared (and often times contested) between various branches of the national government, and between those particular institutions and the branches of the subordinate state governments. The constitutional document thus identifies the major institutions of the public realm (legislative, executive, judicial, state, administrative, and so on), imbues them with more or less precise powers (Article I, Section 8, for example, specifies the powers designated to the U.S. Congress), and considers in a very basic way how they must interact with each other to achieve certain policy objectives.

The U.S. Constitution is not unique in this respect. Other regimes have embraced similar structural models. Germany, for example, boasts a federal republic where regional governments share power with centralized political offices. Similarly, Nigeria and Ethiopia insist that their constitutions generate federal republican systems. Certainly, many constitutions share design features with the American model—bicameral legislatures, independent judiciaries, overlapping and countervailing powers among them—but others have chosen to adopt political structures that appear markedly different than the ones most Americans are accustomed to. New Zealand's political structure is one of those distinctive designs. It derives from its 1986 Constitution and is best described as a "parliamentary monarchy," where a prime minister, a unicameral legislature, and the Queen of England (designated as the "Head of State") share political authority. For obvious reasons, New Zealand's constitutional structure is not like the American example; it more closely resembles the parliamentary style of most Western European nations. It is important to note that New Zealand's constitutional engineers have created their own political order, one that is deeply influenced by the country's colonial heritage.

A contemporary sweep of constitutionalist constitutions reveals that a substantial variety of forms and designs exist; seemingly no two constitutional texts are exactly alike. Still, there is at least one similarity among modern constitutional documents: an acute awareness of the past. It would be exceedingly rare, in other words, to locate a single constitutional text that is not in some sense reflective of its country's historical legacy. One of those many constitutional systems whose design features have been influenced by its recent history is the focus of a short case study below. The story of South Africa's constitutional rebirth effectively illustrates a number of important lessons related to the general principle of constitutional design. Why do framers construct constitutional polities the way they do? Does a constitution that begins its arrangement of political institutions with a description of legislative power mean that the regime's framers favor a legislative-centered government? What point are constitutional draftsmen making when they place institutions in a specific order within the document? Do we learn anything about the founders' priorities or vision when the text opens rather than closes with a list of rights and liberties? Do we learn anything about the politics, culture, and history of a place when constitutional designers choose to adopt certain institutional configurations in favor of others? If so, what are those lessons learned?

Fresh in our memories, South Africa's struggle for constitutional transformation is a useful case study because it not only addresses many of these (and other) questions but its constitutional construction is also a purely modern constitutional construction. The design features of the South African text, including the governmental structure adopted, the detail and length of the text itself, and the penchant for frontloading the list of rights and liberties, is emblematic of so many constitutions drafted in the last half-century. It is, in other words, representative of the type of constitutional design that many contemporary framers now favor. Equally important, though, is the fact that South Africa's constitution elucidates more clearly than most one of the primary themes of this chapter: that a constitutional text will reflect, in its design, the principal aspirations of the polity.

One related lesson evident in the South African illustration that warrants mentioning here involves the relationship between the *process* of drafting the text and the *structure* of the institutions that text creates. Indeed, the relationship between process and structure is crucial, since it implicates the credibility of the entire constitutional instrument. In the modern era, where the legitimacy of so many constitutional texts is anchored to the transparency of the drafting process, it is important to consider how those moments leading up to the opening of a constitutional convention actually affect the eventual design of political institutions expressed within the constitution. That is, to focus entirely on the product of constitutional framing—the specific institutions and how they relate to one another—is to view only a partial image. There should be no doubt that the principle of constitutional design requires that observers pay significant attention to the outcome of constitutional deliberations: Which political institutions are created by the text? How are they arranged? How do they work together to achieve common aims? But that, of course, is not the whole picture. Process affects design, and the South African case is the best example of that. Our brief story begins, therefore, with the events that gave rise to the drafting of a permanent constitutional text in South Africa.

South Africa's Constitutional Design

When South Africans set out to construct a post-apartheid nation, they insisted that their first order of business was to erect a constitutional structure. It would prove an arduous task. The process of engineering a new constitutional order for South Africa was long and complicated, commencing (symbolically) with the 1990 release of Nelson Mandela from prison and the eventual collapse of apartheid. By 1994, however, an interim constitution was in place that set out the rules for adopting a more permanent text. Chapter V of that interim constitution stipulated when a permanent constitution would be in force ("within two years as from the date of the first sitting of the National Assembly under this Constitution"), what body would write it (the Constitutional Assembly), and even the intricate process of ratification (including provisions for supermajorities, simple majorities, and public referenda). Less than three years and one serious judicial setback later, the permanent constitution was ratified.[7] In the words of one observer, "The leaders of all the participating political parties signed the [interim] agreement bringing into effect the single most dramatic political change ever experienced in South Africa. The agreement reached was more than a legal contract: it set the basis for a new constitutional order. It was in effect a peace treaty that sought to relegate conflict and civil strife . . . to the status of a shameful blemish on South Africa's history, and marked the beginning of the democratic era."[8]

The Constitution of the Republic of South Africa, 1996—the permanent text—was thus born primarily out of careful and inclusive deliberation, which in itself represents a deliberate choice on the part of the regime's founding generation. Beginning with the Interim Constitution of 1994, the entire constitutional project consisted of a nationwide conversation about values, goals, and legacies.

It is probably an understatement to say that an enormous variety of groups— including governmental officials, constitutional experts, lawyers, economists, common citizens, traditional regional and ethnic constituencies, whites, blacks, Indians, ex-pats, political prisoners, oppositional parties, members of the African National Congress, members of the predominantly white National Party, members of so many other political parties and organizations (the list is almost endless)—enjoyed a stake in the eventual product of their endeavors. As one participant put it: "To each party the negotiations were as much about constitutional change as pursuing the interests of its constituency. On the other hand, fundamental to the success of the process was its inclusiveness, which clothed the Constitution with the legitimacy it needed as the supreme law. Accordingly, the process was designed to give parties the confidence that they could achieve their objectives through negotiation, and that their success was not entirely dependent on their voting strength."[9]

Altering the design of a political society as complex as the one in South Africa required a shared commitment to a radically different future. That is, for the next phase of the country's history to be successful, South Africa's constitutional draftsmen had to encourage intense collaboration at the same time that they were seeking dramatic change. Most importantly, they had to convince many segments of society of the inherent value of attending to the common good. Consider a few difficulties: How does a country with no experience in universal democratization construct a polity that rests almost entirely on that very principle? How does a majority population that has been disenfranchised and powerless for generations buy into the idea that political power ought to be shared with their oppressors? How does a country without a tradition of constitutionalist government suddenly spawn the necessary faith that is required to lend credibility to the new constitutional experiment? More practically, how does a country decide who warrants a place at the drafting table?

These and many other issues faced the people of South Africa as they contemplated a new constitutional order. One thing was certain: the process of constitutional construction would be deliberate and transparent. The discussions had to be slow, and they had to be visible not only to the South African citizens directly affected by any change in constitutional structure but also to an international community clamoring for free and fair elections. As we now know, the discussions were productive, and they eventually led to an entirely new political design (many describe the South African constitution as a testament to the power of consensus and collaboration). Amid violence in the cities and townships, creeping unemployment, and increasing frustration over lingering apartheid policies, delegates to both Conventions for a Democratic South Africa (CODESA I and II) plotted a strategy for new constitutional governance. To be sure, one of the primary reasons for their success was the painstakingly slow deliberation that occurred because so many interests were represented at the convention. But that was of course necessary in South Africa. As Patti Waldmeier notes, constitutional formation in South Africa is best described as "negotiated revolution."[10]

The Constitutional Text

Turning directly to the particulars of the permanent text, the constitutional description of South Africa's political institutions begins with an acknowledgement of the country's unpleasant past. In fact, one important conclusion that emerges from viewing the entire text is that its design is influenced in many ways by the fear of a return to the kind of intolerance and oppression that necessitated a constitutional transformation in the first place. The preamble, quoted in chapter 3 above, explicitly mentions the historical abuses endured by the majority black population. It speaks of "recognizing the injustices of the past" and "honoring those who suffered for justice and freedom in our land." The constitution's first chapter—titled "Founding Provisions"—also seemingly addresses the country's history of racial oppression. Chapter I, Article 1, reads: "The Republic of South Africa is one, sovereign, democratic state founded on the following values: (a) Human dignity, the achievement of equality and the advancement of human rights and freedoms. (b) Non-racialism and non-sexism. (c) Supremacy of the constitution and the rule of law. (d) Universal adult suffrage, a national common voters roll, regular elections and a multi-party system of democratic government, to ensure accountability, responsiveness and openness." Other provisions articulating the framers' prioritization of the "supremacy of the Constitution," the principle of "equal citizenship," and the importance that all major languages spoken have equal political status, follow.

The tone of these "Founding Provisions" is purely aspirational. They create an expectation of universal equality and individual liberty that spills over into the text's second chapter on the Bill of Rights. Interestingly, the document's Bill of Rights commences with a self-referential statement relating the necessity of a list of freedoms for promoting those values, like democracy, that are essential to the country's reconstituted political experiment. The chapter's first article reads, "*This Bill of Rights* is a cornerstone of democracy in South Africa. It enshrines the rights of all people in our country and affirms the democratic values of human dignity, equality, and freedom" (emphasis added). Continuing, the next article insists that the state must "respect, protect, promote and fulfill the rights in the Bill of Rights."

This entire chapter produces a set of expectations similar to the aspirational claims made in the Preamble and Chapter I. Constitutionalizing the promise to "protect, promote, and fulfill" individual rights is potentially dangerous business, especially when one considers that other expressed freedoms in the document include the "right to have access to adequate housing," the "right to access to health care services," the "right to sufficient food and water," the "right to a basic education" and the right to "further education, which the state, through reasonable measures, must make progressively available and accessible." From the perspective of expectations potentially unmet, it is noteworthy that a 30-page pamphlet explaining the provisions of the complex constitutional charter, and aimed at the mostly undereducated citizens of South Africa, accompanied the public release of the constitutional text. In it, the narrator vows that the "government *must* try to make sure that everybody's basic needs are met!"[11]

The collection of additional rights in Chapter II reads at times like the more familiar grants of freedom found in other constitutional texts. There are provisions for safeguarding the right to free expression, privacy, association, religion, property, assembly, and movement. There is also a provision—found in Article 35 of Chapter II—that resembles the U.S. Constitution's Fourth through Eighth Amendments' protection of the rights of the accused. Coupled with the fundamental right of individuals to "access the courts" found in the text's previous article, Article 35 is exhaustive, covering areas such as the right to a "fair trial," habeas corpus provisions, and the specific protections enunciated in America's "Miranda" warnings. It is important that these rights not be discounted because they are so familiar to us; they too advance the underlying theme that the country's defenses against oppression require the status and authority of the regime's fundamental law.

Continuing, Article 36 and Article 37 are two of four articles that conclude South Africa's Bill of Rights. They are unusual in that together they create a mechanism for South Africa's political officials to limit or check the literally hundreds of rights protected by the Constitution's earlier provisions. Article 36, labeled in the text as the "limitation of rights," explicitly empowers the government in certain rare instances to make "reasonable and justifiable" restrictions on individual freedoms so long as they are done openly and in accordance with "human dignity." Article 37 enables the government to curb the text's extensive list of freedoms during "states of emergency." To be sure, the constitution stipulates that Parliament is authorized to declare states of emergency only in certain situations (when the nation is "threatened by war, invasion, general insurrection, disorder, natural disaster, or other public emergency") and only for a designated and relatively short period of time ("21 days unless the National Assembly resolves to extend the declaration"). Perhaps most interesting is that there is a structural check on the power of the legislature to declare states of emergency: Article 37, subsection 3, claims that "any competent court may decide on the validity of (a) a declaration of a state of emergency; (b) any extension of a declaration of a state of emergency; or (c) any legislation enacted, or other action taken, in consequence of a declaration of a state of emergency." The provision for judicial review of states of emergency obviously complements the text's more general themes of tolerance, transparency, and accountability.

Scrutinizing the more conventional sections of the text—Chapters III–XIV, which design and energize governmental institutions—we see that again there is an almost continuous attempt to remind both citizens and officials of the racial and ethnic troubles that divided the country under apartheid. Immediately, the tone is set for cooperative governance when, in Chapter III, the text speaks of the need for all spheres of government to "preserve the peace . . . secure the well-being of the people of the Republic . . . provide effective, transparent, accountable, and coherent government . . . and, perhaps most importantly, not assume any power or function except those conferred on them in terms of the Constitution." Constituting only one page of the lengthy document, Chapter III on "Cooperative Government" is nicely reflective of the new South Africa, a country whose constitutional form is preoccupied with maintaining principles of fairness, transparency, and justice. There are even clauses in the chapter that mandate "cooperation with one another in mutual trust and good faith by fostering friendly relations, assisting and supporting one another, . . . [and] avoiding legal proceedings against one another."

The text then enters more familiar constitutional territory. The next several chapters involve the division of power among the various government entities, specifically stating which institutions will control which political functions. South Africa's constitution identifies three branches of the federal government, a separate provincial authority, and a derivative local level. The national government is divided into three independent branches—a bicameral Parliament, the National Executive, and the Constitutional Court. Resembling in structure the American system of separation of powers, the South African constitution also includes provisions for the overlap of authority, more commonly known as a system of checks and balances. The powers of the bicameral federal Parliament (consisting of the National Assembly and the National Council of Provinces), for example, are laid out in Chapter IV. Chapter V, in contrast, identifies executive power, beginning with the selection of a single president from the ranks of the National Assembly. Chapter VI describes provincial power, Chapter VII local power, and Chapter VIII the power of the South African judiciary. Altogether, the constitution incorporates a familiar design, for the framers of the South African text took their cues mainly from Western constitutional models.

Chapter IX is most interesting in that it creates State-sponsored institutions whose sole purpose is to "foster and support constitutional democracy." Consider how these constitutionally authorized offices contribute to erasing, or at least numbing, the memory of the country's past. In Chapter IX, Article 182, the Office of the Public Protector is established. This office is constitutionally empowered to investigate any potentially improper government conduct. Similarly, in Chapter IX, Article 184, a Human Rights Commission is set up to "monitor and assess the observance of human rights in the Republic." Perhaps unsurprisingly, the constitution mandates that complimentary commissions will be established in other areas, including ones to "Promote and Protect the Rights of Cultural, Religious, and Linguistic Communities" (Chapter IX, Article 185), to ensure "Gender Equality" (Chapter IX, Article 187), to monitor all elections (Chapter IX, Article 190), and to regulate the media (Chapter IX, Article 192). It hardly bears repeating, but the impetus for giving these offices constitutional status rather than simply legislative authority is to further fortify them to defend the powerless against the authoritarian and often oppressive whims of political leadership.

The Framing Process

Designing the South African Constitution consisted of blending many different constituencies and influences. On the one hand, significant portions of the text have been transplanted from the constitutions of other nation-states; on the other hand, it is all too clear that the text is a unique reflection of South Africa's historical legacy. And then there is the process of drafting the text: the story of South Africa's path to relative constitutional stability provides fascinating insight into the mind of the modern constitutional designer. In the past, the process of constitutional engineering was handled in ways that are noticeably dissimilar to the ways in which we construct constitutions (and constitutional regimes) today. In the first place, constitutional texts are now designed through the process of exhaustive deliberation and, in the best-case scenario, widespread consensus. South Africa's example is just one of many where the perceived legitimacy of the text depends in large part on the inclusiveness of the drafting process. That, of course, was not always the case. As Alexander Hamilton pointed out, constitutions of the past were usually born out of "accident and force" rather than "reflection and choice"; they were, in other words, often the consequence of aggressive political forces seeking to expand their dominion over neighboring territories. Even Hamilton's own constitutional convention can not be considered inclusive; his notion of who may "reflect" on the design of a new constitutional text or "choose" a different constitutional structure did not include a number of constituencies that became subject to the text's principles and rules.

Presently, we know that successful constitutions are often reflections of a country's shared set of beliefs and values. They are typically a consequence of careful planning rather than imperial aggression. Groups (primarily through their representatives) convene to create constitutional documents that reveal the complexities of the modern heterogeneous state. As evidenced by the South African experience, one of the apparent goals of any constitutional convention now is transparency. In any political situation transparency is important enough, but when pursued in the context of constitutional framing, that particular ambition has a direct impact on other components of the creative process. Take ratification, for example. The contemporary insistence on transparency is so powerful that even when there are mechanisms that call for universal ratification—still the favored form of endorsing or legitimizing the document—the process of constitutional formation remains under scrutiny. It is no longer enough to say that the sovereign people retain the authority to approve and (more importantly) reject the proposed constitutional text through ratification; they must also have some role in supervising the actual deliberations that produced the document itself.

As a result, perhaps we are now two steps removed from Hamilton's historical observation. The conception of how constitutional conventions should be organized has changed in the last century. The style of constitutional convention that gave rise to the American text—a constitutional convention shrouded in secrecy—has been discredited in the modern era. It seems reasonable, in fact, to assume that the initial vote to maintain secrecy during the American constitutional convention would, in the present, be viewed with deep suspicion. There is a sense of distrust that seemingly animates many modern constitutional foundings (a sense of distrust, I might add, that perpetuates the need for constitutional limits in the first place). This sense of mistrust reveals not only the difficulty of a framer's task but also the significance of what is at stake. Constitutions are important documents, and their effect on institutions and individuals is genuine. Individuals now demand that the process be open and apparent. That demand may correlate with the experience of many in late-eighteenth-century America who were troubled by the silence surrounding Pennsylvania's statehouse during the summer of 1787. What has changed dramatically, however, is the fact that constitutional framers, unlike in the American example, now consent to those demands.

Such thinking animated the events leading up to the framing of the South African constitution, and with good reason. The divide between the economically and politically advantaged minority and the disenfranchised and powerless majority created an atmosphere of doubt surrounding the construction of a new constitutional instrument. The rules for governing a democratic and just South Africa would eventually emerge in a permanent constitutional document, but initially the rules for governing the transitional period between the end of white rule and the beginning of a post-apartheid regime had to be established. Those guidelines for ordering a transitional government were articulated in the 1994 Interim Constitution.

As it turns out, then, the process of constitution-making in South Africa was actually made up of a *series* of processes. All of the eventual steps that ushered in a new constitutional form were punctuated by the need to be inclusive and discernible. The important work that went into preparing for the constitutional convention—work such as inviting particular constituencies to the table, encouraging them to articulate a vision for a new South Africa, urging critical groups that walked away from the negotiations to return, and so on—was crucial to setting a tone and eventually lending important credibility to the entire constitutional project. In fact, the push for a pre-constitutional constitution—the Interim Constitution—is a direct consequence of the country's anxiety over its history of oppression and the tendency on the part of political leaders to design polities that preserve their authoritative power. Not to be too casual about the terminology, but it should be noted that South Africans, in a sense, demanded the *constitutionalization* of the process leading to the adoption of a permanent constitutional text: they sought to establish specific though temporary rules that, if successful, would pave the way for the establishment of permanent governing procedures.

For our purposes, what is most important is that the South African experience is illustrative of a growing tendency among citizens of new or reconstituted polities to demand that there be clear mechanisms for constitutional accountability. Moreover, these mechanisms are not isolated simply to the drafting process. The change in approach to creating a constitutional polity, from one where secrecy during the constitutional convention is productive and efficient to one where a constitution drafted in secret would lack significant legitimacy, has had a profound impact on the design features of modern constitutional texts. That is, the concern about transparent and deliberative processes has seeped into the tangible products of constitutional documents—the values and institutions themselves. Constitutions are now drawn up in such a way that the governmental bodies created by the text are described in great detail. The powers distributed to these political institutions are carefully outlined, and often the combination of political bodies creates a complex political structure. In short, the level of distrust that now animates all aspects of the creative process has deeply affected the specific design of constitutional polities.

The Relationship of Institutional Order to the Bill of Rights

Returning again to the realm of theory, framers are the architects of new political orders. The texts, therefore, are the blueprints for constructing those institutions that eventually carry out the draftsmen's expressed vision. Cass Sunstein is thus accurate in claiming that constitutions are "pragmatic instruments" aimed at achieving particular structural objectives.[12] They are designed to promote and foster specific ambitions (including, in Sunstein's estimation, the conditions for meaningful democracy), and, as is so often the case in the contemporary political world, if the principal ambition of a political community is the protection of individual rights and freedoms, that too will be reflected in the design choices that eventually make it into the constitutional draft. Surely, the South African example is illustrative of this functional reality. While almost certainly more explicit than most, South Africa's constitution is not distinct on this point.

It is surprisingly true that citizens around the world (and especially in the United States) often forget that one of the primary functions of the modern constitutional text is to order the institutions of the polity in a self-conscious way. Ironically, a principal reason for this occasional neglect can be attributed to the specific design of many current constitutional documents. Anecdotal (and some survey) evidence suggests that citizens in a variety of countries can relate more readily to the concept of individual rights than to the structural particulars of legislative, executive, and judicial branches. They see more easily how they are affected by the specifics and the overall scope of constitutional rights than by the system of political institutions created by the text, and they clamor more loudly for the protections that accompany a constitutional bill of rights.[13] It is thus realistic to assume that a constitution's list of freedoms will inevitably eclipse the more routine and less sexy design features of the text in the minds of the constitution's citizen-subjects. This is especially true now that constitutional framers prefer to place the inevitable list of freedoms at the beginning of the document rather than at the end. Both literally and figuratively, the constitution's role in organizing various political institutions is now overshadowed by the perception that the text's first priority is to identify and protect individual rights. In the modern era, where most polities are judged on their capacity to protect and even promote individual freedoms, it would not be too surprising to see contemporary constitutional framers embrace a model that privileges individual liberty within the nation's fundamental law. The framers of the South African constitutional draft did just that.

History demonstrates that leading off a constitutional document with a list of rights has not always been the preferred practice of constitutional founders. The early American state constitutions typically commenced with a comprehensive listing of rights, but according to Donald Lutz it was not entirely clear that these bills of rights carried the same status as the structural chapters of the document. Lutz writes, "When it finally came time to write state constitutions, Americans frequently distinguished between the bill of rights and the constitution proper. The bill of rights usually came first, as part of or along with the preamble. Then the second section of the document was entitled the constitution, thus leaving open the question whether the bill of rights was part of the constitution."[14] At the time, a number of American constitutional framers, led most vocally by Alexander Hamilton, wondered about the necessity of adding a bill of rights to the text. "The truth is," Hamilton famously remarked, "that the Constitution is itself, in every rational sense, and to every useful purpose, a Bill of Rights."[15] It is in the nature of a constitutional charter, he insisted, that individuals find their greatest protection from the abuses of political authority. Hamilton's principal argument was that because the Constitution grants only limited power to the political branches, and the authority to infringe on individual rights is not among those delegated powers, the structure of the constitutional design made it essentially unnecessary to include a list of rights and freedoms. He insisted that adding a bill of rights to a constitutional text was mostly redundant.[16]

Of course we now know that Hamilton lost that battle: America's present Bill of Rights is the product of a political concession made to Anti-Federalists in exchange for their support during the ratification debates. And yet, for a time, he may have won the theoretical war. By a considerable margin, constitutions drafted during the nineteenth and early twentieth centuries either did not include bills of rights, or, following the American lead, placed those rights at the end of the document. While most American state constitutions maintained the practice of including a statement of rights immediately following the text's pre-ambulatory, or introductory, statement, many of the most influential international constitutions, including the Spanish constitution of 1812, the Bolivian constitution of 1826, the German constitution of 1848, the Swiss constitution of 1848, the Canadian constitution of 1867, and the Meiji (Japanese) constitution of 1889, either omitted a bill of rights altogether or at least began the document with descriptions of the structural designs of government institutions.[17]

As international scrutiny of political abuses intensified and the idea of individual liberty emerged as the dominant universal value, the relationship between bills of rights and constitutions proper changed. Indeed, the present reality that many constitutional draftsmen prefer to locate bills of rights at the beginning of the document is itself a comment on the design of contemporary constitutions. More importantly, it is equally evident that the major point Lutz makes about American state constitutions—that it was not clear whether a list of freedoms at the beginning of the text even carried the same authority as other parts of the document—no longer holds true. If anything, a contemporary constitution's bill of rights is now its most commanding feature. Of the 147 active constitutional texts reviewed, 128 (close to 88%) place a list of rights before any article that discusses the institutional structure of the political regime; all but 19 texts essentially begin with an examination of the individual freedoms retained by the people. Of the remaining 12 percent, only a handful (approximately five) hail from regimes with some recent history of imperial control, national instability, or internal political oppression.[18] The remaining 14 constitutionalist polities whose texts still place the list of rights after the description of institutions have enjoyed relative political stability over the past half-century. One conclusion we are able to draw from these numbers is that constitutional framers, especially those found in historically oppressed regions of the world, presently favor constitutional texts that highlight those declarations of individual freedom that were largely absent from previous constitutional systems.

South Africa is just one of the newly constituted nations that has certified its strong commitment to the principles of tolerance, freedom, individualism, and human dignity by frontloading a list of individual safeguards. Other regimes that have endorsed a similar design statement include many of the former Soviet republics. The Estonian constitution, for example, begins with a preamble and a short chapter outlining the constitution's "General Provisions," which include a sovereignty statement, an adherence to the rule of law, and a declaration of the country's national colors and official language. Then there appears an extensive list of rights and freedoms, including forty-seven separate articles devoted to individual rights. It is not until Chapter IV, Article 59, that the constitution finally turns to the structure of the Estonian government.

Like so many countries in the region—and indeed, across the globe—Estonia has emerged from a situation in which imperial forces dictated the nature of most political relationships. Rights were restricted under Soviet control as everything flowed through the party apparatus. One commentator notes that from the end of World War II until the collapse of the Soviet Union in 1991, Estonia was "a captive nation, existing as a republic, or administrative unit, of the Soviet Union."[19] That same commentator goes on to highlight the "degrading effect that the Soviet system had on the rule of law. Ideology, not law, was king, and the role of law was to serve Soviet ideology. Courts provided what was known as 'telephone justice.' After a trial, the judge would call the party headquarters to find out what to do."[20] Those freedoms most Americans take for granted were not available to Estonians during the period in which their country was occupied by the Soviet Union. Considering this historical backdrop, it is perhaps not surprising that independent Estonia altogether reformed its constitutional charter in 1992 and began its text with an exhaustive list of rights and liberties. The polity's specific constitutional design, in other words, is reflective of its recent historical journey.

Conclusion

At the risk of overstating the point, it might be argued that the changing design of constitutional texts—including the insistence on highlighting bills of rights, the deliberative and transparent nature of constitutional framings, and (recalling themes more thoroughly discussed in an earlier chapter) the abandonment of brief and general texts in favor of detailed and lengthy ones—signals a shift in the design priorities of the modern constitutional document. What was once a blueprint for governance—a design for political order—is now equally and *explicitly* a celebration of the principles of freedom, liberty, equality, and tolerance. Constitutions are still architectural documents aimed at structuring political communities, but they are now far more individualistic in language and purpose.[21] It is true that a constitution is still responsible for constructing a political order, but alongside that duty stands an equally powerful obligation to pacify citizens of the polity who remain constantly fearful of the power of political authority. Throughout history, constitutions have protected personal liberty. What is different about constitutions drafted in the contemporary era is that now announcing the commitment to individual rights and liberties appears to be their principal function.

Although perhaps unique in terms of an historical narrative, the consequence of South Africa's struggle with consensus—the Constitution of the Republic of South Africa, 1996—appears remarkably similar to the traditional model of modern constitutions. Its central feature, in short, is not only the construction of particular political institutions and the ultimate division of power among those separate institutions but also the steadfast defense of individual rights. These are arguably the most common and most obvious features of contemporary constitutional charters. Indeed, constitutions inevitably create and design governmental institutions. They provide the blueprint for how political branches will be arranged, and in doing so, they imbue those institutions with distinctive powers. They also regulate that power in the name of the individual.

Most constitutions around the world have followed the American lead and have fashioned separate legislative, executive, and judicial bodies, giving to each a unique set of powers. Other constitutions have constructed different institutional arrangements—some are legislative-centered, while others are executive-centered; some have powerful judiciaries, while others do not. Still, the point is that one of the primary functions of modern constitutions is to articulate a particular design for the governmental institutions of that polity. They pattern the divisions of government in a self-conscious way. Quite simply, they design polities.

CHAPTER FIVE

Constitutional Conflict

Constitutions spawn conflict. The great irony, in fact, is that constitutions—written in large part to regulate and curtail conflict so as to increase the likelihood of regime stability—have so often been at the center of the world's most intense political and legal battles. Debates over linguistic identity in Canada, sovereignty in Eastern Europe, democracy in the Middle East, ethnic particularism in south Asia, citizenship in southern Africa, economic development in Central and South America, and morality in the United States have all had (or continue to have) a distinctly constitutional flavor. Even multinational constitutions like the unifying charter of the European Union cannot escape controversy. Critics of the EU Constitution cite dozens of reasons for their skepticism; some even insist that the document will create more disunity, inaction, and conflict than would be the case had the member states simply spurned the idea of a multinational constitution when it was originally proposed.

For a few of these countries or regions, one problem may be that the fundamental law has not yet lived up to its hype. It was (or is) viewed by many as an important ingredient of the antidote for a long history of political strife, but it has yet to produce the type of transformative and stabilizing results that many statesmen have come to expect from modern constitutions. Citizens around the world assume that the constitutional document will answer more questions than it poses, and in most cases that is probably true. But constitutions also create conflict where there was none; they manifest tension in areas where the framers either did not anticipate or could not have anticipated that there might be disagreement; they are interpreted in ways that advance the self-interest of political leaders; and they are often so vague and ambiguous that fierce battles emerge about their specific meaning. Perhaps that is why Martin Edelman once portrayed the capacity of constitutions to resolve political conflict in rather sobering terms. "Written constitutions by themselves," he wrote, "rarely answer important political/legal issues. Because the core message of a constitutional text is framed in broad, general principles, few, if any, conclusive answers are provided."[1]

Of course, Edelman is correct in at least the literal sense: constitutions "by themselves" *are* incapable of answering important legal questions and settling divisive political disputes. Instead, institutions authorized to give meaning to the broad general contours of a constitutional text are charged with the duty to mediate most political and legal conflicts. It is here that the interpretive role of government organs like the judiciary cannot easily be separated from any discourse on constitutional functionality. To make constitutions function in their capacity as paramount laws for the governance of a polity requires that institutions carry out their individual responsibilities too. Edelman is thus right to insist that a constitution alone is not sufficient to prevent a majority from trampling on the rights of the minority or for any agent of government to seek greater personal or institutional influence. History has too often demonstrated that constitutional limits—"parchment barriers," as Madison put it—can be just as easily ignored as they are embraced.

And yet constitutions are not entirely useless instruments in a polity's quest to manage legal and political conflict. Institutions interpret the text, and thus they are the polity's first line of defense against political instability. But one of the major functional purposes of a code of laws—one that is perhaps more fundamental (or supreme) than all the rest—is to *guide* or *direct* those institutions in the decision-making process. The whole purpose of choosing a written text over an unwritten constitution is to provide a point of reference—a transparent and discernible touchstone—for individuals and institutions that remain skeptical of the corruptibility of human nature.[2] The hierarchy of laws, beginning with the presumably ratified constitutional text and proceeding downward to derivative and ordinary legislative statutes and enactments, tells a tale: constitutional texts, which create and empower those very institutions that eventually interpret the document and pass those ordinary laws, maintain a certain conceptual authority over their creations, one that is vital to the continued survival of the polity. The absence of that conceptual authority signals the demise of the constitutionalist polity; it begins a process whereby a fully operative or authoritative text turns eventually but inevitably into a sham or façade constitution. In short, once institutional fidelity to the text is lost (an occurrence that happens with disturbing frequency) the constitution ceases to be a credible source of institutional guidance.

That potential disintegration of a constitutional order provides us with an initial avenue into a deeper discussion of constitutional conflict. It is important to recall that the difference between a fully or reasonably authoritative constitution and one that could only qualify as a sham depends almost entirely on the willingness of political leaders to consent to the pre-established rules embedded in the constitutional document. Constitutionalist and nonconstitutionalist charters alike will both be considered authoritative if the sovereign (or, more likely, representatives of the sovereign) abides by the provisions of the text. The common denominator among authoritative or reasonably authoritative constitutions, therefore, is that the institutional directions articulated in the text (Who holds power? How do they get that power? What is the scope of their power? and so on) are, for the most part, followed. When they are not followed, the constitution becomes a virtually useless guide to settling political and legal disputes ("It isn't worth the paper it is written on"). But when those directions are followed, a constitution can provide meaningful guidance for institutions and officials seeking to find ways to manage most types of political conflict. The document does not always answer the questions most required by the polity's political leaders, but rarely does it completely neglect to provide some meaningful guidance. This chapter thus explores the fourth function of the modern constitutional text: its role as an instrument to manage political conflict. It begins and ends with the assumption that a constitutional text may spawn more conflict than it eliminates but that one of its principal virtues is its ability to guide the institutional management of conflict.

Constitutional Conflict: Three Themes

Any discussion of constitutional conflict limited only to a single chapter is bound to be highly (and perhaps irresponsibly) selective. Entire books, after all, have been written on the topic. My fear is that tackling the broad concept by attempting to explain the countless related issues would be far more careless than admitting at the outset that I intend to sacrifice breadth for depth. In the pages ahead, I will explore three of constitutional theory's most enduring themes, all of which in one way or another connect to the central focus of this chapter: (1) the unique nature of constitutions and how that contributes to conflict management; (2) the idea that constitutions are written to promote regime stability; and (3) the paradox of text and time. I will conclude with a separate discussion of the importance of amendability for constitutional maintenance. Citizens and political leaders faced with increasing political and social tension often find comfort in the potential to alter formally the constitutional document. To be sure, each of the following limbs of a more general discussion of constitutional conflict is, in its own right, worthy of an entire chapter or, more likely, an entire book.[3] However, we take them up here in a preliminary and nuanced, though certainly not comprehensive, way.

The Unique Power of Constitutions

I begin with a few assumptions. First, the nature of conflict in political and legal institutions rarely allows for what we might describe as a complete resolution, where complete resolution is defined as the *elimination* of conflict. In the modern political arena, especially when we factor in the current penchant to frame discussion around the absolutism of individual rights,[4] true resolution of conflict is often elusive. Political institutions like the judiciary may resolve cases and declare one party a winner over another, but the various issues that give rise to legal proceedings in the first place—issues ranging from which institution of government owns contested power to substantive issues like whether groups or individuals are able to openly criticize government officials—often recur again and again. Insofar as compromise represents a true resolution, then it is reasonable to assume that we often arrive at a desired destination. But compromise is often elusive. For that reason perhaps a more appropriate way to frame the quest for minimizing conflict is to think in terms of conflict *management*. A constitution is supposed to *manage* conflict in a way that ensures regime stability.

Conceiving of a constitution's functional role as managing rather than eliminating conflict is important because of the second assumption: that conflict, in a contemporary constitutionalist society, is not always bad. As Mariah Zeisberg has noted in her work on the subject, constitutional conflict is not only inevitable but is also necessary for the continued development and survival of the state.[5] Particular types of conflict, especially legal and political battles that somehow advance the promises laid out in the text's preamble, are constructive. A constitution's goal, therefore, is to maximize the constructive conflict and, obviously, to minimize any destructive conflict.

That said, an authoritative constitutionalist text leads a sort of dual existence when it comes to the reality of political and legal conflict. On the one hand, its normative goal is the regulation of conflict through the designation of clearly assigned political responsibilities. There is, of course, a delicate balance between a constitutional text that is too detailed and thus overly constraining, and a text that is too vague or ambiguous to provide meaningful guidance in the management of conflict. Part of the success of a constitution depends on its ability to strike that balance. A constitution's companion responsibility—the other half of its dual existence—centers on the concept of empowerment.[6] A constitutionalist text empowers government agencies to use the document as an instrument to prevent the emergence of untenable or unwelcome power arrangements. Almost literally, institutional actors under established constitutions will cry foul by waiving the text in the face of those governmental officials who they believe are abusing their constitutionally granted authority.

The success a constitution has in managing political discord thus begins with a conception of the relative influence of a constitutional text over the many institutions and public officials in a political regime. A relationship exists between the degree of respect a constitution engenders and the capacity of that constitution to regulate political disagreement. Presently, a constitution that garners widespread support and respect will more successfully negotiate conflict than one that is less capable of winning over the population. The more legitimacy, credibility, and power a constitution enjoys, the more it will command the compliance of the polity's decision makers. More succinctly, political leaders are less likely to ignore the provisions of an authoritative constitutional text if it commands widespread legitimacy. Legitimacy is born from a variety of sources, including a sense that the process of drafting and ratification were honest and transparent and that the text still broadly reflects the moral sensibilities of the sovereign. And yet it is not easy to achieve. The degree of legitimacy that a constitutional charter possesses will no doubt influence the outcome of many legal and political disputes; indeed, a legitimate and respected text is the most powerful tool for constituents whose aim is to combat all sorts of political discord.

What is required is an acknowledgement of the unique force of an authoritative constitutional text. Citizens, public officials, government representatives, and so on, must admit that the constitution is unlike any other expression of the sovereign's general will. They must declare that the constitution is distinct in its singularity and primacy, that it is supreme, and that no other document or set of documents competes with it for the title of fundamental law.[7] If the recognition of the supremacy (or unique force) of a constitution is present among the population, it follows that institutions and officials are less likely to ignore the dictates of the text.[8] The branches of the polity (assuming, again, that these branches fall under a fully operative or authoritative charter) take their cues from the constitutional charter and thus are conceptually beholden to that text as the country's supreme law. That is to say, they recognize their subordinate position to the constitutional document. The fact that it does not always work that way, or that institutions and officials *do* circumvent the provisions of the document, does not alter the status of a constitutional text as the primary touchstone for institutional conflict. Indeed, defenders of constitutional primacy would be right to claim that the text's greatest feature is its ability to guide the institutions of government through many (though not all) political storms precisely because it is the singular act of a completely sovereign people.

Consider the example of Canada. Symbolically, the introduction of a Canadian Charter of Rights and Freedoms—essentially a constitutional bill of rights—to the preexisting fundamental law in 1982 was a powerful statement both about the values of a divided people and about the importance of constitutional authority. For many, there was a felt need for a document that articulated the numerous freedoms retained by the citizenry. The Charter became that centerpiece document. But what is most compelling about the story is that in a very real sense Canadians already enjoyed most of the rights that were eventually embraced in the Charter. Citizens exercised liberties such as the right to free speech and freedom of association, not by virtue of a silent constitutional text, but by parliamentary acts and provincial guarantees. Gil Remillard captures the reality that the Canadian Charter of Rights and Freedoms was largely redundant when juxtaposed against previously articulated safeguards when he writes, "Actually the Charter of Rights and Freedoms sets down few new social, political or economic guarantees for Canadians." He continues: "In certain respects [the Charter] is less extensive than the Parliament's Canadian Bill of Rights, or the Provincial Charters already existing, particularly that of Quebec."[9]

And yet the redundancy of the text was more than offset by the added value that accompanies granting the 1982 Charter full constitutional status. Observers noted with concern that as long as the grant of freedoms originated from legislative enactments, those rights could be curtailed by simple legislative action. As Remillard writes, "Before the passage of the new Charter, rights and freedoms were set forth in simple federal or provincial legislation, thus subject to modification by the government at both levels. Today these rights and freedoms are part of our Constitution and are binding on the Canadian Parliament as well as on the provincial legislatures."[10] As evidenced by the Canadian example, the transference of rights guarantees to a constitutional document is no insignificant act. What Canadians did in altering the place in which rights are expressed was to explicitly recognize the unique force of the constitutional text. In their minds, the constitutional document carries more weight; it is the most powerful and respected source of all political authority in the state. No longer would the national Parliament or the provincial legislatures retain primary jurisdiction over the individual liberties enjoyed by Canadian citizens (although some might argue that power was simply transferred to the judiciary once the Charter was ratified). The constitutional text became the source of the authority surrounding rights and liberties, and that, as this chapter notes, has significant consequences for the management of institutional conflict.

Interestingly, the drafters of the Canadian Charter of Rights and Freedoms also embraced a mechanism that held the potential to temper the impact of newly adopted liberties on the cultural identity of specific groups. The "Notwithstanding Clause," discussed in greater detail in the next chapter, is a perfect illustration of a constitutional provision whose primary purpose is to manage conflict. In fact, the clause allowing provincial legislatures to override the provisions of the constitutional document for a specified period of time (up to five years) permits legislative bodies to essentially opt out of certain constitutional requirements. A province, for example, is empowered to enact a piece of legislation that "operate[s] notwithstanding a provision included in section 2 or sections 7 to 15 of [the] Charter."[11] There is perhaps no greater (or worse) constitutional mechanism to manage the potential for all types of conflict than to allow discontented constituencies to literally suspend those portions of the constitutional text they regard as most troubling. The "notwithstanding clause" was included in the amended Canadian Constitution to do just that.

Before going any further, it may be prudent to consider what is meant by political and legal conflict. What exactly are we referring to when we claim that the constitution is an essential component of a polity's regulatory scheme? Our examination of this question must begin with a simple assertion: a constitution's provisions are nothing more than rules.[12] More accurately, they are, in the words of Larry Alexander, "metarules" in that they differ from other political enactments in their position relative to the day-to-day operations of government.[13] A command that Congress "make no law abridging freedom of speech," while certainly subject to considerable interpretation and often ignored or manipulated by public officials, sets out a rule prohibiting the legislature from interfering with an individual's right to free expression. The clause creates a space—in this instance, a liberal space related to individual thought and expression—where government is not permitted to enter. Illegitimate governmental entry into that space will inevitably and appropriately lead to a challenge based on the alleged violation of the textual clause. Institutions then take over to determine whether a violation actually occurred. The point is that constitutional rules like the one found in America's First Amendment may be more fundamental than other rules in that they are essential to the effective and continued governance of the entire polity; they are, in short, of an entirely different character than the myriad of ordinary rules/laws that regulate our everyday existence. Still, we also must remember that at their core they are still rules.

Embedded within a constitutional text are provisions or rules that empower government agencies to do certain things or mandate certain political or social realities (realities that reflect, say, the will of the majority). The regulation of interstate and/or foreign commerce, for instance, is typically one of the powers reserved to legislative branches by many of the world's constitutional texts. So are the powers to promote national security, ensure territorial sovereignty, raise taxes, deploy the military, and so on. Of course, there are also provisions or rules within that same text that *proscribe* government from exercising certain powers or mandating certain realities (consider again the First Amendment to the U.S. Constitution). Typically, the arena with which constitutional rules are concerned is the arena of politics, though that too may unnecessarily limit the scope of our general definition. At a minimum, a constitution is specifically designed to answer a number of important questions about the architecture of government: Who qualifies as a political official and how are those officials chosen? What institutions of government control which powers and how do those powers overlap or converge (if they do)? Who makes particular political decisions at particular times? How are citizens involved in the political process (if they are involved at all)? Where are the limits of the government's authority to interfere with personal rights and freedoms? What mechanisms exist for the alteration of the constitutional text? And so on. There are obviously dozens or even hundreds of questions like these that any typical constitution should address. The answers to those questions will of course depend on the specific regime. More generally, though, modern constitutions aim to preordain the common rules for political practice prior to emergence of institutional conflict.

Conflict emerges in the absence of clearly defined rules. In other words, conflict arises when so many of the questions related to governance are not clearly or easily answerable by the constitution, when the "metarules" are either not clearly discernible or are susceptible to wild and erratic interpretation. It is impossible, and probably inadvisable, for constitutional framers to attempt to design a charter that seeks to anticipate every minor quarrel that may arise in a complex, modern state.[14] Certain political or legal discord will not easily lend itself to constitutional clarification. The problem is exacerbated when the poor design of a text conspires to make it difficult for institutions like the judiciary to find substantial meaning in the words of the constitution. Obviously, proper management of political conflict will not happen (or will not happen neatly) if the meaning of the text is rendered obscure by social or political forces.

In most cases, however, constitutions are capable of addressing the major thematic differences of the day. Political questions about jurisdiction, power, rights, even morality, are often answered, at least in a preliminary or procedural sense, by the constitutional document. Donald Lutz describes the role of constitutions in managing conflict accurately. His argument is worth quoting at length. "Constitutionalism," he insists,

> represents an advanced technique for handling conflict. Since constitutions make clear the locus of political authority and its basis, they provide an efficient means for establishing the third party, government, that can end conflict. The definitions of a way of life and of institutions to further that way of life tend to knit people together, and the overriding sense of community resolves many conflicts. The distribution of power and the limits of its use tend to structure conflict into predictable patterns. The provision of a publicly known, regularized procedure for decision making takes potential conflict out of the streets and into arenas where calm and reason can prevail. Any constitution that fails to manage conflict efficiently and effectively is seriously flawed.

Take the puzzling debate about judicial supremacy in the United States as a specific example. It is all too clear that the text does not expressly delegate primary interpretive control to the federal courts.[15] Larry D. Kramer suggests that it is "experience" and not the clauses of the Constitution that supports the idea of judicial supremacy in the United States. That is, because the text is silent on the subject (and few individuals in the late eighteenth and early nineteenth centuries were even concerned about the topic) it must be the development of judicial power that has foretold the emergence of judicial supremacy. "What ultimately moved a greater number of Americans to embrace the idea that judges should have the preeminent word on constitutional meaning," he writes, "was experience, which seemed to teach that popular constitutionalism in its traditional form might not work in a society as diverse and dynamic as the United States."[16] In essence, he is arguing that the Constitution cannot be primarily responsible for judicial supremacy because it is silent on the issue, so the only reasonable conclusion to draw is that "experience" has filled the void and declared a winner.

Despite the lack of textual reference to the question, though, one might conclude that the design of America's federal institutions (which of course *is* announced by the text), coupled with the defining character of a constitution as a limitation on the power of the majority, suggests that the largely independent judiciary has perhaps a more compelling claim than any other branch on the power of constitutional interpretation.[17] In other words, the constitutional text may be silent on the subject, but even with that silence we can make certain logical inferences from the nature of the individual text and the theory of constitutional government. In the United States, judicial supremacy may qualify as one of those logical inferences. The judiciary may not have *exclusive* jurisdiction over the interpretation of the Constitution, but it is hard to contest the fact that the structure of government as articulated in the text supports a significant interpretive role for the courts. The American judiciary is specifically designed so as to remain largely immune (or at least isolated) from the passions of a contemporary majority. The other institutions were designed in just the opposite way, as practical reflections of the will of the majority. Does that suggest that we have an answer? Of course not. Few constitutions, if any, answer all questions definitively, and the American text is no exception. What the American constitutional charter does provide to citizens is at least a rational and logical argument in favor of judicial supremacy. Whether or not one adopts that reasoning often depends on many other factors.

Ongoing battles about the proper management of conflict are typically less a product of constitutional defects than of institutional parochialism (of course, that in and of itself may suggest a constitutional defect). That is, political differences may not be purely constitutional differences, although they often envelop and implicate the text. A substantive debate about the sanctity of the flag as a symbol of national unity and pride certainly involves the text, especially in terms of such lines of inquiry as the proper interpretation of the document and the relationship between desecrating the flag and the definition of free expression. Even so, the conflict is primarily a political debate between two or more forces arguing about history, tradition, community, liberty, symbolism, patriotism, and common decency. To be sure, constitutions are deeply concerned about history, tradition, community, liberty, symbolism, patriotism, and common decency; these are in fact some of the many principles that give the world's constitutions their primary energy. What is important to remember when thinking about political debates like the one over the sacredness of the flag is that the constitution acts as the critical reference in the attempt to manage the conflict. Borrowing Alexander's terminology, it is the "metareference" for the entire regime. It may seem patently obvious to most, but the constitution provides direction for institutions managing the disagreement. The constitution always remains in the center of the fracas (that is the nature of primary rules, after all) even when the continuing debate is more accurately characterized as one that implicates institutional interpretations of the text and not the text itself. Authoritative constitutions, in short, manage conflict by occupying a unique, powerful, and even supreme place in the polity.

Constitutions and Regime Stability

All of this is to admit that the role constitutions play in managing political conflict, both at the moment and over time, is complex and significant. Contemporary political societies are difficult to administer; the institutions of a newly constituted regime or of an old polity are often unclear about the scope and breadth of their power arrangements. As a consequence, these political engines are forced to grapple with friction between governmental institutions, conflict between the various levels of a federal structure, and even tension between the competing aspirational values or visions of a "more perfect union."[18] One of the most intriguing conflicts confronting a contemporary polity involves the tension that may arise between the regime's principal public documents. A nation like the United States, where the Constitution competes with the Declaration of Independence for primacy in the minds and hearts of the citizenry, must consider how best to resolve differences in the messages espoused by its fundamental texts. Sometimes the attempt to come to grips with variations in national themes embedded in public documents is tragically unsuccessful—witness the American Civil War.

At the center of these and other conflicts lies the constitutional text. Let us expand the discussion a bit by considering what is at stake when constitutions are incapable of managing conflict. Many scholars have insisted that the primary purpose of a constitutional text is to structure institutions in such a way that political conflict is minimized and regime stability is maximized. Mariah Zeisberg refers to this line of constitutional inquiry as the "settlement thesis."[19] She argues that settlement theorists are "mesmerized by the role of the Constitution in resolving legal disputes," especially when they insist on arguing that a constitution's "*only* purpose lies in political settlement."[20] Among others, she contends that Alexander Hamilton's vision for the American polity rested in large part on the principle that a constitution's primary function was in settling political disputes. In her estimation, the idea that an independent judiciary was constructed so as to remain largely detached from the pressures of political interests is further evidence of the founders' view that the text could, and should, act as the nation's primary rulebook.

Zeisberg's examination of the "settlement thesis" includes a useful evaluation of the reasons why so many observers see conflict management as one of the major features of a constitutional text. She notes, for example, that constitutions provide a stabilizing force for the polity, an original source for political actors to appeal to when political stability is threatened. Insofar as the text orders a political environment through self-conscious structural design and identifies the powers delegated to the various institutions of government, it becomes the single prism through which institutional conflict must pass. That is, the primacy of a constitutional document, acting as the supreme law, means that disputes between governmental agencies, offices, and individuals is often (though not always) resolved by reference first to the provisions of a constitutional text. Often the constitution is not the document that provides the key to resolving the conflict, but it is frequently considered before all other sources are utilized. As the centerpiece of a polity's fidelity to the rule of law, it is the primary source for fixed legal and political rules.

In some sense I may be downplaying the obvious: the legitimacy of constitutional*ist* constitutions rests on their ability to resolve political conflict. If we are to agree that constitutional documents are designed in part to limit the power of the sovereign by establishing preexisting rules that will govern political relationships, then their authority or legitimacy is linked directly to their capacity to maintain political order over time. In Larry Alexander's words, "Constitutionalism implements the rule of law. It brings about predictability and security in the relations of individuals to the government by defining in advance the powers and limits of that government."[21] Similarly, Richard Kay insists that we can measure the effectiveness of a constitutional text by considering how well it promotes long-term planning, or the capacity of institutions and individuals to have faith that their plans will not be disrupted by arbitrary and capricious state action. He argues, "A constitutionally defined government with extensive granted powers is, in some ways, less dangerous than a weak government whose powers are not defined by prior law. . . . The special virtue of constitutionalism, therefore, lies not merely in reducing the power of the state but in effecting that reduction by the *advance* imposition of rules"[22] His point is clear: pre-established, fixed, and transparent constitutional rules are essential for the long-term health of a polity.

The occasionally heated debate surrounding the need for a formal, written constitutional text in Israel nicely illustrates the point. At present, Israel's constitution consists of a series of texts (the 1948 Declaration of Independence, the 1950 Law of Return, the 1952 Covenant Between the State of Israel and the World Zionist Organization, and the Basic Law). But practically since the moment of Israel's modern birth, a number of constituencies have pressed for a more traditional constitutional charter. The country's Declaration of Independence, in fact, stipulates that a formal constitution will be drafted "by a Constituent Assembly not later than the first day of October 1948." The expectation at the time was that a country as potentially divisive as Israel was perfectly suited for the calming and stabilizing influence of a constitutional text. Political order likely would be maximized by the presence of a supreme law that predetermined many of the state's institutional power relationships. However, it was not to be. As we now know, October 1, 1948, came and went, and no constitution was enacted either on that day or any day since.

The absence of a formal constitutional text in Israel has not gone unnoticed.[23] From time to time over the last sixty years, pivotal political, cultural, and religious figures have floated the idea of adopting a constitutional text to add a measure of stability to a notably insecure region. Most recently, former Prime Minister Ehud Barak made the adoption of a constitutional text one of his primary campaign pledges during the 2000 election. Barak's plan for a formal constitution was part of a larger initiative that he called "civic revolution," in which Israel was to undergo significant secular reform. A new, written constitution fit neatly into his proposal primarily because his image for a constitutional document included a number of secular components, including provisions for the protection of individual rights and clear limitations on institutional authority. Ultimately, he was not successful in bringing his dream of a formal, written constitution to reality, but his reasons for embracing the idea were reminiscent of ones that have resonated throughout Israel's half-century of sovereign statehood.

Support for the adoption of a written constitution has always concentrated on a few primary themes, all of which claim some connection to the aim of long-term regime stability. One of the leading experts on Israeli constitutionalism describes the early debate in these terms: "The proponents of a formal constitution [maintained] that a constitution would protect individual rights by establishing written limits on the power of the majority; that it would stand as a symbol of Israeli independence and status within the international community; and that it would serve the pedagogical purpose of educating a diverse population in the political principles of the regime."[24] Opponents suggested that a written constitutional text was unnecessary and would compete with the Torah for supremacy within the religious state. In the minds of such monumental figures as David Ben-Gurion, a constitution with pre-established constraints on the power of the government would make it difficult to maintain the type of policymaking flexibility that a non-secular, particularist regime requires.[25] Consider Menachem Begin's words during the First Knesset: "If the Constituent Assembly legislates a constitution, then the government will not be free to do as it likes."[26] It is somewhat ironic that detractors have successfully argued that a formal constitution in Israel, precisely because it ties the hands of government, would lead to less regime security rather than more.

So far the opponents of constitutional adoption have had the better of the debate. They have managed to quell any significant movement in favor of radical constitutional change. If we focus on the ambitions of those who favor the enactment of a new, formal text, however, we are able to see that much of their platform is directed to the need for greater regime stability and security. The inclusion of a Bill of Rights to Israel's constitution, many insist, would have the effect of reaching out to minority religious and ethnic groups who have long felt oppressed by governmental policies. Likewise, a written constitution that orders the political institutions of the political regime in a reasonably transparent fashion might go a long way toward appeasing communities that believe the largely unconstrained authority of the state has contributed to ongoing violence. To be sure, the debate is much more complicated than I am intimating. There are multiple reasons why some in Israel have sought a constitutional list of freedoms or a more tangible limitation on political power. Yet it is not unfair to suggest that the primary theme of the entire discussion of constitutional transformation is increased regime stability. A constitutional document, some contend, might be one considerable step toward greater peace in the region.

The Paradox of Text and Time

Perhaps the most intriguing puzzle in all of constitutional theory—and certainly one that regularly appears in the literature on constitutional conflict—involves the relationship between text and time. Laurence Tribe, among the most visible constitutional scholars of his generation, was so curious about the relationship that he opted to introduce his famous treatise, *American Constitutional Law,* by exploring it. Less visible though no less talented scholars have also been intrigued by the connection.[27] The puzzle is this: how can a constitutional document, written so many decades ago by individuals who could not have conceived of the complexities facing modern society, still control and constrain present majorities? Why, in other words, should the interests of the contemporary citizenry be controlled by a symbolic (or spiritual) commitment to a text that these citizens had no hand in enacting? Why, Tribe wondered, would a nation "that rests legality on the consent of the governed choose to constitute its political life in terms of commitments to an original agreement?"[28]

Such is the nature of constitutions. Their authority, especially relative to the comparative authority of derivative institutions and constituencies, is always dubious. In a literal sense, most constitutional texts, including the U.S. Constitution, are inherited documents; those who abide by the rules set out in the charter were not literally participants in the document's construction or ratification. Instead, they consent to the stipulations articulated in the text by pledging an abstract and often indefinable oath to the values expressed within and, more intangibly, to the future success of the polity. This oath, as Sanford Levinson implies, likely resembles the type of pledge one takes as a born citizen of a particular nation: it is steeped in a sense of belonging and the need to identify oneself as part of a collective whole—and yet, for many, its bonds are shallow and artificial.[29] They are based on the concept that as long as one physically lives in a particular territory and one does not seek revolutionary reform of the political structure, one tacitly assents to the constitutional guidelines that inform that polity. Fidelity to the text, in short, becomes in large part a simple product of the duties of citizenship.

The situation in the United States is instructive. Inhabitants of the United States demonstrate allegiance to the Constitution, not by continually ratifying the document (although that might be preferred),[30] but by simply acknowledging its fundamentality. Perhaps because of the reverence most Americans have for the country's founding documents, citizens often consent to the authority of the constitutional text by taking its primary features for granted. They unwittingly acquiesce to the centrality of the constitutional charter by refusing to question many of its components or, in the most extreme case, its overall wisdom. As a result, a constitutional dispute in the United States is often centered on particular institutional interpretations of the text and rarely on the Constitution itself. The judiciary, the legislature, or the executive is often criticized for its erratic and unprincipled elucidation of the supreme law, while the Constitution itself remains largely (though not always) immune from the same type of intense scrutiny.

On those occasions when citizens are asked to intentionally confirm their commitment to the values espoused in the Constitution, it is typically done by reciting the "Pledge of Allegiance" or singing the National Anthem at the opening of the school day, at ceremonial celebrations, or at sporting events. The "Pledge of Allegiance" (which is not just a pledge to the Constitution, by the way) is seemingly ubiquitous in certain environments, and for many it is a meaningful expression of one's dedication to the country's primary values. For others, though, the Pledge is routine and hollow. To be sure, a commitment to national identity and the constitutional text is far more complex than can be captured in a few short sentences. One must consider the importance of a shared language, history, culture, celebration, and tradition—even a shared recovery from a regrettable past is a powerful binding agent. The larger point is captured, nonetheless, by remembering the central paradox of constitutional theory: that as soon as a country's supreme law is drafted and ratified, its separation from the actors who conceived of its structure and aspirations, and who literally endorsed its first principles through ratification, begins.

I am certainly not the first student of constitutional theory to ponder the paradox. Stephen Holmes is perhaps the most curious about the subject. He refers to this aspect of the constitutional enterprise as the "discord between majoritarian politics and constitutionally anchored restraints."[31] If constitutionalism insists that certain decisions will be "removed" from the purview of contemporary majorities because they might interfere with individual rights guarantees or governing processes, then the capacity of a democratic people to attend to the common good is clearly restricted. Holmes and others have spent much of their careers contemplating the tension that exists between the principle of democracy, where power is vested in a current people as sovereign, and the constitutional ideal, where that very power wielded by those contemporary citizens is limited in the name of original ambitions such as justice, equality, liberty, stability, and the rule of law. Holmes has hinted that there is something troubling about ordering a political society around the principle of "precommitment." He even goes so far as to conclude that constitutionalism is inherently "antidemocratic" and that the concept of constitutional democracy is a "marriage of opposites, an oxymoron."[32]

The tug that inevitably surfaces between a present majority and a polity's longstanding commitment to a preexisting or original set of first principles is one of many related conflicts that plague contemporary constitutional democracies. The importance of the temporal conflict, however, should not be understated: at the heart of all derivative debates about constitutional conflict lies, in some way, the paradox of text and time. Debates surrounding the institutional arrangement of governing bodies, the scope of power retained by those institutions, and even the moral tension that arises when cultural values become out of step with constitutional values, all put pressure on the enduring quality of a constitutional text. As the distance traveled between the original act of enactment and the present increases, that pressure will also rise. Individuals begin to wonder whether the constitution accurately reflects the will of the present people and whether it still serves its original purpose.

Many scholars have attempted to tackle the temporal question from other perspectives. Joseph Raz, for one, has provided interesting insight into the lasting *authority* of constitutional texts.[33] His central question focuses on how a constitution remains authoritative over time, and his answer admits to the differences between new and old texts. He contends that in all cases constitutions derive their original influence from their principal authors. The legitimacy of a constitutional document, particularly at the exact moment of framing, correlates directly with the moral legitimacy of those tasked with the responsibility of crafting the document. If constitutional draftsmen are viewed as morally legitimate, Raz claims, the product of their endeavors will also be seen as morally authoritative. Over time, of course, the moral legitimacy of the framers may begin to fade, and thus Raz is fittingly curious about how older constitutions can sustain their legitimacy in the long term. Is there an expiration date for constitutions? he wonders. Should there be? In essence, he is asking a variation of the same question that absorbed Jefferson more than two centuries ago: should a polity convene a new constitutional convention every generation because the legality of the text and its constitutive power will inevitably diminish? According to Raz, the answer depends on the particular polity and its peculiar circumstances. The continuing authority of constitutions, he says, will depend on many other factors, including the symbolic value of the document and whether the provisions of the text are morally sound. The quality of a constitutional charter older than a generation or so, he concludes, is contingent on the extent to which that document maintains its moral standing.

Raz's argument about the dependency of *moral* factors on the longevity of constitutions is debatable. What is not controversial is his focus on issues related to authority, temporality, and particularism. The legitimacy of a constitutional document does depend on its capacity to remain, in the eyes of the citizenry, more or less up to date. Its authority, and thus its ability to resolve political conflicts large and small, fluctuates not only with vacillations in the expressed values of a regime but also with time. And each regime is different. Some older constitutions, like that in the United States, still maintain much of their original authority, while others (many of which are no longer around) have lost their influence. In those latter cases, what contributes to the loss of legitimacy varies widely, but certainly in many instances an important factor is the increasing incapacity of constitutions to manage a multitude of political disputes. Political conflict, if left unresolved, can destroy a constitutional regime.

One final point before turning to the process of constitutional amendment: what makes the management of political conflict all the more important is that the credibility of the constitution is occasionally at stake. If political conflict becomes so protracted or the tactics of the political officials become so vicious, political leaders may clamor for constitutional change or dissolution. The recent experiences in South Africa and Canada are illustrative. Each of these countries has witnessed in the past several decades political battles that threatened the continued unification of the state. Each, in a sense, witnessed the toppling of a previous constitutional order and the emergence of a new (or, as in Canada, an altogether restructured) constitutional form. In the case of South Africa, the enduring conflict centered on the marginalization of the black majority; whereas in Canada, the discord revolved around the apparent disenchantment of the minority French-speaking population. In both of these instances the political battle erupted into a full-scale constitutional crisis. In a sense, then, perhaps Tocqueville only captured part of the picture. Speaking about nineteenth-century America, the Frenchman insisted that almost every political question eventually becomes a judicial question.[34] At the moment, it may be more accurate to say that in most of the world's constitutional democracies political questions, whether they intend to or not, inevitably become constitutional questions.

Amending the Constitution

Throughout this chapter we have concerned ourselves with the perennial problem of constitutional conflict. How does the constitution respond to political and legal disputes that arise from its institutional creations? How does a constitution endure when its central principles are no longer reflective of the beliefs held by the present majority? Why is a constitution so crucial to the polity's main objective of regime stability? The answers to these and similar questions have been varied and, to this point, incomplete. It is now time to raise the stakes a bit. What, we might ask, happens when conflict takes on a more threatening posture, when it is so intense, protracted, or politically expedient that literally altering the constitutional text becomes prudent or necessary? In the remainder of the chapter we will consider the issue of conflict as it relates to constitutional maintenance and ask one fundamental question: How does a political society maintain a constitution over time when forces are constantly being exerted to destroy it? The answer, I suggest, can be found in the principle of amendability.

We begin with a few definitions. To amend is to compensate or to make something whole. The word *amendment* itself is defined as "an addition to, or correction of, a document, law, or constitution."[35] The concept hints at the need for renewal or revitalization, that something is broken or incomplete and requires supplemental action to make it whole again. A rather innocuous interpretation of the principle of amendment would suggest that the constitutional break requires only a minor adjustment, one that is satisfied by a single, often specialized, addition to the text. The history of amending the U.S. Constitution, if we begin after 1791 when the first ten amendments to the text were ratified primarily as a package and if we exempt the Civil War Amendments, supports this interpretation. Constitutional amendments have been, for the most part, individual and often isolated attempts to manage specific political, legal, and cultural problems. We need look no further than the amendments ratified in the twentieth century to illustrate the point. Some amendments, like the Nineteenth Amendment, which extended the right to vote to women, have had a profound impact on the body politic. Others, like the Eighteenth and Twenty-First Amendments, which essentially cancel each other out, have not had the same effect. All amendments to the U.S. Constitution that have been drafted and ratified in the twentieth century, however, involve specific, though largely isolated or independent issues.

There is, of course, a more provocative interpretation of the concept of amendment. It comes originally from the prominent historian of the American founding, Gordon Wood. In his seminal work *The Creation of the American Republic, 1776–1787,* Wood remarks that the amendment process is akin to legitimate institutional "revolution."[36] He cites a statement by the American founder James Wilson as capturing the sentiment of the time: "This revolution principle—that, the sovereign power residing in the people, they may change their constitution and government whenever they please—is not a principle of discord, rancour, or war: it is a principle of melioration, contentment, and peace."[37] Bruce Ackerman has made a parallel assertion. His view of the period of reconstruction surrounding the adoption of the Thirteenth through Fifteenth Amendments is that it has come to represent one of America's major constitutional transformations.[38] It did more than just change the wording of the text, according to Ackerman; it altered the entire direction of the polity. The alteration of constitutional sentiments through the amendment process represents a revolutionary—albeit peacefully revolutionary—moment.

In every sense both Wood and Ackerman are correct: the ability to amend the constitution is a powerful, and possibly revolutionary, entitlement conferred by the original sovereign on the present population. In the rather capable minds of these two scholars, the aim of a constitutional amendment is primarily corrective: to alter the text in such a way as to more accurately capture the vision of political life that will help deliver on the aspirations laid out in the document's preamble. That course correction can be subtle or, as in the case of America's Civil War Amendments, it can be "revolutionary." More accurately, it is the process of reconstituting the polity through the act of addition. Amending a written constitution always entails *adding* to the text, even when the ultimate goal of the change is to repeal provisions believed to be outdated or politically controversial.[39]

Before proceeding to a case study examining the profound power of amendability, it is essential to highlight the concept of process, for any robust definition of amendment must also include an important procedural component. It hardly requires mentioning that in most constitutional democracies around the world amending the constitution warrants a more demanding process than does the passage or alteration of simple legislation. The constitutional amendment process, therefore, is often more complicated, requiring a higher threshold for consent or acceptance than simple legislation, which typically requires only majoritarian support.[40] One unique feature of most constitutional amendment processes is that they are theoretically unrestricted. The only regulation on the scope and substance of a constitutional amendment is the sense of self-restraint exhibited by the proposing institutions (typically legislatures) and the ratifying populace. In most cases the fact that a constitution includes provisions for amendment means that, if taken to the theoretical extreme, the text itself can be amended entirely out of existence through internal procedural mechanisms. A fair and legitimate process, even one that presumably requires super-majoritarian support, could conceivably lead to the perfectly legal destruction of the polity's constitutional order.[41] Such a scenario is unlikely to occur in the extreme (although it is conceivable, as Ackerman contends, to imagine amending the constitution in such ways as to effectively transform a polity altogether), but it does demonstrate the power of amendability. Control over the authority to amend the text represents the highest power in a nation's political life.

It seems profitable at this point to conclude the exploration by considering the role of constitutional amendment in shaping the political landscape of a polity outside the United States. Article V of the U.S. Constitution, while deeply interesting and profoundly influential on the world stage, does not represent the most useful illustration for our particular purposes. Instead, we look again to the north, where it can be argued that no nation over the past several decades has wrestled more thoroughly with the idea of constitutional amendment than has Canada.

The Canadian Illustration

At various times in Canada's history, the country has undergone radical constitutional transformation, all without scrapping the original 1867 Constitution and starting anew. Most recently, Canadians fundamentally altered their constitutional document by endorsing the Constitution Act, 1982, whose most famous section includes the Canadian Charter of Rights and Freedoms. Amending the Constitution Act, 1867, to include an extensive list of rights and freedoms has had a significant impact on the politics and culture of a nation struggling with its multicultural identity. Consistent with the theme of this chapter, it has also remedied some political and legal divisions while creating others.

Specifically, Canada's constitutional change has produced two significant consequences. First, it has united the nation's people in some unexpected ways. Recent survey data points to a country that is more comfortable with its linguistic, ethnic, and cultural differences now than it was just two decades ago.[42] The second major consequence of constitutional amendment in Canada relates to the principles of national sovereignty and colonial independence. Amending Canada's original 1867 Constitution to allow for the recovery of autonomous control over any future revisions to the text has at long last released Canada from its colonial legacy. One of the last remnants of British authority over Canada—ultimate jurisdiction over constitutional change—was finally erased when the Constitution Act, 1982, was enacted.

The history leading up to the drafting and ratification of the Constitution Act, 1982, and in particular the Canadian Charter of Rights and Freedoms, is long and complicated. It includes Pierre Trudeau's stunning victory for the Liberal Party in the 1980 elections; the contentious debate surrounding the attempt to "patriate" or modernize the Canadian Constitution of 1867 so as to more accurately reflect the polity's linguistic, ethnic, religious, and regional diversity; and the concerns expressed (particularly in Quebec) about retaining cultural identity in the wake of constitutional reform.[43] Central to the discussion surrounding the apparent need to reform Canada's constitutional order was the contentious and seemingly ubiquitous showdown between defenders of greater federal power and advocates of primarily provincial authority. The debate was especially heated in Quebec, Trudeau's home province and the region of the country most concerned about meaningful provincial autonomy. It is hardly surprising that Quebec, an enclave of French Canadians surrounded by the majority English-speaking population, would express a certain degree of anxiety over any plan that might shift primary decision-making authority away from the provinces and to national governmental institutions.

According to Peter H. Russell, Prime Minister Trudeau's 1980 resurrection from political defeat presented him with an opportunity to fulfill his primary dream of greater national unification through a stronger federal government and a more robust and reflective constitutional text.[44] Trudeau, himself a French-speaking Canadian, recognized that the central problem in Canadian politics revolved broadly around deep cultural divisions. Questions related to federalism, accommodation, provincial autonomy, sovereignty, rights, and so on, were all in one way or another connected to the issue of cultural hegemony. Quebec, for example, posed a problem to those who sought greater national harmony. Leaders like Rene Levesque were instrumental in keeping the Quebec separatist movement at the forefront of Canadian politics. Although ultimately defeated, a number of referenda were proposed that would have made it possible for Quebec to secede altogether from the Canadian confederation.

Trudeau's purpose for adopting a constitutional list of freedoms (incidentally, after his hope for more comprehensive reform was rejected) was based largely on the principle of compromise. His stated goal was to embed a wide assortment of rights into a fragile constitutional system that faced the very real possibility of rupture. Specifically, he sought, and successfully achieved, the entrenchment of standard individual freedoms like the right to free speech, assembly, religion, and certain procedural guarantees. More interestingly, Trudeau envisioned a section that would guarantee broad equality for all citizens, a dream that would eventually become a reality in sections 15–22 of the text. Still, the real revolutionary idea reflected in the text is the inclusion of "Minority Language Educational Rights" beginning in section 23. Here the constitutional framers, inspired by the vision of the country's prime minister, sought a remedy for years of political turmoil over linguistic and cultural differences by using the power of the constitutional document. The specific details of Canada's Charter of Rights and Freedoms, and in particular the important role that personal and cultural identity played in the formation of a new constitutional order, will be discussed later, in chapter 6. For now it is important simply to mention the consequence of Canada's constitutional transformation. Current data reveals an interesting picture about the use of constitutional revision as a means to manage political and legal conflict.

In direct response to many of the potentially destructive political issues facing Canada at the time—including Quebec separatism, minority rights, and cultural identity—the Charter was formally introduced. It managed to accomplish many of the goals Trudeau envisioned. Although the Quebec legislature's initial rejection of the Charter was a setback, current survey research indicates that over the past quarter-century an overwhelming majority of Canadians have come to believe that the list of rights and freedoms is a "good thing for Canada." According to the Center for Research and Information on Canada (CRIC), 88 percent of Canadians now support the Charter. And 72 percent of those surveyed also believe that the constitutional document is adequately protecting citizens from potential government abuse. What is most interesting is that support within the provinces does not seem to vary widely. The western Canadians polled endorsed the Charter at a rate of 86 percent, while in Quebec, arguably the province most affected by the amendment, more than 9 out of 10 citizens polled pledged their sponsorship of the document (91%). In fact, provincial support for the Canadian Charter of Rights and Freedoms was highest in Quebec.[45]

Andrew Parkin of the CRIC has interpreted the survey data. His findings confirm the contention that the Charter has defused a considerable amount of the political tension facing the country over the past several decades. In his words, "The Charter has become a living symbol of national identity because it defines the very ideal of Canada: a pluralist, inclusive and tolerant country, one in which all citizens can feel equally at home. What Canadians like most about the Charter are precisely those aspects that underpin the maintenance of unity—protection of official languages, multiculturalism, and equality rights."[46] As evidence, Parkin points (among other places) to the data that indicates that more than 86 percent of English-speaking Canadians feel that French-speaking families have the right to educate their children in their native tongue, while an even higher percentage of French-speaking Canadians (88%) support the idea of native language education for their English-speaking neighbors.

Of course, this evidence alone is not conclusive. Other factors beyond the enactment of the Charter of Rights and Freedoms are no doubt also responsible for the overall attitudinal development in Canada. Nonetheless, there does appear to be some sense of tangible accommodation brought on by the newly revised constitutional document. Insofar as the Canadian Charter of Rights and Freedoms set out to increase the national sense of unity and provide a degree of stability to a fractured nation, it has succeeded. By almost every measure, Canadians have embraced the amended constitutional text. In the process, they have reconceived their legal and political relationships.

A renewed national unity is not all the amendments to Canada's original constitution were able to accomplish. More intriguing even than the story behind national unification is the role the amendment process played in marking an end to Canada's colonial tradition. The country's original 1867 Constitution had no provision for altering the text through amendment, and thus formal changes to the document were made only with the approval of the British Parliament. Peter Hogg described the rather unorthodox situation as Canada's "imperial amending procedure."[47] In essence, Canadians were left without final jurisdiction over their constitutional text because all changes required approval from the British Parliament. A colonial power, in other words, maintained ultimate jurisdiction over Canadian constitutionalism.

For most of Canada's modern history, the paternalistic amendment process left many citizens uneasy. Canada established her independence from Britain in the nineteenth century, and yet the British monarchy retained veto power over the country's most serious constitutional decisions. Hogg was careful to note, however, that the process was not one that left Canadians entirely without power. A longstanding convention existed whereby the British Parliament would not impose constitutional amendments unilaterally. Textual amendments would be introduced initially by Canada's national or regional governments and then passed before the British legislature for ratification. Consequently, Canadian citizens maintained meaningful control over the direction of their constitutional text, even if the ultimate power rested with the country's original colonial overseer. But still, as Peter Russell noted, "the debate over a Canadian amending formula involved nothing less than the question of who or what should be constitutionally sovereign in Canada."[48]

The power to alter the constitutional text through amendment is essential to the concept of national sovereignty. A country cannot be said to control its own collective destiny without also maintaining jurisdiction over changes—both large and small—to its fundamental law. For many decades, Canadians lacked that authority. Yet as soon as Trudeau and his immediate followers announced a plan for radical constitutional transformation, they implicitly declared their intention to recover sole constitutional sovereignty for Canada. The Constitution Act, 1982, although controversial at first, at least satisfied one concern of a majority of Canadian citizens: it eliminated the imperial check on constitutional amendments. "Part V of the Constitution Act, 1982," says Hogg, "introduces into the Canadian Constitution a set of amending procedures which enable the Constitution Act, 1867, and its amendments to be amended within Canada without recourse to the U.K. Parliament."[49] For the first time, Canadians gained exclusive control over their fundamental law. Adapting to cultural and political changes would now remain within the jurisdiction of Canada's political institutions. The irony in bringing the Constitution Act, 1982, to fruition was that it too had to be accepted by the British Parliament. Canadians, in essence, were required to request permission to recover the authority to control their own constitutional destiny. In many respects, seizing complete jurisdiction over the amendment process represents the culminating statement of Canadian independence and sovereignty. And it happened through the power of constitutional amendment.

Conclusion

When we step back and look at the universe of political regimes today, a few trends become immediately apparent. First, politics remains a highly contested arena, a place where individuals and organizations fight relentlessly for even the smallest power advantage. It seems that public officials and ordinary citizens are regularly contesting the minutest details of political authority. Comparing the strength and vigor of political conflict across time is obviously impossible, but it is not unreasonable to assume that contemporary political and legal differences are just as nasty and vicious today as they once were. The constant battle to establish oneself as an actor in the political process has not waned in the past several generations. If anything, more and more institutions and individuals are vying for less and less political and legal turf.

There appears also to be no respite in the public's cynical attitude toward politicians. In many Western cultures especially, governmental officials are suspicious characters, viewed by ordinary citizens as attracted primarily to the power that accompanies the job and rarely to the call for public service. Not often in contemporary politics is an elected official seen as purely altruistic, a statesman who entered the political arena not for personal gain but for the collective good of the population. It is a sad commentary on contemporary politics that politicians are constantly defending their honor.

Relatedly, another trend in contemporary politics appears to be an increased demand for greater governmental accountability. Interest groups dominate much of contemporary politics, and often their advocacy takes on the appearance of oversight. They are the current watchdogs of the political world. Even in those polities where interest groups do not enjoy relatively open access to political institutions and officials, other organizations (like the media) are quick to take on the responsibility of scrutinizing all types of governmental action.

The broader point revealed by this watchdog mentality and by the other trends mentioned above is largely reminiscent of James Madison's concern regarding the true nature of man. He believed that "men were not angels," that they were easily tempted by the prospect of increased power, and that they could not be trusted. Troubling for Madison was that government, which he insisted is "the greatest reflection on human nature," deals almost exclusively in the currency of power. To the primary architect of the American Constitution this reality was disconcerting, but it also presented interesting possibilities for political design. His complex response to the wariness of placing power in the hands of easily corruptible humans was to create "auxiliary precautions"—constitutions, in other words—that are aimed at combating the worst impulses of humankind. These constitutional texts, he remarked, are indispensable tools for managing the type of conflict that inevitably arises in political systems not administered by angels. The Virginian understood, in short, that one of the primary functions of a constitutional draft is to manage political and legal conflict.[50]

Madison's strategy for dealing with conflict is now wildly popular. In direct reaction to the wave of political and legal conflict over the last few centuries, countries have consistently turned to constitutional documents to help manage their feuding institutions. In just the past fifty years more than half of the countries of the world have founded new constitutional regimes on the principle that codified rule can provide meaningful benefits to fractured polities. As faith in the rule of law has swept across the globe, many nations have crafted constitutional texts that aim to increase transparency and provide adequate guidelines for political jurisdiction. These constitutions, that is, were adopted so as to attack the pervasive problem of political and legal conflict. Some have been successful and some have not. What is remarkable is the almost universally shared belief in the ability of constitutional texts to manage institutional disputes. When faced with profoundly damaging disagreements, regimes like Canada have resorted to constitutional change as the principal way to transform the polity. The goal is always the same—increased regime stability—and the remedy adopted by political regimes around the world has become increasingly consistent. In the end, many constitutional framers have taken seriously the admonition expressed by Publius more than two hundred years ago: "The subject [of constitutional formation] speaks its own importance; comprehending in its consequences nothing less than the existence of the Union."[51]

CHAPTER SIX

Constitutional Recognition

⌗ ⌗ ⌗

Referring to the plight of linguistic, ethnic, racial, and religious minorities in many contemporary societies, James Tully once remarked that these "communities" are often frustrated by a lack of cultural and constitutional recognition.[1] Culturally, groups such as the Zulus and the Ndebele in South Africa were, until recently, largely ignored in many of the republic's most prominent public and private institutions. Under apartheid, they were not allowed a voice in the development of a South African society dominated by the Afrikaners and English. Constitutionally, groups such as the non-Jews in Israel or the non-Catholics in Ireland are also (admittedly in a different way) discounted when it comes to shaping the broad contours of the political environment. Their voices are also muffled when discussions about the future direction of the polity arise. Their contributions toward achieving a polity's collective aspirations, that is, are less recognized than are the contributions from other, fuller members of the political order. Joav Peled, in comparing separate ethnic groups in Israel, noted that non-Jews enjoy a reduced status or type of citizenship—one that, in contrast to Jews, does not permit any meaningful contribution to the nation's collective good.[2]

At the center of many ethnic differences around the world is the principle of recognition, the concept that, if it is to have constitutive power, one's identity must be acknowledged and protected by those who do not share it. Collective identity is a powerful force in the modern world; it is by definition the glue that binds individuals to each other and to a specific region or particular country. But when one's identity is marginalized or even outright ignored, tensions between those unrecognized groups and those in power inevitably emerge. Those tensions are evident in virtually every corner of the globe, from North and South America to Africa, Asia, the Middle East, and Eastern and Western Europe. Moreover, they regularly result in violence. Minority groups often clamor for assurances that their political aspirations will be met, and when they are not (or because of the clamoring itself), violence typically erupts. Civil Wars, ethnic cleansing, targeted political violence—these are often the consequences of a lack of political and constitutional recognition.

The problem of a lack of political recognition is also evident in nonviolent disagreements among particular groups. Take Canada, for example, where pockets of the French-speaking community in Quebec often lament that they have little control over the constitutional destiny of the entire country. As a distinct linguistic minority (and a paideic community in Robert Cover's terminology),[3] francophones consistently maintain that they cannot adequately participate in the existing institutions of the dominant society but must instead either assimilate to the general character of the larger population or—as a number of Quebecois find appealing—secede altogether from the union. What is more, the problem of constitutional isolation is exacerbated by the fact that the 1867 constitutional text is one that was imposed on the citizenry by the English monarchy during the period of colonial rule, and not, as in the United States and other modern regimes, designed by those who were to be governed directly by its principles and commands.[4]

In fact, many contemporary Canadians insist that they have not yet found the necessary constitutional ingredients to make their country's major cultural and linguistic differences more manageable. Prior to the ratification of the 1982 Canadian Charter of Rights and Freedoms, prominent public officials (including Prime Minister Pierre Trudeau) argued that the country had not constructed a viable constitutional document that was capable of engaging both linguistic groups in a single common purpose. On this point, Tully has suggested that because Canada's original constitutional text fails to recognize its second largest community, the document cannot be considered a success in any meaningful sense of the word.[5] He notes that in order to be effective as a constitutive tool, a modern constitution ought to recognize all ethnic, cultural, and religious groups, if not equally, then at least in a way that impedes the type of conflict that has historically threatened to tear Canada apart.

The lack of recognition experienced by many of the world's paideic communities, including francophones in Canada, obviously has serious constitutional consequences. If we are to believe that a modern constitutionalist constitution's greatest challenge, and its greatest triumph if successful, rests on its ability to *constitute* a citizenry, then many ethnic, religious, linguistic, and racial groups around the world have reason to doubt the power of constitutions. The most difficult task of a modern constitutional text is finding a way to establish political and social order—to bring populations of disparate peoples together in a structured, ordered community—when the human instinct calls out for just the opposite, for individuals to be free to do exactly as they choose and not to be bound by arbitrary connections based on national interests. The lesson of many social contract theorists is that humans are not naturally inclined to modify their behavior for the greater good even if environmental circumstances dictate that they should. A constitution-like agreement, in fact, is needed for those reticent individuals even to make the transition from a state of nature to a civil society. And yet one central purpose of a constitution is to create that ordered society, to engineer and cultivate a common purpose among individuals who may not be inclined toward unification, and to modify or shape a population's identity to reflect the interests of the collective. Citizens must agree to endorse certain central principles of the constitutional document, and that is often a tall order. Many French-speaking Canadians, for example, still cannot endorse the principle of assimilation. The same was true of most southerners on the eve of the American Civil War. In both instances the original constitutional draft failed to adequately constitute the entire citizenry, thus creating in both nations a constitutional crisis of significant proportions. In one case the resolution of that constitutional crisis called for civil war; in the other it called for the principle of constitutional recognition, the fifth function of a modern constitutional text.

In its simplest form, constitutional recognition refers to the practice of modern constitutional texts to embed or implant specific protections for minority groups within the constitutional document, to literally recognize a distinct group by textualizing some form of protection for that group in the nation's fundamental law. But simple definitions are not sufficient here. The concept of constitutional recognition relates to numerous ideas and themes surrounding the entire constitutional enterprise. It implicates issues such as collective identity, nationalism, assimilation, and transformation. It includes political, economic, social, religious, ethnic, racial, and other forces that have the capacity to tear regimes apart. In the end, though, recognizing minority groups by referencing them and their particular identities in the constitutional draft is a favored practice of many recent constitutional framings, and for that reason we turn now to a more complete working definition.

Defining Constitutional Recognition

To measure the success of a constitution by exploring the extent to which it establishes and shapes a population in a particular image—the extent to which it constitutes a citizenry—is really to ask about the transformative authority of constitutional texts. Earlier we spoke about the considerable power of constitutional foundings to destroy an old citizenry and create a new one. The central conclusion of chapter 2 is that constitutions can be influential vehicles to help define conceptions of citizenship and identity within a given polity. This discussion builds on that chapter by examining the recent trend among many constitutional polities to use *already existing* constitutional texts as a means to enfold particular sub-polities within the larger political order. For many groups that cannot easily find a voice in the political process—groups like African Americans or francophone Canadians—the most effective (or at least symbolically effective) way of entering the political dialogue is somehow to embed one's group identity within the extant constitutional instrument, to alter that document in an effort to reflect changing social and cultural dynamics but not to seek an altogether new constitutional design. The present discussion thus recognizes that constitutional transformation does not always occur at the literal birth of a nation. Constitutional transformation can happen at almost any point in a polity's historical arc; it can emerge from grassroots movements aimed at altering the defining features of a political society, from governmental initiatives that have a profound affect on an entire population, or from longstanding beliefs and practices that finally achieve constitutional status. The common feature among all constitutional transformations, however, is that they result in the fundamental reshaping of political and social norms.

Perhaps no scholar over the past three decades has contemplated the nature of constitutional transformations more than Bruce Ackerman. In his two-volume *We the People* series, Ackerman describes those profound constitutional moments in which an American populace agreed to transform its polity in fundamental ways. These moments, he insists, have the effect of a constitutional founding, and yet they are not accomplished by meeting in specially designed drafting conventions or penning new constitutional charters. According to Ackerman, constitutional transformations occur in several ways. Most obviously, they emerge through the process of constitutional amendment, through the literal alteration of the text to reflect changing cultural, political, and social perspectives. More rarely, however, they arise from a series of decisive political events that introduce a radically new understanding of the constitution. The passage of the Civil War Amendments in the United States, he says, is an example of the type of transformation initiated by textual change; the Supreme Court's endorsement of New Deal legislation beginning in 1937 is an example of the type that occurs through less formal means.[6] In George Thomas's words, Ackerman's notion of constitutional transformation recognizes that "the people, in a genuine act of popular sovereignty, ratify new constitutional understandings, giving us a new constitutional regime."[7] The hope is that eventually all citizens will embrace that new understanding, thus completing the transformation. The main point in Ackerman's theory is that states, institutions, communities, government officials, and private individuals within a particular polity all view the political society through different lenses once the transformation takes place.

Despite his primary interest in the American experience, Ackerman's theoretical arguments can be universally applied. It is clear that moments of constitutional transformation can occur almost anywhere. The Yale University political scientist speaks of moments of "higher lawmaking" in which constitutionalist polities redefine themselves in profound and meaningful ways.[8] The American constitutional scheme is not the only one capable of promoting, allowing, or enduring such a constitutional transformation. Of course, it has managed to accomplish all three. Again, one need only look to the history immediately following the passage of the Thirteenth, Fourteenth, and Fifteenth Amendments to the U.S. Constitution to see evidence of a radical alteration of constitutional meaning. These amendments have not always been successful at constituting a new population free from all forms of discrimination, but by virtue of their addition into the constitutional document they have come to represent the type of transformation Ackerman is talking about.

And yet, like that of the Civil War Amendments, the story of many constitutional alterations around the world has been one of attempts to enfold previously marginalized groups into the political process, to literally reference safeguards for minority groups within the constitutional document. Some of the most interesting constitutional transformations occurred recently in Eastern Europe. It is well known that loosening the grip of Soviet hegemony in Eastern Europe accompanied a feverish attempt to modify the constitutional forms that had previously dominated the region. Stephen Holmes and Cass Sunstein write that the transition from Communist regimes to more democratic ones was accomplished, in part, by amending the existing constitutional documents. Their description of the events hints at the power of constitutional transformations and the importance of constitutional recognition:

> Throughout the region, the unstitching of the hammer and sickle from uniforms
> and banners was accompanied by the deletion of the clause that appeared in every
> Soviet-era constitution stipulating the leading role of the Communist Party. And
> this was only the beginning. The denouement of the Polish Round Table Talks in
> 1989, for instance, was the amendment of the 1952 Constitution to bring it into line
> with the compromises struck between Solidarity and the party. Similar attempts to

codify a swiftly changing balance of social forces occurred throughout the region. And it was not inappropriate that the greatest political transformation of this century was decorated by, or embodied in, constitutional amendments. Communist-era constitutions were repeatedly amended, of course. But to found a new regime through the strategic use of the amending power, which was never the purpose of earlier modifications, represents a wholly non-Bolshevik method for reacting to and promoting social change. The old order was not overthrown but simply negotiated and codified away.[9]

An equally interesting constitutional transformation recently came to pass in Canada, where a majority of Canadians ratified a comprehensive set of constitutional additions that radically redefined the nature of the constitutional polity. The 1867 Constitution, which did not adequately recognize the country's largest paideic community, was amended in 1982 to account for the polity's heterogeneous and increasingly fragile existence. Here the concepts of recognition and transformation converge. Indeed, the principle of constitutional recognition is deeply embedded within the framework of constitutional transformations. Often the higher lawmaking that occurs in contemporary constitutionalist regimes involves the recognition of previously marginalized groups. The most profound constitutional transformations in the United States, South Africa, Eastern Europe, and Canada all occurred because of attempts to integrate isolated groups more squarely into the political landscape. The constitutive feature of modern constitutionalist texts has now become more explicit: rather than relying on universal rights guarantees to bind a polity, constitutional amenders are singling out particular groups as deserving higher degrees of constitutional recognition.

Although at first glance it may seem that the concept of constitutional recognition is simply a shorthand version of the principle of tolerance, the two ideas differ in several important ways. Tolerance, defined as the *acceptance* of the differing views of others, is a broader, more general concept. It can refer to almost any circumstance in which the actions, beliefs, values, and/or characteristics of individuals (or, more likely, groups of individuals) are permitted to continue with relatively few public restrictions. A majority's tolerance of a minority's religious beliefs, for example, is symbolic of a general philosophy (based on liberal ideals) that a political society will flourish if individuals and groups are largely free to pursue their own conceptions of the good. Similarly, a state's tolerance of an individual's unorthodox views—say, when that individual angrily protests against the policies of the state—is symptomatic of that same notion of forbearance.

By comparison, constitutional recognition is a far narrower concept. It is defined as the *acknowledgement* of the existence and rights of differing communities within the larger polity through the mechanism of constitutional authorization. More specific than clauses that safeguard universally protected freedoms, provisions in a constitutional text that qualify as recognizing group identity are ones that isolate the characteristic (or characteristics) that set the groups apart in the first place. The Fifteenth Amendment to the U.S. Constitution, for example, prohibits the denial of the franchise based on *racial* characteristics. Many specific provisions of the Canadian Charter of Rights and Freedoms empower francophone Canadians to continue their *linguistic* and *cultural* heritage even in the face of obstacles imposed by national political policies. In each example, the text literally identifies the marginalizing characteristic in an effort to remedy the discrimination of the past.

Accordingly, constitutional recognition may be a narrower conception, but it can be a far more powerful idea when compared to the principle of tolerance. Its power is derived from its connection to the fundamental law. The idea is that accepting a group's identity is made more forceful by virtue of its inclusion in the country's most important public document. The polity announces a degree of embeddedness of the previously excluded group when it goes to the trouble of amending its constitutional document. As such, constitutional recognition represents both a symbolic and a tangible moment in a polity's history. Its symbolism is manifest in the reality that a previously marginalized group is able to point to a clause (or clauses) of the constitutional draft as representing an entrance into the political dialogue. Unfortunately, such recognition often remains symbolic (for a time) because, as with the Fifteenth Amendment extending the right to vote to all citizens regardless of race, the actual practice of acknowledging group rights often does not immediately reflect the amendment's promise. It took more than a century and the passage of the Civil Rights Act of 1964 for most African Americans to finally realize the freedom to vote.

Yet in some sense the inclusion of a clause or clauses recognizing distinct group identities marks a tangible change in the direction of the polity—a transformation, in Ackerman's words. Ackerman describes such a shift that occurred as a consequence of the Reconstruction Amendments. After the inclusion of the Civil War Amendments, it became much more difficult to ignore the pleas of black Americans. Majorities could not discriminate without violating the constitutional instrument, for black Americans were now equipped with constitutional ammunition. They were fortified by the additions because they could, after ratification, depend on the assistance of the third branch of the American government. Indeed, the Thirteenth, Fourteenth, and Fifteenth Amendments empowered the judiciary as the great defender of the minority voice. It may have taken a number of generations to realize its purpose, but the Court did eventually embrace the constitutional mandate asserted in cases such as *Brown v. Board of Education,* 347 U.S. 483 (1954).

The Civil War Amendments supposedly shield blacks and other minorities from arbitrary and sometimes discriminatory policies by safeguarding them from entrenched majorities. Specifically, the amendments (along with the Bill of Rights) limit the authority of the majority by prohibiting certain forms of regulation. In the same way Congress "can make no law abridging freedom of speech," the Fourteenth Amendment precludes states from treating people in fundamentally irrational ways, especially when the distinction is based on immutable characteristics like race. It is the judiciary that is charged with the responsibility of overseeing the relationship between the majority (as represented in governmental institutions) and the minority, for it is the institution of the judiciary that was designed precisely to combat the will of the collective peoples. Publius wrote in *Federalist* 78 that the judiciary must be infused with a particular style of power, one that could withstand the force of majority rule. Strict independence from the other two branches as well as the general populace, he argued, was the crucial ingredient in achieving a level of authority commensurate with the judicial mission.[10]

Outside of the United States, illustrations are equally prevalent. The passage of the South African constitution denotes a radical shift in the vision for that country's future and for the lives of those who were so ruthlessly oppressed. As Mandela indicated more than a decade ago, the ratification of a new South African constitution, with a number of clauses that specifically recognize distinct linguistic, ethnic, racial, and regional identities, represents a "rebirth," a "new road" for the entire polity. Citizens now point to that historical moment as representing the beginning of a new and modern South Africa. Similarly, Canada's image for its future was reconceived with the passage of the 1982 Charter of Rights and Liberties. Ratification of the comprehensive amendments meant that French-speaking Canadians would (at least symbolically) enjoy a greater degree of recognition in political and cultural circles.

Recognition of this sort is not easily achieved. Often the groups that are clamoring for a voice in the political process are minorities who, rightly, ought to be excluded from monopolizing any conversation about the common good. But being heard is far different than dominating the conversation. It is one thing to cry foul when a minority group controls the debate unfairly; it is a fundamentally different thing when that same minority group is ignored altogether. That is why constitutional recognition requires more than simply extending the vote to previously disenfranchised groups; indeed, *constitutional* recognition is not equivalent to *political* recognition. Constitutional recognition requires at a minimum the capacity of certain individuals and groups to contribute to the nation's public good and, perhaps more importantly, the belief on the part of those same underrepresented groups that their arguments about the good are being heard and taken seriously.

Such recognition can come in the form of rights—free speech, freedom of assembly, and so forth—that are jealously guarded by the citizens and the institutions of power alike. It is more powerful when it comes in the form of specific provisions within the constitutional text that grant special (or at least protected) status to particular groups. At its core, constitutional recognition can only truly be achieved when the acknowledgment emanates directly from the legitimate and authoritative constitutional text. By this measure, Canada's 1867 Constitution has failed miserably. It all but ignored an important member of the nation-state when its framers refused to consider the contributions of certain francophone thinkers and the extensive presence of French-speaking citizens generally. As such, it cannot be said to engage fully 25 percent of the current Canadian population, a problem that has given rise over the last quarter of a century to the very real possibility of national disintegration and the broader movement to change the constitutional text in a way that better recognizes Canada's many ethnic and linguistic minorities. Canada's constitutional history presents the richest account of a polity struggling with the principles of constitutional recognition, and for that reason we turn to it once again.

Canadian Constitutionalism: A Case Study

Much has been written in recent decades comparing Canada and the United States, and among the major conclusions suggested by these studies is the finding that, constitutionally, the history of Canada differs in fundamental ways from that of its southern neighbor.[11] When evaluating the two regimes, one is immediately struck by the fact that Canada has had two major founding moments—one in 1867 when the British North America Act was drafted, and one in 1982 when the Canadian Charter of Rights and Freedoms was added to, and fundamentally transformed, the original 1867 document.[12] In contrast, the core of the U.S. Constitution was adopted at a singular moment in American history and has been altered (but only slightly) at various times since the end of the eighteenth century.

The consequence of this disparity can be detected in the differing attitudes Canadians and Americans have toward their respective constitutional charters. On the one hand, Canadians are currently battling over the very future of their constitutional regime, questioning the document's true efficacy as a constituent tool and its longevity as an organizing political document. In the United States, on the other hand, where the two-hundred-year-old text seems firmly entrenched, the major skirmishes now tend to be political rather than constitutional, derivative rather than fundamental.

What is more, Canadians have struggled with the issue of ratification since the introduction of the British North America Act. Because of their experience as a colonial arm of the British Empire, the citizens of Canada have enjoyed little say in the formation, interpretation, and development of their political regime. The actual process of consent as a means of engaging and binding a citizenry to one another and to the institutions created by a constitutional text has been preempted in favor of colonial domination and control. In the United States the issue of consent was resolved, at least in part, by Article VII. More importantly though, the ratification process was used in the United States as a way to unite the citizens to their governing charter. Americans have, either actually in the period immediately following the Constitutional Convention or figuratively as enduring constituents in the constitutional project, agreed to live under the rules and procedures outlined by the Constitution, something that cannot be said for Canadians.

Such dramatic contrasts make for widely divergent constitutional developments. Like so many countries around the world, Canada is governed by a constitutional document that makes many of its citizens uneasy. Its problems are macro-constitutional, involving the text itself. Canadians are constantly inquiring as to what should be done to make their constitution more effective as a collective tool. How can the constitution embrace French Canadians, for example, and if it cannot, should the text be scrapped in favor of another? Similarly foundational and basic questions have not been seriously asked in the United States since the mid-nineteenth century. That is to say, the U.S. Constitution is not perpetually on trial whenever policy differences arise. Major public disagreements in the United States are refereed precisely by the constitutional document, almost as if it were the one thing that remains constant and ensures regime stability. Hence, problems in America tend to be more of the micro-constitutional nature—those that involve issues of partisanship and policy, but not specifically those that question the very foundation and existence of the political society itself.

The Constitution Act, 1867

The original Canadian constitution was born mostly out of fear.[13] Among other things, Canadians in 1867 feared the continued expansion of British imperialism beyond the status quo, the problems associated with internal political disorder, and the type of provincial or state disunity that mirrored the one threatening the survival of the United States in the mid-nineteenth century. Of course, constructing a political order out of fear is not unusual. The framers of the American constitutional order were frightened by both the tyranny of British rule and the more intangible oppression that often accompanies majoritarian control, and as a result they drafted a constitutional text that reflected these worries. Similarly, countries such as South Africa, Poland, Germany, and post-Communist Russia have, over the last half-century, formed political regimes and built political institutions that seek to minimize the possibility of turmoil and despotism.

What is peculiar about the Canadian situation, however, are the circumstances that led up to the Quebec Conference of 1864 as well as the ones that have shaped Canadian constitutionalism since that founding moment. For most of Canada's early history she was just another pawn in the vast European imperial system. Controlled by both the British and the French at various times, British North America promised the great natural resources that accompany a largely unexplored land as well as the further opportunity to expand European political and cultural hegemony. In the first half of the nineteenth century, most inhabitants of British North America were fairly content with their current colonial arrangement. Expanded colonial rule in the form of additional restrictions on trading and commerce was perhaps troubling for some, but there was also a pervasive sense of loyalty and security that came with membership in the British Empire. That is to say, pre-independent Canada did not share the same animosity toward the mother country that dominated the American revolutionary period. An end to colonial rule in Canada was not established through revolution as it was in the United States, nor was it realized by a complete overhaul of the major political institutions. Other influences mandated a subtle change in the political environment and the creation of a new political order.

The colony had witnessed a number of internal struggles between French loyalists and their British counterparts in the eighteenth and early nineteenth centuries, the result of which was a considerable tension between the two linguistic and cultural communities. British subjects in Upper Canada most often relied on the aid of the English monarchy to quell uprisings by French Canadians, while the

French in Lower Canada could also rely (albeit to a lesser extent) on the support of the French establishment. But the consequence of this ongoing dispute was significant political disharmony. British subjects were constantly wary of their French neighbors, while the French believed that their distinct way of life was being suppressed by the stronger British presence. Add to this internal conflict the difficulties affiliated with a land so vast that any type of informal governmental control was, at best, challenging, and what one had in the early to mid-nineteenth century was a precarious and potentially ominous political situation.

The proposed remedy for these problems was the British North America Act of 1867, which has come to be known as the Constitution Act, 1867, Canada's first written constitution. In many ways a response both to the fractured federal style of government that gave rise in the United States to the Civil War and the developing animosity between the two dominant linguistic identities, the British North America Act of 1867 attempted to order Canada's political universe by solidifying a shaky confederation between the major provinces and the Maritimes.[14] It did so by promising a stronger central government, a parliamentary system, and a limited notion of federalism modeled after the principles of unity and cooperation and in contrast to the more American theory of partition.[15] The main purpose of Canada's 1867 constitution was to strengthen the fragmented ties that bound French-speaking and English-speaking Canadians or, at the very least, to provide a political structure that could ensure peaceful coexistence. Canadians had glimpsed the dissension in the United States that generated the Civil War and thus believed that a distinct constitutional order—one that was for the most part unrelated to that which structured the United States—could better ensure unity.

Unfortunately, the reality in Canada since the founding has been anything but harmony. Instead of easing the conflict between English-speaking and French-speaking Canadians, the 1867 Constitution Act has in fact exacerbated the tension. Since 1867 the constitution has been unable to properly order the citizens of Canada and provide them with a shared constitutional heritage, something that is essential for most modern multicultural nations. Part of the constitution's ineffectiveness derives from its peculiar form and its technical rigidity, but another significant factor lies in the fact that it exclusively reflects British hegemony.[16] It is, according to three members of the founding generation, a constitution that does not "derive from the people," but rather has been "provided by the Imperial Parliament" in England.[17] The constitution does not, in other words, originate with the consent of the citizens in the way most other modern regimes have begun. Instead, the 1867 Constitution has been imposed on the people by an extrinsic source.

Consequently, those who are governed by the British North America Act of 1867 have never fully agreed to live under its rules and procedures; they have never, in other words, formally ratified the document. Such a condition is not overly disturbing for the average English-speaking citizen because the document's main principles, ideas, and commands reflect a primarily British way of life. The 1867 Constitution, however, does not similarly acknowledge the presence of French-speaking Canadians, and thus consent—or the lack of it in this case—takes on additional significance for that particular group. The document cannot provide the means—ideological or otherwise—to bind the French community to its more populous neighbor. In fact, the 1867 Constitution does not adequately recognize any group that does not share the same heritage and tradition as the descendants of Great Britain. The public institutions created by the 1867 Constitution are modeled broadly after the British style of governance, while that particular instrument in modern constitutions that often supplies some kind of political voice for minorities—a list of rights and freedoms—is missing from the original Canadian charter.[18] The result is a principally British document that many French-speaking Canadians could not conceivably ratify in the mid-nineteenth century and cannot fully support now.

The fact that a significant percentage of the Canadian population cannot endorse the existing constitutional text is, to say the least, troubling. If the principal thesis of this book is accurate, constitutions are documents that perform multiple functions. Aside from the obvious ordering of institutions, modern constitutions are supposed to articulate aspirations, reflect cultural priorities, and unite communities by initiating a compact or covenant between peoples, some of whom share nothing more in common than a geographical border. The U.S. Constitution embraces almost all of these objectives. The Preamble to the American constitutional text sets out a number of aspirations, while the original charter and its additions reflect the founders' penchant for the principles of liberty, self-government, and moderation. Moreover, America's constitution manages to bind different groups loosely together to form one unified nation, and it does so by staying largely neutral to differing cultural practices. People can come from various parts of the world and preserve their particular cultures while at the same time acclimating to broader American customs. America's status as a nation of separate peoples rests precisely on the theory that both citizens and institutions share, above all else, universal values—ideals such as freedom, democracy, representation, and sovereignty. All are principles that promote the notion of participation, or the mentality that each American can contribute equally to the realization of a common good, and none are specific to a particular cultural or linguistic identity. What makes them so much more authoritative is that each of these universal values finds its particularized origin in the Constitution itself.

In contrast, contemporary Canadians have not yet found the necessary constitutional ingredients to make their country's major cultural differences more manageable. Canada has not, that is to say, constructed a viable constitutional document that is capable of engaging both linguistic groups in a single common purpose. The original 1867 constitutional instrument, absent the addition of the critical Canadian Charter of Rights and Freedoms, could not easily manage the growing uneasiness of a population burdened with differing linguistic identities.[19] Something had to give. And thus Canadians turned to the project of constitutional transformation—of constitutional engineering—as a remedy. Insofar as constitutions help to manage conflict—often using constitutional recognition as a means to manage that conflict—amending the fundamental law to better reflect the country's heterogeneity was warranted.

The Canadian Charter of Rights and Freedoms

The year 1976 is significant in Canadian constitutional history, for it is in 1976 that the Parti Quebecois—a political party committed to the independence of Quebec from greater Canada—gained its first majority in the Quebec legislature. For some time francophones in Quebec had been advocating the ideas of national bilingualism and individual rights—ideas that were central to their political agenda—but with little success among the larger Canadian citizenry. Very few English Canadians took the French seriously in its plea for a renewed constitutional organization, partly because French leaders in the provincial legislature had very little with which to bargain. What could the French-speaking citizens offer the rest of Canada in exchange for either a new constitutional convention or some form of political recognition? The French were concentrated in Quebec, and even though they held some collective political power, their numbers still constituted a national minority and their leaders were mostly unwilling to anger the members of the national government in Ottawa. Pierre Trudeau had brought Quebec's grievances to the capital a few years earlier and had enjoyed some success, partly because he was personally committed to continued unification of the provinces. Still, his successes were never completely satisfactory for the more extremist population back home in Quebec.[20]

It was not until the Parti Quebecois found itself in the majority in Quebec's National Assembly that talk of meaningful constitutional change took on added significance. French-speaking Canadians still had little to offer the rest of Canada, but what Quebec had now was a political representative that was committed to independence, and with the threat of secession by the French growing more and more imminent, English-speaking Canadians realized that fundamental change was necessary. The 1867 Constitution simply did not recognize the people of French descent or the distinct culture that came with that particular heritage. The consensus throughout all of Canada was that somehow the French separatists must be accommodated or Canada would be split apart along linguistic lines. Yet it also stood to reason that in the attempt to appease the independence movement, English Canada should refuse to hand over all authority and surrender its majoritarian position. That too would be unfair. Thus in 1982 Canadians looked to solve their growing political problems by altering the 1867 Constitution to include a schedule of rights and liberties.[21]

Dubbed the Canadian Charter of Rights and Freedoms, the document guaranteed those freedoms that so many of the world's people have come to take for granted. Rights such as freedom of speech, free exercise of religion, and freedom of assembly were now safeguarded by the modified Canadian constitution. The document also proposed that every Canadian should enjoy, among other things, the "right to life, liberty and security of the person,"[22] the right to "move to, and pursue gainful employment in, any province,"[23] and the "right to equality under the law."[24] But the introduction of constitutional freedoms and the articulation of clear limitations on governmental power are not the only achievements of the Canadian Charter of Rights and Freedoms. The 1982 Charter also enabled the French-speaking community to enter Canada's constitutional dialogue and actively participate in the determination, promotion, and protection of the common good, something it had been effectively blocked from doing since the country's formal founding in 1867. The addition of individual rights into the Canadian constitution did much to shift what Alan Cairns has characterized as a "governments' constitution"—one whose primary purpose was to design institutions and arrange political procedures—to a "citizens' constitution," where the people could now share in the determination of Canada's collective future.[25]

The 1982 document permitted participation from all minority groups by creating a zone or area where the majority cannot legally interfere. The true value of a positive grant of freedom is that it prevents the majority from manipulating and regulating people's ideas and relationships, particularly those that may challenge the dominant majoritarian (or governmental) policy. This obviously is critical for any minority group trying to influence the collective political process because it allows that group to speak and act virtually unfettered and without fear of retribution. In Canada, minority French-speaking citizens were shut out of any meaningful constitutional and political dialogue prior to the formulation of the Charter precisely because they constituted a minority group and there was no constitutional provision that shielded them from the policies of the majority. After the inclusion of a list of rights and liberties within the constitutional text, however, French Canada enjoyed new and potentially more potent political authority.

The Canadian Charter of Rights and Freedoms specifically empowered French-speaking Canadians by creating certain provisions specially designed to shield that single minority group from the English majority. Article 15, for example, grants equal protection to all citizens, "in particular, [without regard to] race, *national or ethnic origin,* colour, religion, sex, age or mental or physical disability."[26] In addition, Articles 16–22 protect French as one of the official languages in Canada, granting it "equality of status" and mandating that it, along with English, shall be used "in all institutions of the Parliament and government of Canada."[27] Finally, Article 23—titled "Minority Language Educational Rights"—states that all citizens of Canada whose first language is either French or English shall enjoy the right to an education in that same language.[28]

These are not simply token grants of freedom intended to silence somehow the entire French-speaking community and in particular those for whom secession is a very serious option. Language is the single most prominent method of public identification, and its continued use and recognition is central to the perpetuation of a distinct culture. Cultural survival, that is, depends primarily on the ability to communicate in a language that connects a people to their past and assures those same people that their offspring will have an uninterrupted future. The provisions in the Charter protecting the French language go a long way toward accomplishing the goal of cultural survival. Certain public institutions would now carry on their business in both English and French, while students in various parts of Canada could now celebrate their particular heritage by being educated in their native tongue. Even road signs and other public announcements (mostly in French-dominated Quebec) would now reflect the constitutional change.[29] The intended result of all this was some kind of public admittance that recognition of French culture—as a distinct part of the larger Canadian legacy—was of serious importance to English Canada. That recognition is not nearly as potent if it does not also include constitutional authorization.

The Impact of Constitutional Recognition on Judicial Power

Two immediate comparisons between blacks in the United States and the French in Canada are obvious by this discussion. First, it is quite clear that prior to the ratification of the Canadian Charter of Rights and Freedoms, French-Canadians could locate no tangible connection to the Canadian constitution. No specific provision of the British North America Act of 1867 spoke directly to the French in the same way that the Civil War Amendments symbolically empowered blacks in this country. Following the addition of a list of rights and liberties, however, the French could no longer as easily complain of a lack of textual recognition, for they were now protected by specific provisions safeguarding their language and, to a lesser extent, their culture. But as was the case in the United States prior to the mid-twentieth century, textual recognition does not always translate into constitutional recognition. African Americans could point endlessly to the Civil War Amendments in their attempt to highlight the injustices of certain legislative policies, yet such accusations would not have made any impact had they not been accompanied by the legitimacy and authority of the American judiciary. In Canada, Quebecois are presently at the stage where they require significant judicial support.

Secondly, the inclusion of a list of rights and liberties in the Canadian constitution further infuses the judiciary in that country with the added responsibility of judicial review. Like in the United States after the ratification of the Civil War Amendments, the federal judiciary (in Canada and elsewhere) takes on the primary role of protecting the constitutionally recognized identity. In other words, constitutional recognition often means a greater role for the judiciary in maintaining the type of paideic insularity that warranted a constitutional amendment in the first place. Both positive rights—ones that are expressly granted to the citizens through the constitutional text—and negative rights—ones that exist because the state is prohibited from encroaching in certain areas—place direct limitations on the power of the state, and in particular on the power of those institutions that represent the majority.[30] The judiciary, as the state's most prominent counter-majoritarian institution, thus becomes the guardian of these rights and subsequently of the minority groups that require rights protection. Its status, in other words, as an institution (somewhat) insulated from the political process, gives it the independence necessary to counter the country's majoritarian departments and, as a result, to shield minorities from the sometimes-oppressive tendencies of certain majorities.

To date, the Canadian courts have not been altogether receptive to francophone demands. Neither were American courts receptive to African Americans immediately following the ratification of the Civil War Amendments. French-speaking Canadians cannot yet point to a single major victory that has been achieved through traditional judicial channels. There are many underlying reasons for this lack of success, not the least of which involves the question of timing. The time, many might argue, is not right for French Canadians to embrace the courts. The courts' willingness to use judicial review as a means to protect minority interests is still relatively ambiguous, while the number of cases exploring the critical provisions of the 1982 Charter remains comparatively low.

In addition, some have speculated that the "notwithstanding" clause—the clause in the 1982 Charter that permits Parliament or the legislature of each province to *override* certain constitutional provisions—takes some of the burden off of courts to protect distinct linguistic minorities.[31] The original aim of section 33 was to solidify the principle of parliamentary supremacy that pervades Canadian politics. The notwithstanding clause allows provincial governments, in short, to ignore particular provisions of the 1982 Charter (say, the right to free speech) for a fixed period of time (renewable five-year cycles). The hope is that by allowing legislative overrides, regional distinctions will be more effectively protected and questions of constitutional import will be addressed, not by the independent judiciary, but instead directly by the peoples' representatives.

The reality has been somewhat different; provinces have seen the clause as an opportunity to entrench cultural norms. Quebec, in particular, has used the "notwithstanding" clause to promote a French way of life within the province; its legislature has used the broad protection afforded provincial governments to further certain policies. Less than three months after the 1982 Charter was declared, for example, the Quebec legislature repealed all provincial legislation and then promptly reenacted each law, but this time with a special statute that invoked section 33. The strategy allowed Quebec to avoid the limitations—both procedural and substantive—imposed by the newly ratified constitution.[32]

Yet despite its apparent appeal, the notwithstanding clause has not lived up to its promise. It has not satisfied many French-speaking Canadians of their wish to anchor certain linguistic and cultural traditions within the constitutional text, nor has it persuaded half the population of Quebec to abandon its call for independence. The reasons for the failure of the clause are clear enough: the language provisions of the 1982 Constitutional Charter (sections 16–23) are exempt from the reach of section 33, and thus Quebec cannot avoid an English presence by simply legislating bilingualism out of existence.[33] Secondly, invoking section 33 comes at a very real political price. To override entrenched rights like the right to free speech is to risk widespread popular disapproval; people simply do not take lightly the elimination of their fundamental freedoms, even for a short time. Mark Tushnet has further added that section 33 "lends itself to such a narrow reading" that its impact on actual governance is dubious.[34] Add all of these factors together, and one can conclude that the notwithstanding clause has not eliminated the need for supplemental institutional—and perhaps judicial—intervention.

In the end, this constitution remains a source of great concern for many French-speaking Canadians; the francophone community has never ratified it. The inclusion of a particular provision that allows provinces to sidestep or override constitutional safeguards has clearly not yet appeased even the most moderate French separatists. A fairly recent referendum on the issue of independence failed, but only by the narrowest of margins.[35] Many French still feel that their cultural identity is largely ignored and that, as a distinct linguistic community, they are not adequately recognized. Paralleling the plight of African Americans in the midcentury, Quebec's quest for constitutional recognition therefore will likely move beyond the words of the text and into the nation's courtrooms.

The current status of the Canadian judiciary presents serious opportunities for minority groups in Canada. Prior to the introduction of the Canadian Charter of Rights and Freedoms, the primary task of the Canadian Supreme Court was to interpret federal laws and review governmental procedures. Rarely did the nation's highest court even consider the question of rights and liberties. With the advent of a schedule of rights, however, the judiciary can now engage in the process of judicial review; it can check the will of the majority by refusing to enforce legislation that conflicts with the federal constitution. And with that authority comes the very real possibility for enhanced constitutional recognition. The Civil War Amendments presented African Americans with an opening and, perhaps more importantly, provided them with a strategic roadmap for achieving substantial constitutional recognition. French Canadians now have that same opportunity; it is up to them to begin drafting a more aggressive plan of action.

Conclusion

As vocal as French Canada has been about the absence of constitutional recognition, very few would contend that English Canada ought to relinquish its control of the country's democratic institutions. The French are not advocating a shift in power from one linguistic community to the other; they simply want to be recognized as a "distinct culture" within the larger polity and to be given meaningful representation in Canada's political process.

When all was said and done, certain Quebec independentists were not completely satisfied with the constitutional recognition achieved by the Charter. The schedule of rights was ratified by the English provinces, but Quebec's National Assembly ultimately opposed adoption, citing the absence of any expression of self-determination within Canada's majoritarian institutions as the major reason for rejection. Language and education rights were fine, according to most French Quebecois, and certainly a step in the right direction. But in order for French separatists to consent to any constitutional document, greater representation in Canada's policy-making centers would have to be ensured. It was not sufficient that francophones could now safely enjoy their way of life within Quebec; they were now determined to find a significant and powerful voice in the larger political process. For the French to embrace the Charter of Rights and Freedoms, the feeling was, English Canada would have to invite them to enter Canada's political dialogue and provide them with the means to participate actively, and perhaps equally, in the determination of a collective good.[36] Words in a constitutional document were not sufficient to satisfy French Canadians in the same way that the words of the Civil War Amendments themselves did not adequately protect African Americans. Something else was required.

And yet the type of recognition secured by a specific set of constitutional provisions is essential because it creates for French Canadians a tangible connection to Canada's governing charter. They are now able to see how the constitution relates to them and how they, as a distinct minority group, are empowered and protected by its commands. They are, in short, bound to the rest of Canada's citizens by these specific additions. In many ways the theoretical security gained by the Canadian Charter of Rights and Freedoms constitutes but a feeling for francophones, a spirit that the nation's fundamental law somehow includes them. The data cited in an earlier chapter revealing that roughly nine out of ten Canadians are pleased with the Charter of Rights and Freedoms attests to this spirit. This is the essence of constitutional recognition. Prior to the ratification of the 1982 Charter, French-speaking Canadians could find no meaningful status within the constitutional document. They had no collective voice in the political process and thus could make no contributions to the common good. As a distinct minority and as individuals within that minority group, they had to rely for that voice on the kindness and altruism of certain political leaders, some of whom enjoyed comparatively short political careers.

CHAPTER SEVEN

Constitutional Empowerment

⌗ ⌗ ⌗

Of all the noteworthy paradoxes of the modern constitutional age, one of the most interesting is the one that highlights the seemingly schizophrenic nature of the constitutional instrument itself. A constitution is a *limiting* agent, a device charged with the task of restraining the various institutions of the polity by establishing rules and guidelines prior to the commencement of a new regime's political life. But it is also an *empowering* agent, created for the very real purpose of ennobling or authorizing those same institutions to act in the name of the sovereign. A major theme running throughout the *Federalist Papers* attests to this point: Publius regularly reminds us that if the American Constitution is to be truly successful it must attend to both functions; it must simultaneously limit *and* "energize" the very political branches it creates. For proof, we need only consider the words of Alexander Hamilton who, writing as Publius, noted that "energy in the executive is a leading character in the definition of good government."[1]

We should not be altogether surprised that the dual character of constitutions is so often shrouded behind genuine concerns about achieving a certain degree of constitutional*ist* government. That is, the schizophrenic nature of modern constitutions is made evident primarily because the limiting function seems so dominant at first. For many founders, politicians, practitioners, and ordinary citizens, the constitutional text represents a shield, a first line of defense against the nastiest impulses of political leaders. The demands of these various constituents are actually quite simple: a successful constitutionalist text, they say, ought to bridle the ambitions of political officials as well as the institutions they control. It should effectively manage conflict, while also ensuring that no single political branch becomes too powerful and thus too abusive.

It should hardly astound anyone that a major goal of many contemporary political regimes has been to cultivate a sense of constitutional limitation. Still, what is more telling is that the call for limitation through textual constitutionalism is now growing even louder. Polities that differ in almost every conceivable way almost universally look to the constitutional instrument as one of the primary means to prevent the rise of potentially tyrannical authority. Political draftsmen from the northern and southern hemispheres alike now rely on the principle of writtenness, of limitation through formal constitutional means, as a necessary barrier to arbitrary rule. It is not an exaggeration to suggest that there has been an almost revolutionary explosion in the birth of constitutional regimes over the last century, and part of that explosion is due to the "global faith" that polities now have in the restraining function of constitutional documents.[2]

But by the same token, the perception that constitutions perform the principal task of limiting political authority only captures part of the picture. Indeed, a constitutionalist text cannot adequately function if its sole purpose is to limit the power of the sovereign. It must do more. As Stephen Holmes has remarked, "In general, constitutional rules are enabling, not disabling; and it is therefore unsatisfactory to identify constitutionalism exclusively with limitations on power."[3] Earlier in the article he writes with more specificity that a "democratic constitution does not merely hobble majorities and officials. It also assigns powers (gives structure to the government, guarantees popular participation, etc.), and regulates the way in which these powers are employed (in accord, for example, with principles such as due process and equal treatment)."[4] Holmes's purpose is to suggest that one should not discount the fact that a primary function of a constitutional document is to infuse the institutions of the polity with the necessary force to operate effectively and efficiently. Constitutions, in short, empower institutions.

This chapter will explore the *authorizing* function of a modern constitutional text—a constitution's role as the primary mechanism to *empower* public institutions to enact legitimate and credible policy in the name of the sovereign. It is meant as a companion to the next chapter, where we revisit and expand on the definition of constitutionalism. Together, these two chapters explore the issue of political power: in one instance, the need to ensure it; in the other, the need to limit it. Throughout the lengthy discussion, one central line of inquiry involves the extent to which the limiting function of constitutions is closely linked to a constitution's empowering function and vice versa. In other words, does the fact that a constitution is charged with the task of creating a structure of political institutions and then empowering those institutions to make policy decisions in the name of the public good somehow advance its role as an instrument whose aim is to limit political authority? Similarly, does a constitution's job to constrain or control the various institutions of the polity actually enhance its credibility, thus enabling the institutions under its watch to gain more authority? These are complex questions, and their answers may not be immediately evident. Yet they are important questions, and to the extent that we can answer them, our understanding of modern constitutional theory will be enriched. Toward that end, we begin with a story.

The Exchange Between Thomas Hutchinson and John Adams

The year is 1773, and the British colonies in America are creeping ever closer to open rebellion. The colonists have been subjected to a series of insulting taxes aimed not necessarily at commercial regulation but instead at revenue generation. The British have largely altered their policies regarding colonial taxation from ones based primarily on the need to coordinate trade among the various geographical entities to ones based principally on obtaining much-needed income. As a result (and unsurprisingly), the cry for no taxation without representation is beginning to echo throughout colonial towns and villages. To add insult to injury, within the next twelve months colonists will witness, in chronological order, the Boston Tea Party, the passage of a series of legislative enactments (dubbed the Intolerable Acts) aimed at punishing the colonists for subversive behavior, and the official commencement of armed conflict at Point Pleasant, Virginia. Dissatisfaction with the way British officials are treating colonists is starting to prompt calls for full-scale revolution. The British in the American colonies are, to put it mildly, uneasy.

At the precise moment in which tempers are flaring and British tax policies are inciting expanding circles of protestors, a higher-level skirmish is taking place. No less intense than the episodes of violence on the streets of colonial America, this battle is being waged not with guns but with words. It is an intellectual exchange of the first order, and it pits some of the ablest constitutional and legal minds of the time against one another. Letters are being written by colonists decrying the lack of representation in the British Parliament, while newspapers are running editorials that highlight abuses by the British Crown. Pamphlets are being distributed to ever-widening audiences that seek to rally support for independence and for the general cause of liberty. Thomas Paine's *Common Sense*, in fact, becomes the widest read publication of the time. Meanwhile, on the other side of the Atlantic, British officials are equally impassioned about the virtue of their philosophical and political positions. They constantly remind the colonists of parliamentary supremacy and of the fact that all in North America are subject to the British authorities. There should be little doubt that during the late colonial period, as during the early Republic just a few years later, some of the most subtle and informed constitutional dialogue took place.

One particularly famous exchange occurred between the Royal Governor of Massachusetts, Thomas Hutchinson, and John Adams, a practicing lawyer who would later become arguably the most familiar face of the revolutionary period. Adams, though not a member of the Massachusetts House of Representatives at the time, was asked by that body to respond to several constitutional arguments posed by Hutchinson. The dispute began with the announcement by Hutchinson in 1772 that from henceforth the salaries of Massachusetts' judges would be paid by the Crown rather than, as was more customary, by the colonial legislature itself. Concerned that he was losing control over various institutions in the American colonies, the king in Parliament believed that usurping authority over judicial salaries would at least render the state courts subordinate to his command. His *official* position, of course, differed. Publicly, King George III stated that all judges within the colonies hold their offices only with his consent, and therefore it is both legal and appropriate for their salaries to come out of his coffers.

Several of the colony's leaders were incensed. They claimed that the new fiscal relationship would remove any degree of independence from the state's courts. How could colonial judges remain objective if the Crown was effectively scrutinizing their legal decisions? For more than a century the principle of self-rule had been embedded in the minds of the colonists and the political practices of the colonies. Samuel Adams, the most notorious rebel of the time, confronted Governor Hutchinson with particular demands aimed at reversing the Crown's decree, including one that called for an open meeting with the Massachusetts colonial legislature. Hutchinson, a loyal subject of the British Crown, refused the demands. He essentially told Samuel Adams and his followers to "mind their own business," to which Adams responded by forming powerful grassroots organizations—committees of correspondence, he called them—whose purpose was to disseminate information to other towns and cities in an attempt to fuel anti-British sentiment.[5] These committees of correspondence would soon emerge in all of the colonies, and their self-declared purview over British abuses expanded. In territories across the thirteen colonies, members of the committees of correspondence were increasingly critical of a large number of British policies and actions.

But back in Massachusetts the confrontation over judicial salaries continued uninterrupted. From the perspective of the colonists, the controversy was principally about the power of colonial legislatures against that of the Royal governors and the Parliament in London. Hutchinson's announcement that the British would control salaries and appropriations ostensibly amounted to a substantial loss of colonial authority. Consequently, the Massachusetts General Assembly issued an ultimatum. The legislative body "offered the judges their salaries in their usual form" while also "threatening to impeach them if they should dare to accept a penny from the Crown."[6] On many judicial benches around Massachusetts the choice—to risk impeachment if paid by the Crown—was alarming. On the one hand, these officers of the Court knew that to accept payment from the colonial legislature was to defy the Crown. But on the other hand, to take money from the king was to jeopardize one's career and, if tensions escalated, to be seen as a loyalist. The talk on the street was that a relatively minor conflict of this sort might lead to open warfare. Governor Hutchinson's response to the rising level of tension was to "call for two special joint sessions of the General Court in order to pacify the towns and to explain why Parliament must retain supreme authority over all British dominions."[7] He understood that ultimate authority resided in London, not Boston. At this point, Hutchinson commenced a theoretical and constitutional argument based on sovereignty that would be countered a few months later by John Adams.

Essentially, Hutchinson voiced concern over the wisdom of promising loyalty to two separate sovereign bodies: the colonial legislatures and the British Parliament. He insisted that it would be illogical, under any theory of good government, to permit citizens to pledge allegiance to separate representative entities. In fact, constitutional government could not be sustained if subjects could pick and choose which sovereign body to listen to. In the present case, he remarked, those Massachusetts citizens who recognized the colonial legislature as the primary institutional authority were simply ignoring the hierarchical nature of governmental power. Under a constitutional monarchy, the power of Parliament is supreme and all other offices are, in varying degrees, subordinate. He insisted that the principle of parliamentary supremacy confirmed one primary rule: that sovereignty was whole and absolute, and thus it could not be shared or divided among different offices and institutions. All British citizens, regardless of their geographical home, were subjects of the primary sovereign, and thus colonial legislative assemblies in Massachusetts (or any of the other colonies) were authorized to make policy only insofar as the British Parliament empowered them to do so.

His arguments about absolute sovereignty were (and are) powerful; indeed, they implicate the entire constitutional project. At the time they were part of a larger belief that colonial charters, those constitutional forms that established and ordered the pre-revolutionary governments, represented grants of authority that disseminated directly from the British Crown in Parliament. Conjuring up the image of the original formation of the Massachusetts colony, Hutchinson proclaimed to the Massachusetts House of Representatives that, "when our Predecessors first took possession of this Plantation or Colony, under a Grant and Charter from the Crown of England, it was their Sense and it was the Sense of the Kingdom, that they were to remain subject to the Supreme Authority of Parliament."[8] His point was that the notion of parliamentary supremacy is revealed through the act of constituting colonial charters and establishing colonial governments. The authority of the British government over and above all colonial governments is actualized by the fact that Parliament established the colonies in the first place. As Governor of Massachusetts, he is an officer of the British Empire; the original charter, in fact, declares his position. His authority is made legitimate because the British Parliament elevated him to the executive office. The colonial charter, in short, is the principal evidence that the sovereignty of the British Parliament should not be questioned. Whatever authority the colonial governments possessed was made possible because it was delegated from the original parliamentary source.

In Hutchinson's mind, the rule of law suggests that there is but one power granting authority. It is, of course, the Parliament, he says, and thus all derivative bodies—including the colonial legislatures—are empowered only to the extent that the sovereign in Parliament grants them control. Those charters infusing colonial governments with the license to make public policy in the name of the sovereign, he claimed, maintain their legitimacy precisely because the British Parliament maintains original and exclusive authority; without Parliament's agreeing to authorize or empower the colonial governments in the first place, those institutions cannot be considered credible.

John Adams was not convinced, at least not with the succession of power defended by Governor Hutchinson. He agreed that the colonial charters were subject to a single authority, but it is not Parliament that is supreme, he said; it is instead an altogether different source. He insisted that the colonial governments are legitimate precisely because they are beholden to British constitutional principles. It is the *Constitution*, Adams claimed, that represents the original and exclusive source of power. Constitutional documents—like the English Bill of Rights and the Magna Carta—occupy a position of authority even greater than the king or Parliament. His evidence? The Parliament in London (as well as the Crown) is no less accountable to those same British constitutional principles; members of Parliament are also limited by the rule of law. Thus, insofar as the tax policies that are being thrust upon colonial citizens violate those basic constitutional tenets as laid out in such provisions as those found in the historical defini-tive texts, the authority of Parliament to demand acquiescence defies reason. As James Otis, a powerful colonial figure of the mid-eighteenth century said, "An act against the [British] Constitution is void."[9] The Parliament is a creature of the British constitution in much the same way that the colonial charters, although drafted and distributed by Parliament, ultimately derive their power from the British constitution.

Adams's words are clear on this principle. Speaking of the original charters granting lawmaking power to the colonial governments, he says that "the laws of the colonies should be as much as possible, conformant in the spirit of them to the principles and fundamental laws of the English Constitution, its rights and statutes then in being, and by no means to bind the colonies to a subjec-tion to the supreme authority of the English Parliament."[10] These charters, he says, "are repugnant to the idea of parliamentary authority"; their legitimacy is tied directly to the legitimacy of a constitutional monarchy.[11] Adams goes on to weave a complicated philosophical argument about the nature of sovereignty itself. He challenges Hutchinson directly on his claim that there cannot be two sovereign authorities within the same jurisdiction. No, Adams responds, there cannot; but the arguments presented by Hutchinson are flawed because they as-sume a faulty premise—that colonial governments are subordinate to parliamen-tary supremacy. Adams's contrasting position suggests that colonial legislatures throughout the entire British colonies (and not just in North America) are sub-ject to the same single head—the Crown—and that all institutions are account-able to constitutional principles. In response to Hutchinson's largely rhetorical question about whether "the two legislative bodies will make two governments as distinct as the kingdoms of England and Scotland," Adams replies: "Very true ... and if they interfere not with each other, what hinders but that being united in one Head and common sovereign, they may live happily in that connection and mutually support and protect each other?"[12]

Adams's main point is that all government institutions are beholden to the higher authority of the British constitution. Even King George III himself, the Massachusetts statesman argues, is subject to the general principles announced in the English constitution. The British constitution confers authority on Parlia-ment, which, in turn, conferred authority through the colonial charters on the state assemblies; and it is these legislative bodies that control local matters, in-cluding the payment of salaries and the imposition of taxes. The legitimacy of lo-cal taxation, in fact, derives from the legitimacy of the constitution, says Adams. The Massachusetts colonial legislature is authorized to impose taxes on subjects within its jurisdiction for two reasons: first, because the legislative body has been empowered to do so through a grant of power originating in the English constitution; and second, because the practice does not violate those constitutional principles that mandate fair and reasonable representation by those constituents subject to the taxation. The primary philosophical argument by those colonists, including John Adams, who voiced opposition to the lack of representation in the British Parliament was *constitutional* in nature: taxing the colonies without providing an avenue for opposition amounts to an illegal act precisely because it violates one of the first principles of England's constitutional structure.

The intellectual battle between Governor Hutchinson and John Adams helps to illuminate one of the core functions of the modern constitutional text. These organizing instruments—whether unwritten like the English constitution or parchment documents like most contemporary constitutions—are constructed to enable or energize institutions to act in the name of the sovereign. One task of a modern constitution, in other words, is to empower the political branches of the regime—to literally grant them authority—so that they may legitimately, and with some expectation of popular approval, carry on the business of ordinary politics.

The eighteenth-century argument about the flow of sovereign authority was an argument centrally about constitutional empowerment. Constitutional empowerment refers to the act of creation and distribution: a constitution creates political branches (in our historical case, the Parliament in London as well as the colonial governments) and then, by distributing various powers to them, authorizes the products of their deliberations (the allocation of salaries to state court judges). A constitutional conflict occurs when multiple institutions claim control over the particulars of a specific governmental policy. That was the case with regard to the allocation of judicial salaries: Hutchinson and Adams believed that different institutions claimed rightful authority to pay Massachusetts' state judges. Constitutional empowerment is thus also a component of constitutional maintenance. Doubtless most framers who set out to constitute a polity imagine that their design will endure over time. A necessary factor in ensuring the durability of a constitutional order, therefore, is to produce a set of political institutions that enjoy the degree of legitimacy that derives only from the polity's fundamental law.

Constitutional Empowerment

In a typical constitutionalist regime, absolute power originates with the sovereign (which presently often amounts to, and is described as, "the people"); but conceptually, it does not remain there. The process of constitution-making and the subsequent ratification of the text alter the relationship of the sovereign to its exclusive authority. If the sovereign begins the process with unlimited power, the constitution symbolizes the delegation—the distribution or giving up—of some of that authority to the various institutions of the polity. So, for example, the American Congress, as made clear by Article I of the U.S. Constitution, possesses certain sovereign power, while the federal executive (Article II) and judiciary (Article III) possess different sovereign power. Subordinate jurisdictions like the American states also retain certain constitutionally distributed sovereign power. To be sure, the sovereign always retains exclusive authority to abandon or scrap the current constitutional form (a practice that happens with relative frequency around the world), but as long as the present constitution remains in existence, the sovereign's once absolute and unchecked power is both regulated and scattered. Part of that overall regulation of authority comes from the sovereign's commitment to self-conscious limits. Insofar as the sovereign pre-commits to certain limitations on its decision-making power outlined within the constitutional text, its capacity to mandate particular policies is constrained.[13] The sovereign (through its representatives in office), for example, may not legally empower government agencies to censor particular messages if the constitutional document protects the right to free speech. Similarly, the sovereign may not choose to embrace a national religious denomination if the text forbids it. Indeed, one of the primary reasons to adopt a constitutional text in the first place is to force the sovereign to agree to the self-conscious limitation of its power.

And yet another equally valid reason to adopt a constitutional text is to do just the opposite: to *legitimize* or *authorize* those institutions fashioned by the constitutional design, and thus to lend credibility to the practice of everyday politics. The transfer of sovereign power through the constitution to the institutions of government also infuses those governmental bodies with the authority to enact government policy legitimately or credibly. Institutions of a constitutionalist polity (majorities, legislatures, chief executives, courts, etc.) require legitimacy. In order for their actions or policies to be seen as justifiable, defensible, or valid, those agencies themselves must be viewed as meritorious; they must be considered lawful and reputable in the eyes of the public. So how does a governmental institution like a court or a legislature obtain the type of legitimacy necessary for its rulings and policies to be followed? Certainly, credibility can be achieved over time through the process of historical longevity. Assuming that it attends to values such as justice, fairness, neutrality, and equality, an agency that exists over a long period of time will more likely than not enjoy a solid reputation. Time, in other words, can help to shore up the credibility and legitimacy of a polity's political institutions.

Beyond the historical piece, however, a governmental institution acquires legitimacy directly through the constitutional text. Most accurately, a constitutional design provides a necessary but not sufficient condition for institutional legitimacy. When the constitutional document that created and empowered that institution warrants a high degree of respect, the enactments of the institution carry greater weight. In other words, if those who are subject to the policies and enactments springing from ordinary governmental branches see that the constitution is legitimate and that the original distribution of sovereign power from the text to the branches is fair and appropriate, the policies that eventually emerge from the branches of government will also be seen as legitimate.

Of course, ratification is a key element in the process of gaining and maintaining constitutional legitimacy. Without it, the credibility of the constitution in the eyes of constituents is dubious. Canada's constitutional experiment is again a worthy illustration. The original 1867 text, which was not ratified formally by all citizens, did not immediately enjoy the type of status that other constitutions have. Perhaps unsurprisingly then, a significant portion of Canadians sought either major constitutional reform or, in the absence of a new constitutional design that acknowledged the importance of individual rights and cultural recognition, constitutional dissolution and separation. In that example, a portion of the population eventually saw the constitutional document as illegitimate, and thus they also questioned certain policies emanating from various national institutions. The credibility of the constitutional text, therefore, directly affects the legitimacy of the institutions it produced.

As such, the constitutional act of engineering institutions through the allocation of sovereign power is important.[14] In fact, the designation or transfer of power through the constitutional text to the institutions of the polity is precisely what Hutchinson and Adams were fighting about more than two hundred years ago. For them, the crux of the debate was less about the scope of colonial authority than about which institution conferred original power on the colonial assemblies and thus which institution was constitutionally empowered to pay judicial salaries. Hutchinson maintained that the British Parliament retained original sovereign power, while Adams insisted that sovereignty in a constitutional monarchy originates in the constitution. In a sense, Adams argued, the political institutions of the polity are only practical reflections of the sovereign—they are not the sovereign itself. Parliament may be powerful (a point Adams willingly conceded), but it is not identical to the sovereign—it cannot be said to retain unchecked authority over the constitution. As evidence of the strength of his position, Adams reminded Hutchinson that the members of Parliament are subject to the laws of the constitution in precisely the same way as any other member of the British Empire, including the king. If the principle of the rule of law means anything, Adams concluded, it means that men are inferior to the decrees of a constitutional system.

Regardless of whether he was correct in his assessment of sovereign power during the last quarter of the eighteenth century, it is Adams's position that most accurately reflects the character of the modern constitutional experiment. The assignment of authority to specific political institutions so that those offices are empowered to make policy in the name of the sovereign is a necessary feature of contemporary constitutions. All power derives from the sovereign, and in a constitutional scheme that power is managed—distributed, in other words—by the constitutional document. By definition, a constitution orders the political world in a self-conscious way. Part of that task is to identify the powers that will be delegated to the various institutions of the polity. This is not to suggest that a system of separation of powers is a necessary component of a constitutionalist regime, but rather to point out that enabling government institutions is a vital function of a modern constitutional text. The British constitution, Adams insisted, empowered the colonial legislatures to pay judicial salaries, and the effective functioning of the state courts relied on that fundamental principle.

Consider, briefly, one contemporary example. Like most constitutions nowadays, the Polish constitution (which was enacted in 1997) includes a detailed description of the various duties or powers retained by the institutions of the federal government. Chapter IV, Articles 95–125, for example, refer to the authority of the Polish House of Representatives (*Sejm*) and the country's Senate. Resembling Article I of the American Constitution, Chapter IV identifies the specific powers delegated to Poland's legislative unit. Provisions are in place for the selection of legislators (Article 98), for the introduction of legislation (Articles 118–23), for the scope of legislative duties (Article 104), and for the place of political parties in the selection process (Article 100). Additionally, the constitution stipulates that the House is empowered to declare war (Article 116), deploy troops (Article 117), and impose taxes by statute (Article 217). From a comparative perspective, it is interesting that certain powers typically designated to legislative

offices are not granted by the Polish constitutional text. The authority to regulate regional commercial activity, for instance, is nowhere explicitly delegated in
the lengthy constitutional charter. The silence itself is revealing of the breadth of
constitutional empowerment.

One important inclusion in the constitutional document, however, is the provision found in Article 125 that literally empowers the legislative branches, the
judicial branch, and the public at large to resolve important and substantive political problems. This article involves the authority to call national referenda on
"matters of particular importance to the state": the power to "order a national
referendum shall be vested in the House of Representatives (Sejm) . . . or in the
President of the Republic with the consent of the Senate." And yet it goes further
to mandate that the national referendum, once approved, is binding, provided
that at least half of those eligible to vote actually turn out. At that point, the
country's highest judicial tribunal has authority to review the substance of the
referendum and either endorse or reject it. Three constituencies thus have a direct role in the realization of the country's most important substantive issues; the
constitution mandates that all three will participate; and it empowers any of the
three to put a stop to the process. The key point raised by this illustration is that
the constitution is specifically designed to empower various institutions to enact
public policy, all in an attempt to maintain a fully functioning political order.

Keith Whittington understands this feature of constitutions with unique clarity. For him, as for Stephen Holmes and others, the constitution is both a source
of guiding principles and an empowering agent: "The Constitution is often understood less as a set of binding rules than as a source of authoritative norms
of political behavior and as the foundation of governing institutions; it perme-
ates the substance of political action, establishing not only the boundaries of
permissible action but also the standards of action. The Constitution not only
constrains; it also empowers."[15] Later, he is even more explicit. About the features
of a constitutional document, he writes, "In instituting various organic structures, the Constitution also distributes political powers among them through
enumeration, designation, prohibition and reservation, all of which are means
of specifying the functioning of political institutions."[16] His point is to suggest
that constitutions energize political institutions through the obvious process of
"enumeration" and "designation"—the *granting* of authority—as well as the less
obvious process of "prohibition and reservation"—the coordinating and *with-
holding* of political power. By giving institutions certain powers and reserving
others, constitutions empower those institutions to practice politics in legitimate
and credible ways.

Doubtless Whittington recognizes that constitutions provide legal guidance for institutions. That guidance comes in the form of what he describes as "authoritative norms" and "standards of action." Yet he also recognizes that constitutions go well beyond the simple process of guiding public offices. If we are to believe that constitutional meaning is "constructed" by most major political institutions (including, but not limited to, the judiciary), Whittington insists that we should comprehend the constitution as an empowering agent. Insofar as nonjudicial and judicial actors are involved in the construction of constitutional meaning, these actors relate to the text in interesting and important ways. They shape the constitution through their actions. Indeed, Whittington notes that constitutional constructions are distinct from ordinary judicial interpretations. He defines moments of constitutional construction as occurring when the understanding of the constitution is "unsettled" and when there is a need to establish "standards" for future political conduct. He further suggests that these constructions alter and influence the meanings of constitutions in the same way that significant judicial interpretations alter or influence our constitutional perspectives. Some of the many constitutional constructions he identifies within the American context are the introduction of the legislative veto, the indoctrination of judicial review, and the creation of certain executive departments.

More important is Whittington's recognition that constitutional constructions are not possible without enabled or empowered institutions. His general conclusion is that "the Constitution empowers political actors to alter their social and institutional environment."[17] A modern constitution like the one that orders the American polity energizes the political institutions to do the real work of politics, to carry on the ordinary operations of a complex state. In turn, those institutions alter constitutional meanings. They effect changes in our understanding of the constitutional order. The result, implies Whittington, is a metaphorical dialogue between text and institutions about the very nature of political practice. The document creates the political bodies, and, assuming they are powerful enough to generate a credible reputation, those institutions then manage to shape the text through the construction of constitutional meanings. Almost any functioning constitutionalist text around the world provides evidence of this dynamic.

Constitutionalism through Empowerment

A workable constitution will classify not only the ends sought by the sovereign but also those institutions and practices that will help foster the necessary conditions for ultimately achieving those ends. Typically, the ends or ambitions embraced by constitutional draftsmen are embedded in the text's preamble. The establishment of justice and/or liberty, the protection of individual rights and/ or equality—these are the common principles announced in present-day constitutions. Indeed, they are the goals sought by constitutionalist governments all over the planet. And yet the articulation of common values in the constitutional preamble is not enough to make them real. A modern constitution recognizes that it is the institutions of the polity that must be empowered to help to achieve the goals articulated throughout the document, so long as they work within a designed framework that recognizes the importance of limited or constrained authority. In other words, once the goals of a polity find a home in the constitutional document, the process of achieving those goals begins, and it begins with energized and empowered institutions. While describing the adoption of the American text in the late eighteenth century, Philip B. Kurland and Ralph Lerner nicely capture this point. "In the plainest terms," they write, "there could be no grounds for expecting justice, tranquility, and the rest [of the aspirations identified in the Preamble] to prevail in America until there was a national government with energy enough to secure the preconditions for justice, tranquility, and the rest."[18]

It is indicative of the complexity of the modern constitutional experiment that some of the most influential founders of the post-Enlightenment era have insisted that an energized or powerful set of political institutions is required to achieve limited and stable rule. Those writing as Publius, for example, argued that in order to maximize individual freedom, government stability, and national security, a powerful national government was needed.[19] The experience of the weak Articles of Confederation, which set up comparatively impotent political institutions, convinced Hamilton, Madison, Jay, and other framers, that the key to a stable and enduring polity was not to constrain governmental branches but to give them the necessary authority over governmental functions to ensure rough equilibrium. In *Federalist* 1, Alexander Hamilton asserts this point: "The vigor of government," he says, "is essential to the security of liberty." Later, in *Federalist* 23, Hamilton implores readers to support a constitution that is "at least equally energetic with the one proposed." Furthermore, he insists that within the explicitly written allocation of authority each branch ought to enjoy exclusive power over its domain. The legislature enjoys the power to declare war, for instance, and that power is not shared with other branches, said Hamilton. Of course, the brash statesman from New York also understood that the other branches of government—which also enjoy exclusive jurisdiction over their expressly granted powers—would, if powerful enough, counter the impulses of the other branches to amass too much control.

And therein lies one of the secrets to the limitation of authority through constitutional empowerment. A written constitution will confer authority on the institutions of the polity and, in the case of the American text and many others, that authority can even be defined as exclusive, or residing entirely within one sphere. Nonetheless, the enumeration of powers within the fundamental law also implies the absence of authority in places where the text is silent. Constitutions may grant specific powers to legislative, executive, and/or judicial branches, but the very nature of a written charter suggests that what is not explicitly granted is not given. James Wilson, one of the most important of the American constitutional draftsmen, is very clear on this point. In a speech calling for the ratification of the text, Wilson defended the transfer of considerable political power to the newly devised national government by reminding the audience that the federal Constitution should only be seen in relation to the state constitutions, and that all power "which is not given [by the proposed Constitution] is reserved [to the states]." To reiterate the point, he simply reminds the audience that from the perspective of the states the opposite is also true: "All power which is not reserved is given."[20] It is interesting to note that, eventually, the Tenth Amendment inserted Wilson's reminder directly into the constitutional text.

Even Chief Justice John Marshall had to admit, in a case in which the High Court envisioned congressional power as virtually boundless, that the character of a constitutional text suggests an automatic limitation of certain powers. In the case of the expansive "Necessary and Proper Clause," he was quick to remind us that the language of the text reveals its limitations: "Congress is not empowered by [the clause] to make all laws, which may have relation to the powers conferred on the government, but such only as may be '*necessary and proper*' for carrying them into execution."[21] Furthermore, he admits that there are places where the text literally announces restrictions on governmental power (Article I, Section 9; the Bill of Rights; etc.). Finally, he remarks, all written constitutions include implied powers, but the process of textualizing or documenting the fundamental law, if it is to mean anything, must admit to a certain defined scope; not everything is possible under a written constitutional charter.

Hamilton's assertion in the 84th *Federalist* that the "Constitution is itself, in every rational sense, and to every useful purpose, a bill of rights" is also instructive here. His specific arguments have been well rehearsed both in this work and elsewhere. First, he insisted that the addition of a list of freedoms to the American text was unnecessary or redundant because the very nature of a written constitution prohibits government institutions from exercising powers not expressly delegated by the instrument. Second, he and others made the related argument that the inclusion of a list of rights within the constitutional instrument is, in fact, dangerous because it implies that government retains all powers except those specifically limited by the rights guarantees. A Bill of Rights can have the opposite effect than what was intended; it can produce a belief that governments need only ensure the protection of explicitly articulated rights.

It is this more subtle argument that emerges from the dialogue between Hamilton (writing as Publius) and his Anti-Federalist opponents that warrants further attention. Scholars have suggested that the Anti-Federalist endorsement of a bill·of rights had (and still may have) the potential to backfire, that the existence of a textual bill of rights, rather than enhancing freedoms, will stifle or limit the very liberty opponents of ratification so passionately defended. According to Herbert Storing, "The basis of the Federalist argument was that the whole notion of a bill of rights as generally understood is alien to American government. It was derived from Britain, where there was no written constitution and where individual liberties were secured by marking out limits on royal prerogative."[22] Storing then goes on to suggest that the primary reason for opposing the inclusion of a bill of rights in the constitution was, in fact, to preserve liberty itself. The key to freedom was (and presumably still is) a robust and energetic government that understood the scope of its power and that recognized the limits incurred by a preordained constitutional instrument. Quoting Publius in *Federalist* 63, Storing writes, "The friends of the Constitution . . . feared that an undue concern with rights might be fatal to American liberty. 'Liberty may be endangered by the abuses of liberty.'"[23]

The implication of all of this is that a constitution that does not include a concrete list of freedoms (yet is ratified under the Hamiltonian assumption that a constitution is "itself a bill of rights") has the potential to cultivate a greater degree of liberty than one that literally embeds rights within the text.[24] That is so because of the automatic limits that accompany a textual constitution. The idea that the very character of a written constitution restrains political power also applies to individual rights, so that the freedoms not constitutionalized by their inclusion in the document are viewed as presumably less fundamental or even as unavailable to the general population. Certain Federalists were concerned that the placement of rights in the fundamental law would give the impression that they amounted to privileges bestowed on the citizenry by government and not, as was intended, a natural element of the human condition. Benjamin Rush admitted to this perspective. He wrote, "'As we enjoy all our natural rights from a pre-occupancy, antecedent to the social state,' it would be 'absurd to frame a formal declaration that our natural rights are acquired from ourselves.'"[25] In part, the controversy surrounding the right to privacy is a legacy of that philosophical outlook.

Two main points arise from this discussion. First, a written constitutionalist text automatically implies the limitation of power. Insofar as constitutionalist documents are, by their very nature, concerned with the regulation and management of self-conscious restraints on the capacity of the sovereign to exercise its will, they will follow a principle that sounds a good deal like the one espoused two centuries ago by James Wilson. Indeed, it was Wilson who "pointed to the fact that the general government would possess only specifically enumerated powers" and those implicit powers that accompanied them.[26] Second, and more important for our present purposes, a constitution that empowers or ennobles the institutions of the polity to act in the name of the sovereign has a better chance to cultivate the preconditions necessary to achieve those aspirations declared by the text's preamble. In order for a polity to realize its primary ambitions, it must admit to a certain degree of energy in its political branches. Infusing political institutions with legitimate and credible power—power that begins with the unchecked sovereign but is then transferred through the constitution to the institutions of government—can have significant benefits for the newly constituted polity. The most obvious example involves liberty. To establish the preconditions for a genuinely free society, the institutions of the polity must be powerful enough to maintain and protect them. No political or constitutional theorist said it better than Rousseau, who understood that the transition from the state of nature to civil society, rather than leading to less individual freedom, was a principal ingredient in the enhanced liberty of the newly constituted citizen. He wrote, "To the benefits conferred by the status of citizenship should be added that of moral freedom, which alone makes a man his own master. For to be subject to appetite is to be a slave, while to obey the laws laid down by society is to be free."[27]

CHAPTER EIGHT

Constitutional Limits

The time has come to revisit, and develop more fully, the notion of constitutionalism. For many, the *primary* function of a constitutional document is not necessarily captured in the seven chapters above. A constitution's principal role, according to these observers, is not to articulate the polity's aspirations, or to empower the main political institutions to enact public policy in the name of the sovereign, or even to design the regime's political institutions in a self-conscious way. These are all important, but they are not the modern constitution's primary function. Instead, the chief purpose for preparing a constitutional text is to act as an insurance policy against the possibility of random and arbitrary political rule. It is to establish a supreme authority—an instrument universally recognized as the fundamental law—in the hope that the polity will eventually inculcate the principle of limited government and the rule of law. The main reason to draft a written constitutional text in the first place, some say, is to provide a tangible barrier to the impulse of the sovereign (or, more accurately, practical reflections of the sovereign within the institutions of government) to turn against the comparatively powerless population. All other concerns of a constitutional document are essential but secondary. Consider the words of the nineteenth-century U.S. Senator John Potter Stockton. Constitutions, he said, are "chains with which men bind themselves in their sane moments [so] that they may not die by a suicidal hand in the day of their frenzy."[1] The seventh and final function examined, therefore, is that of constitutional limitation, the role of modern constitutionalist charters to identify specific limits on the power of the sovereign. Its importance as a central function—perhaps *the* central function—of the modern constitutional experiment warrants its place as concluding the general examination of constitutional functionality found in this volume.

To be sure, modern constitutionalist constitutions *are* texts that aim to achieve a meaningful degree of restrained or limited political rule. As Cass Sunstein has written, "Constitutional provisions should be designed to work against precisely those aspects of a country's culture and tradition that are likely to produce most harm through that country's ordinary political processes."[2] Even so, their other functions are no less important, nor can they be said to derive somehow from the broader principle of constitutionalism. What is probably most accurate is to claim that the mechanism of limiting political authority through textual means represents the greatest innovation of political rule in the post-Enlightenment period. Gordon Wood suggests that the American experiment with constitutional governance—where many of the historical ideas about limited government finally came together—represented a radical change in the way humans viewed political order. Referencing Thomas Tudor Tucker's extraordinary 1784 pamphlet, *Conciliatory Hints, Attempting by a Fair State of Matters, to Remove Party Prejudice*, in which he "clearly and cogently" describes "just how far Americans had departed from the English conception of politics," Wood writes: "In a brilliant passage, Tucker summed up what Americans had done in two decades to the conception of a constitution: 'The constitution should be the avowed act of the people at large. It should be the first and fundamental law of the State, and should prescribe the limits of all delegated power.'"[3] For Wood, as for Tucker, constitutionalist government through textual limitation represents the eighteenth century's unique and remarkable contribution to the practice of politics.

Scott Gordon agrees: "The most significant feature of political organization is not that the nation-state has supplanted all other forms, nor that the domain of the state has grown so large, but that ways have been found to control its coercive power."[4] The historical development of the idea of constitutionalism, culminating in the modern penchant to rely on a single written instrument to constrain political power, is a remarkable story. In most cases constitutions are now seen as the polity's primary touchstone against arbitrary government. Their framers imagine mechanisms that will help ensure that tyrannical and oppressive governmental rule is unlikely to emerge, but it is largely the responsibility of the document itself, and the credibility that text carries both domestically and internationally, that will deliver the goods. Doubtless, other forces, including the economy, the country's political tradition, the social fabric of the society, and so on, will contribute significantly to the prospect of a constitutionalist constitution taking root in a particular place. And yet all of these factors would mean little if the text itself did not embrace constitutionalist ideals. The document must be the initial source of inspiration; it must act as the original point of reference for politicians and ordinary citizens to use when attempting to manage potentially abusive political authority. Controlling coercive power, although certainly not easy and always fraught with controversy, has been the primary mission of most constitutional framers since the end of the eighteenth century.

Examining the principle of constitutionalism requires that we juggle a number of related conceptual ideas. The heart of this chapter will be devoted to a theoretical understanding of constitutionalism, but to have confidence that any description of constitutionalism is more or less complete, we need to think beyond the realm of abstract theory to other aspects of the constitutional enterprise. It seems appropriate to begin, therefore, with a brief history of the concept of constitutionalism. When and where did the idea originate? How has it changed over the centuries? Then, as part of the examination of the theory of constitutionalism, I will first explore the relationship between constitutional limits and the human tendency to act self-interestedly, and then the connection between constitutions and social compacts. Finally, I will end the chapter by contemplating whether a polity requires a *written* constitution in order to qualify as constitutionalist, concluding with a brief discussion of the role of the judiciary in helping to realize a constitutionalist polity. Is it possible, we should ask, to conceive of a political regime that adheres to the principle of limited rule but still allows its government agencies to alter and implement constitutional rules with simple majoritarian support? Would that qualify as a constitutionalist polity? Does that polity need an independent judiciary in order to check the authority of the other branches, or is independence still not enough to ensure constitutionalism? These and other questions will be addressed below.

Historical Development of Constitutionalism

According to one source, "constitutionalism is descriptive of a complicated concept, deeply imbedded in historical experience, which subjects the officials who exercise governmental powers to the limitations of higher law."[5] Even though the term *constitutionalism* first appears only in the first half of the nineteenth century,[6] the idea dates back many centuries, at least to the Ancients. Both Plato and Aristotle were concerned with the ordered structure of political and legal institutions, and the relationship between political power and higher law. Neither conceived of constitutions exclusively as formal, written documents; that would not become popular until after the American constitutional experiment in the late eighteenth century. And yet Aristotle in particular wrote extensively about "constitutions," defining them as "the organization of offices in a state, by which the method of distribution, the sovereign authority is determined, and the nature of the end to be pursued by the association and all its members is prescribed."[7] He is famous for claiming that certain constitutional orders—democracies, monarchies, oligarchies, and so on—are more appropriate for certain polities and that the success of a new political regime will depend in part on its compatibility with a specific constitutional form. For Aristotle, the "constitution" represented the "most general aspect of law," the broadest principles of the civil body politic, and the "life of the city."[8] It informed the work of the legislator whose responsibilities included crafting laws and decrees that would conform to the polity's general constitutional values.

Other philosophers of the ancient period contemplated the image of constitutional order, but it was during the Middle Ages that the term *constitution* more consistently reappears. It takes on a somewhat sharper focus in that the concern of most medieval jurists was to establish the limitation of political power under a religious conception of higher law. First, a sixth-century ruler of Constantinople, a man named Justinian, commissioned a group of ten jurists to codify the laws of his empire. The task was difficult and lengthy, but the result was impressive. The "Book of Laws" identified a "total of 4,562 enactments, all carefully arranged by subject matter and following the roughly twelvefold organization laid down in the ancient Twelve Tables (451 B.C.)."[9] Justinian labeled the collection the *Codex Constitutionum*. Although technically not a constitution in the sense that it did not structure the institutions of the polity, Justinian's book of laws would later be considered around Europe as the definitive collection of the Roman Law. The collection would also come to represent the entirety of man's law at the time. Later, Thomas Aquinas would write about the natural law—the higher law established by God but known by reason—and its ability to limit the authority of the king. In *Summa Theologiae*, Aquinas implores future citizens to obey the laws set out by rulers and rulers to obey the dictates of reason. The problem, as Aquinas saw it, was that comprehending the breadth of God's law (the law of reason) was next to impossible.

The introduction of Magna Carta in 1215 marked a significant development in the concept of constitutionalism. To that point, constitutional government was almost never limited government; the sovereign's grip on political power was more or less boundless. Take Aquinas' principal lesson as an example. He admits to being able to conceive of the limitation of power, but the practical reality of limited rule was far more difficult to achieve. Constitutional limits were not enforceable short of outright revolution. With the signing of Magna Carta, however, a sovereign authority agreed, for the first time in history, to specific and tangible limits on its power. Those limits came, not from a higher power—a God or deity—but rather from a collection of subordinate citizens. Moreover, that agreement was announced in the form of a written text, a contract of sorts between King John of England and his barons. The king, embroiled in an ongoing war with France, sought to raise money and troops for the military campaign. Unfortunately, support was not easy in coming, and John was forced to resort to increasingly tyrannical measures to realize his objectives. These abusive measures included the confiscation of estates, the imposition of unjust taxes, and even the seizing of children as a means to ensure that certain subjects remain in line. After a military defeat in the town of Bouvines in 1214, John imposed yet another tax, and the barons signaled that they had had enough. They confronted the Crown with a series of demands that amounted to a set of grievances against the king. Their concerns centered on two major areas: the administration of justice and the imposition of taxes. In all, close to sixty-five demands were made.

King John agreed to them all, and in the process consented to significantly more transparent limits on his own authority. The Great Charter, in a sense, replaced God as the higher law to which existing political power would be accountable. That overall shift—from a non-secular notion of higher law to a secular one and from an unwritten to a written experiment in limited rule—represents a key development in the modern understanding of constitutionalism. There has been some debate in the literature about whether Magna Carta qualifies as the first written constitution. On the one hand, it resembles a constitutional document insofar as it articulates a vision for governance that includes shared legislative and executive responsibilities. It also identifies rights and obligations. Yet on the other hand, its structure does not resemble contemporary constitutions. It is a petition. The list of grievances that constitutes the Magna Carta probably more closely mirrors America's Declaration of Independence than the Constitution. Yet regardless of whether it qualifies as a constitutional text in the modern sense, the Charter's profound historical importance lies in its attention to the principle of constitutionalism. Moreover, the idea stuck: over the next two hundred years, British rulers reconfirmed the details and spirit of Magna Carta no less than forty-four times.[10]

Modern Constitutionalism

If asked to review almost any moment in the past four centuries, one will inevitably find evidence of man's continuous battle against the evils of arbitrary political rule. Both at the beginning and at the end of the seventeenth century, for example, the most powerful and stable regime in the world—Great Britain—was embroiled in conflicts over just such an issue. The first quarter of the seventeenth century saw intense battles between the British monarchy and the country's Parliament, culminating in several successful attempts by the Crown to dissolve the legislative body. In response, parliamentary leaders condemned the Crown's actions, claiming that they violated the most sacred principles of British constitutional law. The rebuke by legislative officials eventually forced Charles I in 1628 to consent to the Petition of Right, a document spearheaded by Sir Edward Coke, a member of Parliament and one of the most respected legal minds of the time. The Petition, which sought to identify the rights and liberties of British subjects in relation to the prerogatives of the Crown, was in many respects successful in restraining the authority of the king. Still, its overall force was marginal until sixty years later when a similar battle erupted between Crown and subject. The consequence of the Glorious Revolution of 1687–88 was another constitution-like document. The English Bill of Rights (1689), in addition to articulating more rights and liberties possessed by British citizens, further structured the relationship between the ruler and the ruled in Great Britain. The Bill of Rights, like the Petition of Rights and Magna Carta, was aimed at restricting the unlimited authority of the monarchy. It too was successful at a certain level.

The eighteenth century, of course, is principally known for its examples of discontent over the perceived abusive authority of the state. Revolution in the name of more popular government was a fairly widespread practice in the mid- to late eighteenth century. The American and French Revolutions, although dramatically different in many ways, were both based on the principle that popular sovereignty—rule by the many—ought to replace monarchical control, or rule by the one. In the American context, the contract between ruler and ruled was violated repeatedly, leading eventually to the Declaration of Independence and the call for a new self-governing structure. After that, the debate centered on more parochial concerns, like whether the proper design for government ought to concentrate power in the hands of a distant centralized government or whether the bulk of power should properly reside at the local level. But even then the thread running throughout the debates about the overall effectiveness of the Articles of Confederation or the wisdom of adopting a new constitutional order was one of controlling or regulating political power. Pauline Maier, the eminent historian of the American founding period, accurately describes the worldwide phenomenon. "Every age," she says, "has some major issue that people understand as kind of an agenda for that generation; in the eighteenth century it was the problem of government."[11] Good government to those in the eighteenth century most often meant constrained or restricted government.

Even when political communities were not in the process of carrying out violent rebellion, contracts were drawn up to help bridle the power of government officials.[12] The Mayflower Compact of 1620 marked an agreement between settlers at New Plymouth on the coast of what would become Massachusetts. The document's historical significance for the development of constitutional government should not be understated. Most particularly, it represents a "covenant" between individual citizens of the colony as well as between the collective community and God. The covenant is a compact or a contract whereby the settlers agreed to live by certain established and agreed-upon rules. Many of the passengers on the Mayflower believed that without a formal agreement over the broad scope of political authority the prospect of ordered rule would be elusive.[13] Thus they sat down to the task of constructing a meta-political document that would create a "civil body politic." That text—the Compact itself—represents a significant contribution to the development of constitutionalism in the United States. In 1802 John Quincy Adams described the agreement as "the only instance in human history of that positive, original social compact."[14] By that he meant that the Mayflower Compact represents the primary historical example of an original covenant in which citizens of a community consent to live under particular rules. In that sense, Adams said, the Mayflower Compact foreshadowed the introduction of other constitutional documents.

So did American state constitutions. Between 1776 and 1800 all states in the newly independent America experimented with drafting constitutional texts. In all, twenty-nine separate charters were adopted by the former colonies during that period, and an additional two were written for the unified country. Donald Lutz notes that these constitutions focused on two related commitments: to a system of popular governmental control, and to a system of limited political power.[15] Not surprisingly, constitutions drafted in the nineteenth and early twentieth centuries have also subscribed to the principle of governmental limitation through constitutional textualism. The lengthy Spanish Constitution of 1812, for example, details the variety of powers retained by the various governmental bodies. Similarly, the Mexican Constitution of 1917, which includes an extensive bill of rights, a division of powers among the legislative, executive, and judicial branches, and a scrupulously detailed description of the specific powers distributed to each branch, appears equally concerned with the principle of limited political power.

Contemporary examples of attempts to control the excesses of governmental power through constitutional means are evident in almost every country of the world. From the most oppressive regimes to the least, it seems the pressure for more governmental accountability, more liberty, and more objectivity in the exercise of political power is constant. Popular sovereignty is so admired at the moment that any government that justifies its continued authority through the use of oppressive action or force is swiftly condemned. Consider Nelson Mandela's words to the Constitutional Assembly in 1996 immediately after it had completed its task of drafting a new constitutional charter for South Africa: "Long before the intense moments of the last few days," he noted, "you, the representatives of the people, had decided that open and accountable government will be reinforced by co-operative governance among all tiers. And thus, we strike out along a new road, in which the preoccupation of elected representatives, at all levels of government, will be how to co-operate in the service of the people, rather than competing for power which otherwise belongs not to us, but to the people."[16] Almost every contemporary constitutional framer could utter Mandela's words, for they are not entirely unique to South Africa's situation. Indeed, the constitutionalist sentiments expressed by the Nobel Laureate are timeless.

The Theory of Constitutionalism
The Problem of Human Nature

Perhaps the easiest way to resurrect the theoretical discussion of constitutionalism from its brief introduction in the first chapter is to recall that the principle refers to a subset of constitutional texts whose main commitment is to the ideal of *limited* political rule. The concept of constitutionalism is actually based on a rather pessimistic, though probably fairly accurate, view of human nature.[17] Limiting the power of those with the capacity to wield it randomly, and for the benefit of their own self-interest, lies at the root of any conception of constitutionalism. History has demonstrated that humans, when given the chance, have a tendency to abuse power and oppress those without the capability of adequately protecting themselves. One need not look very far to see illustrations of political tyranny, oppression, and seemingly unchecked political authority. The most famous examples of tyrannical government have involved monarchies or aristocracies where political authority was conveniently concentrated in the hands of the few. And yet we should not forget that majorities are as capable of abusing their authority as any other political institution. The idea of constitutionalism is a direct response to the perceived corruptibility of the human instinct, regardless of what decision-making structure is in place.

It is perhaps unsurprising, then, to note that the tension between the human impulse to think self-interestedly and the requirement that modern democracies cultivate civically minded citizens has confounded many of the modern era's greatest political minds. No one was more attuned to that particular paradox than was James Madison. His intellect and vision for the United States is particularly instructive here. It is generally understood that the shy, diminutive Virginia statesman was the principal architect of the U.S. Constitution. And insofar as the American constitutional text has become one of the paradigm examples of a modern constitutionalist document, Madison's understanding of the concept of constitutionalism is worthy of considerable attention.[18] He thought seriously about the theory of constitutionalism even if the term itself likely never passed his lips.

For Madison, as for all good constitutionalists, framing legitimate political order begins with a comprehension of what could go wrong. Shortly before the opening of the Constitutional Convention in May 1787, Madison wrote his famous "Vices of the Political System of the United States" in which he expressed concerns about the structural features of the American polity under the Articles of Confederation. One concern he identified was that of self-interest, or more accurately, what he described as "faction." He noted that, if left unchecked, factions (which he defined as groups with shared interests opposed to the common good) are a cancer on organized societies. Most revealing is that he frames his discussion of the problem of faction around the prevailing perception of the human condition. "A still more fatal if not more frequent cause [of injustice]," he wrote, "lies among the people themselves. All civilized societies are divided into different interests and factions. . . . In republican government the majority however composed, ultimately give the law. Whenever therefore an apparent interest or common passion unites a majority what is to restrain them from unjust violations of the rights and interests of the minority, or of individuals?"[19] In essence, Madison is asking what prevents a majority from tyrannizing the minority. Certainly not the human penchant to act selflessly, he is forced to admit.

His classic admonition in the 51st *Federalist* that men in power cannot be trusted and thus require clear constitutional restraints echoes the character of his thoughts in the essay on "Vices." It too represents an important component of his overall vision for the United States insofar as he turns to constitutionalism as the mechanism to manage the destructive tendencies of human self-interest. "But what is government itself," he asks, "but the greatest of all reflections on human nature? If men were angels, no government would be necessary. If angels were to govern men, neither external nor internal controls on government would be necessary." "In framing a government which is to be administered by men over men," he continued, "the great difficulty lies in this: you must first enable the government to control the governed; and in the next place oblige it to control itself. A dependence on the people is, no doubt, the primary control on the government; but experience has taught mankind the necessity of auxiliary precautions."[20]

Constitutions, Madison understood, were one of a few "auxiliary precautions" that might regulate man's natural appetite for power. The primary purpose of a constitution, he thought, was to help control the worst impulses of the human spirit. Madison insisted that the compulsion to act self-interestedly, especially when combined with the sense of power that accompanies political authority, inevitably leads to the rise of arbitrary government, the first stage of a polity's degeneration into oppression and tyranny. One of the principal requirements of modern constitutionalism, therefore, is that constitutions somehow limit or regulate the power of a self-interested sovereign. In other words, a constitution is charged with the responsibility of constraining a polity's rulers. Such constraints can be achieved through a variety of different mechanisms, including a system of overlapping powers and/or a list of individual rights. But curtailing a leader's impulse to act self-interestedly or in opposition to the common good is the true mark of constitutionalist government.

Always the pragmatist, Madison was aware of the risk he and the other American framers were taking. He knew that the use of constitutional texts as the primary method of regulating political authority was a fresh and quite revolutionary development in the "new science of politics."[21] He also understood that constitutions alone—"parchment barriers," in his words—were not sufficient to control the power of governments.[22] Still, they were essential. Constitutional polities required additional mechanisms beyond simple texts that would ensure the limitation of political authority. A written text itself would manage to establish constitutionalism because a document of expressed powers automatically set a limitation on power: whatever was not delegated in the constitutional document, government did not have the power to do.[23] But other mechanisms, including a system of separated powers, a structure that required checks and balances, a list of freedoms, frequent and fair elections, and so on (assuming they were successful at checking political power), could further ensure the grounding of constitutionalist beliefs in the citizenry.

In his examination of the principle of constitutionalism, Madison was profoundly influenced by history. He recognized that prior to the Enlightenment there were very few examples of documents that had the necessary force to bridle the virtually unlimited power of the sovereign.[24] This was a period in which the rule of men subjugated the rule of law. During the reign of monarchs in England, the king or queen held almost complete control over their subjects. They could tax indiscriminately, impose ex post facto laws, or punish criminals with a severity that would make even the harshest contemporary sentences look like mere slaps on a wrist. There were, in fact, few avenues for citizens to escape the often arbitrary and merciless power of the Crown, and those avenues that were available were mostly a meaningless "fiction."[25] Again, it is useful to consider Bolingbroke's definition of constitutionalism in the early eighteenth century: "By constitution we mean, whenever we speak with propriety and exactness, that assemblage of laws, institutions and customs, derived from certain fixed principles of reason, directed to certain fixed objects of public good, that compose the general system, according to which the community hath agreed to be governed."[26] He speaks of "institutions and customs," "reason" and rationality, as the principal force to combat the strength of the state; he may as well have been speaking of ghosts.[27]

Of the prevailing definition of constitutionalism, Madison was deeply skeptical. He did not agree that customs, or the assemblage of ordinary law, were enough to control the might of sovereign power. He also knew that the nature of sovereignty had fundamentally changed. His recent experience observing the heated dialogue surrounding the legitimacy of America's revolt against unfair tax policies solidified his understanding of the issue. George III, through his representatives in the colonies, had insisted that the Crown was the true sovereign and that the entire colonial holdings of Great Britain rightfully fell under the broad title of the "British Empire." In his view, the colonists were subjects of his rule; the colonial charters, which the British Crown had instituted and approved, he insisted, were further evidence of this imperial arrangement. The response from figures such as John Adams was that there is no legitimate conception of a "British Empire." An empire suggests that sovereignty resides in a single titular head. The British system of governance, said Adams, is more accurately described as a *constitutional* monarchy, where both the Crown and Parliament share power and are ultimately beholden to a constitutional structure that sets boundaries on their authority. For evidence, Adams and other revolutionary-era leaders pointed to the realignment of power during the Glorious Revolution, when the British Parliament asserted greater influence.

Corresponding to the recalibration in power from a single monarch to the general population, the principle of constitutionalism could take on a more robust form in the late eighteenth century. No longer was it acceptable to trust that political leaders (whether they be kings or majorities) would act with benevolence; measures, it was thought, were needed to ensure that the sovereign's power was controlled. What was once perceived as a reasonably powerful limitation on the power of the king—namely, his divine relationship with a vengeful God—would not work in a system of governance where power resided in the collective peoples. Madison was aware that in some cases written agreements between monarchs and subjects had successfully curbed certain types of political power in the past. He and other framers wanted to use that principle on a national scale. In *Federalist* 10, Madison argued that a large-scale republic, ordered and limited by a written constitutional document, would go a long way to ensuring the existence of fair and just government. Thus, beginning in the United States, the measures favored by Madison and others to constrain public authority typically took the form of constitutional texts.

The Need for Transparency

The U.S. Constitution is a product not only of the period in which it was written but also of a powerful belief in the strength of the binding contract, especially the contract formed between the people and their governors.[28] The document is actually the manifestation of the opinion, articulated in the Declaration of Independence, that good government should derive its "just powers from the consent of the governed." At its core, the text's complex arrangements and subtle language reveal the framers' interest in minimizing the likelihood that the general agreement between the people and their representatives might dissolve, thus inviting the possibility of oppressive or arbitrary rule. The participants at the constitutional convention successfully managed to create structures—not just separation of powers and checks and balances, but also fixed terms of office, the use of oaths, strict rules of qualification, and so on—that would not only keep representatives mostly accountable to their constituents but would also enable political leaders to make meaningful policy choices. For these reasons many now contend that the American Constitution is the paradigmatic example of a modern constitutionalist charter.

But it is not the only example. Many regimes have followed America's lead and framed constitutional charters that combine the various elements of modern constitutionalism. The independence movements of former Soviet bloc countries, or the postcolonial experiences of many African regimes, reveal that constitutional transformations in the twentieth century have been undertaken primarily in the name of greater liberty. Madison's concern about the tendency of political officials to abuse the common citizen has been realized in many nations lately. Moreover, his response to that concern has been widely respected. Even places where the cultural and political setting has been shaped by centuries of authoritarian rule (for example, Iraq) are now seen as fertile ground for experiments in constitutionalist government. Often these attempts to impose constitutionalism and democracy around the world are unsuccessful, but it says something about the potency of constitutionalism that we believe we can force it on countries that do not have the proper infrastructure to support it.

The attempts to modernize political regimes through constitutionalist measures have followed a similar formula; in other words, contemporary constitutionalist texts all share in common some fundamental and essential characteristics. I have written elsewhere that a modern constitutional text attuned to the principles of constitutionalism now requires a high degree of transparency.[29] That is, the rules for governance must not only be clear and understandable, but they must also be fixed and unwavering.[30] Three principles will ensure that those rules remain largely stable—externality, discernibility, and *self*-conscious limitation.[31] *Externality* refers to the fact that the constitution must exist apart from the political institutions it creates and empowers. It must be a distinct entity altogether; it cannot, as was the case under Bolingbroke's classical definition of constitutionalism, exist entirely within the mind(s) of the sovereign or the traditions of the culture.[32] Thomas Paine understood the principle of externality best when he wrote, "A constitution is a thing *antecedent* to a government; and a government is only the creature of a constitution."[33] He understood that a lack of separation between political leadership and the primary source of restraint—the constitutional text—makes it far too tempting for those in power to either change their minds or ignore tradition. So did Madison, who wrote, "The authority of constitutions over government, and of the authority of the people over constitutions, are truths which are at all times necessary to be kept in mind."[34] At the time, Madison was contrasting the American Constitution with the unwritten British constitution, which he saw as clearly violating the principle of externality. The British constitution was crafted and altered by Parliament. Simple and ordinary legislative acts were (and still are) the essence of the English constitution. There is little distinction between the constitution and the acts of government in England.[35] A more traditional modern constitutionalist regime, in contrast, must recognize that its government institutions are not to be confused with the constitutional text; they take their cue from the constitution and are thus guided and limited by that document. But they are not one and the same.

The second principle—*discernibility*—is also required for a constitution to qualify as constitutionalist. Tied closely to the concepts of knowability and recognition, discernibility refers to the idea that subjects of the sovereign must be made aware of the text and its particular provisions in order for that document to adequately shield the populace from government's propensity to oppress. A constitution whose particular message is hidden from those who most need its protection does not perform its central protective function. Such was the main defect of classical versions of constitutionalism: constitution-like restraints were often concealed from public view. Even in those instances when the monarch was supposedly constrained or limited by his or her association with God, those who were subject to the sovereign's decrees were largely unaware of the specifics of that relationship and thus were mostly helpless when attempting to challenge or question political authority. Accordingly, the clear announcement of the nature and particulars of governmental restraints is an important component of modern constitutionalism. The point, in short, is to provide citizens with some recourse—some form of ammunition—in the event that government abuses its authority. As Gordon Schochet has said, "The existence of knowable rules provides an important check on the activities of governing officials. Where their interpretations of constitutional permissibility are questioned, there exists a public standard to which to refer."[36]

The third and final characteristic of modern constitutionalism—*self-conscious limitation*—insists that the sovereign itself impose clear limitations on its own power. Whether political power is organized in the form of a monarchy, an aristocracy, or a majority, it is imperative that the sovereign itself (or, in the case of representative government, practical reflections of the sovereign) identify areas in which it cannot intrude. Those limitations must be established at the moment of founding (or through the amendment process or through constitutional constructions) so that, in conjunction with the principles of externality and discernibility, the rules of political governance are mostly fixed and stable. Moreover, those rules must also apply to those officials who are responsible for crafting ordinary law. As Publius argued in *Federalist* 57, the possible rise of institutional tyranny is diminished considerably if government representatives "can make no law which will not have its full operation on themselves and their friends, as well as on the great mass of the society."[37] Obviously, therefore, those limitations must also be grounded in the constitutional text; they cannot derive simply from ordinary legislation. Jon Elster captures the essence of this necessary qualification when he writes that constitutionalism "refers to limits on majority decisions; more specifically, to limits that are in some sense self-imposed."[38]

Altogether, the three principles of modern constitutionalism aim to combat those bad qualities of human nature that Madison was convinced would inevitably creep into and infect modern politics. Exploring the American constitutional example once again allows us to see that all three principles are present: (1) the document exists externally from the institutions of government it creates; (2) despite requiring a good amount of interpretation, it is mostly discernible in that its broad contours are relatively fixed and stable; and (3) the ratifying populace— both at the founding and, through tacit consent, at present—has agreed to a number of restraints on majoritarian power. Gazing beyond America's borders, we can also see that other constitutions—from the Filipino text to those that have emerged over the past decade in Eastern Europe—have similarly subscribed to the three primary tenets of modern constitutionalism. It seems that much of the world has begun to acknowledge the virtues of constructing a polity from the doctrine of modern constitutionalism.

Constitutionalism and Compact

Next, our theoretical examination of the principle of constitutional limitation—that is, of constitutionalism—turns to the relationship between these fundamental documents and the concept of the public or social compact. A social compact is a particular form of agreement fashioned between two or more individuals/groups in which each consents to give up particular rights in exchange for certain important guarantees. As defined by Ronald Pestritto and Thomas West, the term "implies that human beings are by nature free individuals, so that any legitimate government must be formed by the people's free choice—a *social compact* based on their voluntary consent."[39] The definition is important because, in the Enlightenment and post-Enlightenment eras, many constitutional framers have been influenced by the arguments of the major social contract theorists, especially the one espoused by John Locke in his famous treatises on government.

Locke believed that political order was originally formed when man, primarily out of an interest in self-preservation, was forced to emerge from a state of nature into civil society. The moment of transition occurs when the formerly uninhibited beings, fearing a loss of property or life, consent to particular rules centered on the idea of collective security. In exchange for the increase in personal security, individuals agree to relinquish certain rights they retained in the state of nature. They believe they are better off surviving in a community with fewer natural rights than perishing in the state of nature where no formal laws exist to prevent one individual from essentially destroying another.[40] The agreement to exchange certain rights for security, according to Locke, constitutes the first social contract. As a conceptual matter, it is an important transitional moment for human governance and one that has serious implications for constitution-making. The social contract, said Locke, becomes the basis for the formation of a newly envisioned polity. The agreement is the chief mechanism that binds each citizen who enters the community and tacitly agrees to live under its recently established social regulations. In short, the social contract becomes the first organizing document of the polity.

By reordering the relationship between the first parties to the social contract, Locke's conceptual agreement takes on quasi-constitutionalist form. The particulars of Locke's original social contract are not complex. Individuals existing in the state of nature make several significant choices, beginning with the decision to surrender a measure of personal freedom. Simultaneously, those individuals make an important collective decision as well: to become a community with laws that not only bind the citizens together but also restrain them from continuing the type of behavior that made life in the state of nature so perilous. They agree, in other words, to constrain or control power within the newly constituted civil organism. No longer are the signatories to the contract empowered to abuse others who have similarly agreed to the contract's fundamental directives. Thus the original social contract, as Locke envisioned it, is a covenant resting chiefly on the constitutionalist ideal. It is a rudimentary compact to be sure, but its major benefit—increased collective security based on the principles of consent and stable, transparent rules—smacks of modern constitutionalism.

Without diminishing Locke's considerable influence on the formation of Enlightenment and post-Enlightenment constitutional texts, we should be especially careful about terminology when we move from a discussion of the abstract (the state of nature, the social contract, etc.) to one that is a bit more concrete (involving actual constitutions). More to the point, it is important to use the term *compact* and not *contract* in our discussion because, as Donald Lutz correctly remarks, there is a sizeable difference between the two concepts. It is, in fact, Lutz (among others) who reminds us that seventeenth- and eighteenth-century citizens would not have used the word *contract* in the constitutional context.[41] They would have used the term *compact*, which he defines as a large group of individuals who agree to come together to form a political society based on the principles of collective responsibility and mutual consent. One of the oldest constitutions still in use—the 1780 Constitution for the Commonwealth of Massachusetts—nicely illustrates the point. Its preamble begins, "The body-politic is formed by a voluntary association of individuals; It is a social compact by which the whole people covenants with each citizen, and each citizen with the whole people, that all shall be governed by certain laws for the common good."

A contract, Lutz posits, is a far more narrow or privatistic conception. A contract typically involves two or more parties concerned about "a specific point" and not (as with a compact) about the broader notion of community building. In Lutz's words, "a contract [is] a restricted agreement between relatively small groups of people and [does] not necessarily have the status of law. A compact [is] an agreement between a large group of people creating a new community based upon their own consent."[42] Put differently, a contract is the manifestation of a shared agreement by particular stakeholders whereby each acknowledges certain responsibilities to the other, but who do not similarly require a commitment to an ongoing political community. A compact, on the other hand, *does* require that sort of civic commitment.

More telling, perhaps, is the claim made by Lutz that a contract may be enforceable as law, but it is not in and of itself a law. Unlike a contract, a compact represents an authoritative agreement made by the sovereign that amounts to the type of limitation on power that defines a constitutionalist text. A contract is not a document that organizes or orders the relationship between the parties to the agreement, but rather it stipulates a single transaction or arrangement. There is no doubt that both contracts and compacts have certain similar qualities when considered as part of the dialogue on constitutionalism. Both, for example, include the important principle of mutuality. The primary difference is revealed, however, when considering the nature of the relationship between parties to the agreement. Gordon Wood accurately characterizes the view, which became initially evident during the American constitutional framing, that the metaphor of the contract no longer works because the parties to the constitutional deal are not the ruler and the ruled but individuals emerging from a state of nature and, together as equals, agreeing to abide by certain fundamental principles.[43] A constitution is a sort of social compact, molded in the Lockean sense, and existing prior to the formation of the polity's government institutions. If successful, it binds the citizenry to each other and the polity itself. The central idea is best summarized by several eighteenth-century Americans who, quoting the Massachusetts Constitution of 1780, insisted that state constitutions actually *were* "social compact[s] by which the whole people covenants with each other, and each citizen with the whole people, [so] that all shall be governed by certain laws for the common good."[44]

Even the term *compact* itself evokes a constitutional image: "The word's root meaning," says Lutz, "[is] knitting together or bringing the component parts closely and firmly into a whole"[45]—a constituting, in other words. A compact also implies a certain longevity—a commitment to an *enduring* agreement—that is not similarly suggested by the term *contract*. The word carries a certain gravitas; it brings to mind a seriousness of purpose whereby the parties to the agreement make a pact with each other that is based on a higher principle than just a simple economic transaction. Again, the Mayflower Compact that tied the members of the Plymouth Colony to each other in the seventeenth century is a good example. It was fashioned under a binding and collective oath to God. Its main purpose was to publicly announce the Pilgrims' intention to "covenant and combine ourselves into a civil body politic, for our better ordering and preservation, and furtherance of the ends aforesaid." The Compact goes on to say that the members of the Colony pledge "to enact, constitute and frame such just and equal laws, ordinances, acts, constitutions and offices, from time to time, as shall be thought most meet and convenient for the general good of the colony, unto which we promise all due submission and obedience." Perhaps unsurprisingly, the Mayflower Compact is considered a precursor to the American state and federal constitutions and is still viewed as one of the seminal public documents in all of modern history.

In its contemporary form, then, a constitutional text represents a mutual agreement or compact between several distinct groups. The most obvious is the agreement between the sovereign, as manifest in the traditional democratic institutions of government, and those who are subject to the ongoing power of the sovereign. This relationship involves the classic division between majority and minority. It should be recalled that in order to qualify as constitutionalist, a constitution requires that the sovereign agree to the *self*-conscious limitation of its power. That agreement is made under the assumption that few would choose to live in a world where a permanent majority exercised unconstrained authority if there was a chance that they might end up in the minority. Accordingly, out of a sense of fairness, the modern constitution represents a compact whereby a majority agrees to the ongoing protection of the minority.

The second agreement is a bit more abstract. It concerns the compact made between the original ratifying populace, the current population, and any future citizens of the polity. The substance of that agreement resembles the one above insofar as it too is based on the regulation of political power and authority; but this one is purely intergenerational. A founding generation agrees to introduce and promote the first principles of the polity, and all future generations agree to carry on those (broad) governing values, at least as long as the text remains authoritative or is not amended to reflect new values.[46] Confirming the metaphor of constitution as compact, Thomas Paine once remarked that an action contrary to the constitutional text is "power without right."[47] The exercise of authority by representatives of the sovereign is subject to the original contractual arrangement made when the constitutional document was ratified. Exercising power beyond the specific provisions of the text is thus seen as a betrayal of that original agreement. Although conceptually abstract, this type of compact is perhaps more clearly evident than most others when reviewing the actual constitutional text. The intergenerational compact often appears in the form of preambulatory promises. The Preamble of the U.S. Constitution, for instance, begins with the pledge to "form a more perfect union . . . for ourselves *and our posterity.*" Other constitutional preambles make similar promises.

If we combine those two conceptual agreements with the one Wood explained above, it seems evident that a modern constitutionalist regime founded on the idea of popular sovereignty rests on the principle that a general compact exists between the people and those who represent power. The various clauses of a constitutional text mark the details of the compact; certain powers have been distributed to particular institutions, but certain powers have also been withheld. A constitutionalist regime requires that power be limited and that the constitution as compact specify which powers governmental institutions control and which they do not. Often the limitations on governmental power are recognized only within the gaps of a constitutional text, in the places where the text is silent. More often, however, those limitations are noted by a combination of gaps and clauses (typically in the form of a list of rights and freedoms) that identify areas of authority that cannot be breached by government institutions. The U.S. Constitution's Bill of Rights, with its negative articulation of individual freedoms, is the most commonly cited example.

A considerable number of texts drafted in the last forty years have accepted the idea of the constitution as social compact. To the extent that a compact refers to a document used to "organize a people, create a government, set forth its basic values, and describe the institutions for collective decision making,"[48] almost every Western regime around the world has embraced the concept. The principle of constitution as social compact, however, includes something more: a shared commitment to individual citizens and the overall body politic. The most obvious evidence can be found in the words of the texts, particularly when we revisit several of the constitutional preambles explored earlier. The Polish and Czech constitutions, for instance, echo the sentiment of the eighteenth-century Massachusetts speaker above by prioritizing a shared "obligation to the common good." They imply that one of the prerequisites of a good polity is the public commitment each inhabitant makes to his or her fellow citizens, and, more intangibly, to the future advancement of the regime itself. The social compact articulated in the South African constitution is one based in large part on the principle of equality. The message of the preamble is that all South Africans—black, white, Indian, and so on—suffered from the injustices of the past and that we are now, under this new fundamental law, agreed to move forward as equals, bound by a compact based on liberty, equality, democracy, and, above all, dignity.

Conclusion: Constitutionalism and Textuality

At the risk of sounding a bit hyperbolic, it can be said that the American decision to locate the organization, structure, and authority of an expanded republican government in a single written instrument changed the political world. By all accounts, it was a radical experiment in national governance. The concern over the possible rise of tyrannical rule exhibited by colonists during the American Revolution focused their attention on alternative methods of organizing and restraining power. To that point in history, no national constituency had tested the capacity of a codified fundamental law to constrain political power on the scale the American Framers were imagining. A single written constitution, the American framers believed, would provide far greater security against the abuses of political authority than would the more traditional approach of relying on the common law, especially when one considered the complexity of ordering a geographical territory many times larger than that found either in Great Britain or in the individual states. The experiment was so innovative and logical (and, it should be added, comparatively successful) that all but a tiny handful of political regimes have chosen to forego it since the late eighteenth century.

It was a different social contract theorist who helped shape the minds of America's founding generation when considering the virtues of a written constitutional charter. Thomas Hobbes, writes George Thomas, was acutely aware of the importance of a written constitutional text over and against the unwritten model. According to Thomas, Hobbes "insisted upon written fundamental law that could be deciphered by 'every man' against unwritten law that was based on the 'artificial reason' of judges."[49] Writing in the seventeenth century, Hobbes was offering a radically new view of constitutional government: all else being equal, he argued, written texts are infinitely more capable of bridling the power of the sovereign than unwritten texts, which must rely for their success and longevity on the infallibility of very fallible human judges. Maximizing the principles of justice and liberty, thought Hobbes, requires preestablished codified rules. The common law does not similarly deliver an appropriate level of justice, said he. It suffers from the vice of being infinitely malleable and subject to the passions of those residing in positions of power.

The Hobbesian quote, along with the American experiment, concerns one of the most perplexing questions in all of constitutional thought. We conclude this chapter by asking: Is it possible to achieve a constitutionalist system of government without a corresponding formal constitutional text? That is, the fundamental question is whether limited political power is truly possible in a regime that opts not to adopt the principle of constitutional textuality. We have already described the requirement of a modern constitutionalist government. In order to qualify, a constitution must be external to the polity's government institutions, discernible to those in subordinate positions, and committed to the idea of self-conscious limitation of power. The question is, can a polity that rests legitimate authority on an unwritten constitution still realize these features? Can it practice constitutionalism without a formal constitution? These and other questions related to the virtues of maintaining a written constitutional text inevitably focus our attention squarely on one of the few remaining unwritten constitutions in the world today: the British constitutional system. Therefore, to England we now turn.

The British Constitution

Arguably one of the most famous and widely scrutinized constitutional systems in the world can be found in Great Britain. The oldest constitutional order currently in existence, the British political design has been admired and emulated for many centuries. To provide a brief glimpse into the historical importance of the British constitution, consider the words of William Gladstone, an eighteenth-century Englishman whose comments on the qualities of both the British and American constitutions were widely quoted at the time. The written American Constitution, Gladstone concluded, is "the most wonderful work ever struck off at a given time by the brain and purpose of man." The British constitution, though, "is the most subtle organism which has proceeded from the womb and long gestation of progressive history."[50]

There can be little doubt that Gladstone's sentiments are still timely. The architecture of the British political system, and especially its embrace of a common law tradition, has been deeply influential around the globe. In part because of the connection of many former British colonies to the European power, the English system of government is still evident on almost every continent. Described as a constitutional monarchy, the specific political design in contemporary England combines parliamentary supremacy with energized executive and judicial rule. The nation's parliamentary structure, with lower and upper houses, a prime minister, a governing cabinet, and so on, remains broadly popular among newly independent states. And yet Gladstone's comparison is not literally accurate in the present era: it is not too much of an exaggeration to suggest that Britain's *constitutional* influence no longer matches its political importance. The country's effect on constitutional foundings in the past century has been significantly diminished by the fact that it still maintains an unwritten constitution in a world dominated by formal constitutional charters. Presently, it is one of only three remaining polities that do not boast a formal, codified text. Together with Israel, the English are in fact the only Western society that has never experimented formally with constitutional textuality.

The same cannot be said for the American constitutional experiment. Its constitutional influence is now unquestioned. It is noteworthy, for instance, how often the language of the American text appears in contemporary national constitutions. Many countries have adopted America's structural model for the separation of powers and its constitutional safeguards regarding individual rights. Its greatest effect on other nations, however, can be found in its simple decision to use the mechanism of textuality to constrain political power, the idea that constitutionalism now requires a formal, written text. Students of American politics learn very quickly that one of the most (and perhaps *the* most) effective means to forestall the rise of tyranny is found in the textuality of the Constitution itself. It is infinitely more difficult to abuse power when the rules of the game are previously laid out in a single written document. And yet we should not be so hasty as to discount the unwritten constitution as a viable design for limited government. Perhaps an unwritten constitution in the British tradition *can* ensure the same degree of controlled power that so many have attributed to the written design. Perhaps an uncodified constitution can be constitutionalist.

The British constitution is actually made up of a complicated series of legislative initiatives, judicial opinions, social norms, and public documents (such as the British Declaration of Rights) all falling under the broad label of British constitutional law. Akhil Amar describes it in less-than-flattering terms. "The vaunted English Constitution," he remarks, is "an imprecise hodgepodge of institutions, enactments, cases, usages, maxims, procedures, and principles that [has] accreted and evolved over many centuries."[51] The body of law that constitutes the British constitution is, in fact, as intricate and extensive as any in the world. The intricacy of the legal system, however, does not detract from the power of the law; the requirement that there be some fixed meaning to the constitution in order for it to be transparent and stable is met in Great Britain by that regime's steadfast commitment to the rule of law. Still, the conception of constitutionalism in England, unlike that in the United States, is premised on the belief that a single formal text is not necessary to ensure regulated or controlled power.

Briefly comparing the philosophical foundations of the British and American constitutions provides us with insight into the broader discussion of the relationship between constitutionalism and textuality. The first noticeable difference between the two constitutional models involves the source of authority. A written constitution like that found in the United States rests on the opinion that authority should derive from a single source, a tangible document that exists over and above the democratic institutions of the polity. The Constitution in the United States is that country's single organizing instrument. Part of its original mandate was to identify the powers of the various branches of government and thus, in a very real sense, its purpose was to create the very institutions that now carry out its stated aspirational goals. Logically, therefore, the Constitution maintains a certain authority over the institutions of the polity.[52] The institutions of the polity take their cues from the constitutional charter, not the other way around. Americans have become "enthralled," Gordon Wood says, with their unique idea of a constitution as a "written superior law set above the entire government against which all other law is to be measured."[53]

That particular conception of a constitution is further realized by some of the choices the American framers made more than two hundred years ago. Their view of the constitutional text as the paramount source of authority, for example, influenced their design for amending the document. Article V stipulates that altering the text requires an extraordinary effort on the part of the sovereign. Amending the U.S. Constitution is not accomplished through a simple vote of the majority in Congress, but rather through a complicated process that demands the endorsement of multiple overlapping super-majorities. In order for a proposed amendment to achieve the necessary support for addition into the constitutional text, it must garner support, first from either two-thirds of both houses of Congress or two-thirds of the state legislatures calling for a constitutional convention and then from three-quarters of the states. A change in the constitutional document is viewed as such a significant endeavor because the effect on the institutions of the polity is so considerable. As the *only* reflection of a completely sovereign people, the constitutional text in the United States is truly the supreme law of the land.

The original decision to design a constitutional text without a corresponding list of rights or freedoms is further evidence of the American framers' commitment to the principle of constitutional textuality. The debate for many members of the founding generation focused on the necessity of adding a bill of rights to the original text. Many Anti-Federalists supported the addition, while a seemingly equal number of Federalists opposed it. A constitutional clause that prohibited government from exercising powers it could not claim to enjoy was, according to many Federalists, an absurdity. Why, Alexander Hamilton wondered, was it so imperative to mention that "Congress shall make no law abridging the freedom of speech" when the constitutional text never delegated to Congress the authority to interfere with that right in the first place? Likewise, the government was nowhere empowered to deny any persons the right to an "impartial jury," so the articulation of that right in the Sixth Amendment was largely redundant. A written constitution, Hamilton famously noted in the 84th *Federalist*, is itself a bill of rights. The virtue of a textual constitution, he concluded, is that the parameters of political power are clearly marked by the words of the document: whatever is not mentioned is not retained.

An unwritten constitution rests on an altogether different set of philosophical assumptions. First, the Parliament in England is supreme; it is the primary base of sovereign authority for the entire nation. Under a common law system its enactments automatically enjoy constitutional status. It too is a single source of authority, but unlike in the United States its relationship to the constitution is conceivably as an equal, not inferior, institution. Some, like former colonial Governor Thomas Hutchinson, insist the Parliament is the highest power in Great Britain and the country's constitution is mostly a product of governmental and cultural initiatives. A constitutional change in England does not require the extraordinary demonstration of sovereign unity mandated by the American text. Altering the British constitution is accomplished by a simple majoritarian vote in Parliament or by a judicial ruling in the country's appeals courts. Legislative power over the always-developing constitution is thus comparatively and theoretically unrestricted. If the majority in Parliament wishes to enact particular legislation, and that enactment is not viewed by the judiciary as incompatible with precedent, there is very little to constrain the will of the current majority. In contrast to a country bound by a tangible written constitution, the British constitution is thus not "set above the entire government against which all other law is to be measured."[54] Instead, it is largely a legislative creation.

Second, citizens of Great Britain benefit from the protection of the Declaration of Rights, the Bill of Rights, Magna Carta, and other formal, quasi-constitutional compacts defining the scope of individual liberty. This is so because the authority to grant rights that is vested in the Parliament is always tempered by the possibility (however unlikely) that the legislative body can take them away at any time, and through ordinary procedures. But the historical magnitude of Magna Carta, the Petition of Right, and similar documents makes them practically impervious to parliamentary regulation.

Recently, the British House of Lords ruled on a case that lies at the heart of this discussion. The decision in *A v. Secretary of State for the Home Department*, declared that the European Convention for the Protection of Human Rights and Fundamental Freedoms (which had been incorporated into English law via the Human Rights Act of 1998) enjoys constitutional status alongside the Great Charter and other codified texts.[55] This judgment represents a remarkable moment in British constitutional law not only because it reconfirms the power of the judiciary to enforce individual rights against parliamentary decrees but also because of the Court's decision to transplant an international declaration of human rights squarely into the English constitution. The case involved the indefinite detention of non-British nationals identified by English authorities as possible terrorists. British officials argued that §23 of the Anti-Terrorism, Crime and Security Act of 2001 permitted the state to hold suspected terrorists for an unspecified amount of time. The Court rejected that argument, insisting that the European Convention for the Protection of Human Rights and Fundamental Freedoms prevents Parliament from denying basic liberties to individuals residing within Great Britain. The Court's opinion noted that the Convention should be considered a pseudo Bill of Rights for England and is consequently a material limitation on the power of the sovereign.

The formality of certain portions of the British constitution aligns more closely with the written nature of America's constitutional charter, and, perhaps not surprisingly, these documents help to influence the scope of personal rights in that country. More to the point, one key to the protection of individual rights in England, and thus one key to the country's brand of constitutionalism, can be found in the defense of certain fundamental documents by the country's judiciary. Although currently in flux because of the passage of the Constitutional Reform Act of 2005, the British judiciary consists of a number of different tribunals and a clear division between civil and criminal courts. The nation's highest appellate courts rest in one of the houses of Parliament—the House of Lords, to be precise—and the intermediate appeals court located in the Court of Appeal. All of the country's tribunals, though, rely on the authority of the codified law (through legislative enactments, historical documents, and the common law) to safeguard the individual rights of British citizens. Whatever degree of constitutionalism the British system achieves (and it is a significant amount) is due in large part to the country's judicial authorities.

It is thus all the more curious that, at first glance, the British judiciary is not what Americans would describe as "independent." The nation's highest court, after all, is also its upper legislative chamber. For many scholars of the law, the idea that a political regime could sustain the principles of constitutionalism without a judiciary that is meaningfully isolated from the political currents of the moment is preposterous. The thinking is that once the judiciary loses a degree of independence, it also loses its capacity to keep the other more democratic institutions like the legislature and the executive from potentially abusing their authority. Its ability to restrain the abusive tendencies of the legislative and executive branches is tied directly to its independence. Moreover, a constitutionalist system is in jeopardy if there is not at least one institution that acts as a watchdog overseeing the actions of a self-interested majority.

The British experience suggests otherwise. First of all, the judiciary's apparent link to the legislative department is misleading. More than three hundred years ago, the Act of Settlement (1701) fixed the British courts' independence from the other branches of government by legislating that judges should hold their office during good conduct. The parliamentary act stipulates that jurists maintain their positions without royal interference; the judges cannot be punished or prosecuted for decisions made in the course of the law.[56] Predating the major details of Article III of the U.S. Constitution, the Act of Settlement established a subtle, though meaningful, division between the legislative offices and the judicial authorities. Hence, insofar as the judiciary (in both England and the United States) is the primary interpreter and protector of the rights of citizens, its principal role is a constitutionalist one: it must check or bridle the power of the majority. Although there is no single source that we can point to as the definitive English constitution, the institutions of that polity, including the country's judiciary, are still capable of defining the boundaries of political power.

In the end, the British constitution—unwritten though it is—manages to achieve at least two of the three major requirements for modern constitutionalism. No unwritten constitution can claim to exist apart from the government institutions of the polity, and the constitution of Great Britain is no exception. The principle of externality is thus left unmet by the current design of the British constitution. Still, England can boast that its constitution is more or less discernible. Its constitution is made up of hundreds of years of codified law, judicial decisions, social customs, and other related institutions. It may be a "hodgepodge," but it qualifies as a discernible collection of rules in the same way that the comparatively brief and compact American text qualifies. Insofar as the rules of England constrain or regulate the power of the government, the constitution of that country meets the criteria for knowability. Political leaders and ordinary citizens alike are capable of understanding the British constitution, and what is more, they are both authorized—encouraged even—to use its boundless provisions to help preserve a high degree of political accountability. If the true test of constitutionalism is a polity's ability to control the vices of human nature when they metastasize within the institutions of government, the British constitution passes.

The nature of Britain's political design also guarantees some measure of *self-conscious* limitation of power. All types of political institutions, from the Crown to the houses of Parliament, regularly reassert their allegiance to the values articulated in the nation's major historical agreements. More accurately, the principles espoused in Magna Carta, the Bill of Rights, the Act of Settlement, and so on, undergird the entire foundation of the British political tradition. Now we can add the European Declaration of Human Rights to that list. And yet even if British citizens could not count on the protection of these seminal treatises, there are other mechanisms, including the country's resolute commitment to the principle of the rule of law, that ensure that constitutionalism will continue to find root in the British system. In addition to the frequent reaffirmation of the major public documents announcing limits on the sovereign's power and the fidelity to the rule of law, the simple fact that the British are dedicated to free, fair, and regular elections is evidence of an essential sovereign pledge to the peaceful transition of power. Surely, the fact that the current (and temporary) majority, if voted out of office, will peacefully relinquish control of political power is one of the most significant characteristics of contemporary limited government. It alone certifies a reasonably constitutionalist existence.

Constitutional Futures

❊ ❊ ❊

A great many polities across the globe have scrutinized the American experience in constitutional formation when setting out to create their own constitutionalist regimes. They have understood that individual foundings will differ because political, social, cultural, racial, economic, transnational, agricultural, and ecological factors all contribute to the type of constitutional order that emerges in a specific geographical location. Yet they also recognize that some of the transitional moments experienced by the citizens of the confederated states around the time of the American founding resonate with their experiences. Moreover, several of the values embraced by the American founders and the ends sought by a new constitutional polity in the United States are ones that resemble the principles they too wish to embody. As South Africa struggled (or rather struggles) with its constitutional birth, for example, Nelson Mandela echoed the words and thoughts of such American statesmen as James Madison and Alexander Hamilton. In his 1994 inaugural address, as he took his seat as the country's first post-apartheid president, he spoke of the importance of a constitution for embedding values such as liberty, equality, democracy, and the rule of law within a newly fashioned polity. He repeated those ideas two years later as he addressed the country on the recent adoption of a new constitutional charter. After spending most of that speech praising the delegates to the framing convention for their attention to democratic principles, consensus building, and reconciliation, he reminded them that this constitution ultimately "reaffirms our commitment to the rights of citizens and the need to build genuine equality across the board."[1]

Like Madison, Mandela also recognized that a constitution could help to achieve many of the ends sought by ordered government. The seven functions of a modern constitutionalist draft described in this book all aim to imagine, create, and manage a workable political community. Together, they help to put the words of a constitutional text to work in the service of fashioning a distinct political world; a constitution seeks to produce worlds out of words. If we recall the earlier discussion about constitutional transformation in chapter 2, arguably the premier reason for adopting a new constitutional text is to remedy the defects of the old political order. In the United States, the Constitutional Convention occurred in large part because of general dissatisfaction with the effectiveness of the Articles of Confederation to deliver some of the primary ideals fought for during the American Revolution. South Africa's original apartheid constitution, although undoubtedly far less defensible than the Articles of Confederation, was scrapped for the same reasons: it too would not deliver the necessary political, cultural, and ethical infrastructure for a new and distinct polity. A fresh constitutional text was needed to mark the symbolic end to disenfranchisement, discrimination, and authoritarianism. It was also needed to clearly identify those principles that would carry the new political order into the future.

South Africa's recent experience in constitution-making is, in many ways, familiar. The current generation has witnessed arguably the greatest explosion of constitutional foundings the world has ever known. In virtually every corner of the globe, new constitutions are being written and old constitutions are being radically amended. Over the last eighteen months, for example, several countries—including Bahrain and Croatia—have adopted and ratified fundamentally new constitutional texts. Add to that the large number of countries around the turn of the twenty-first century that embraced alternative political orders, and what emerges is a rich body of founding debates and new constitutional charters. In Eastern Europe, southern Africa, South America, and even in pockets of the Middle East, it seems people are trying to generate new worlds out of the power of constitutional words.

The drafting of so many constitutional documents points to a number of interesting generalizations. Troubling, of course, is the fact that the alarming rate of new constitutional births suggests that so many polities are struggling with internal stability. And yet it is equally important to see this reality in a positive light. For whatever reason and in whatever capacity, constitutions seem to be helping nation-states cope with their problems. Indeed, there seems to be an increasing reliance on the constitutional form as a primary means of ordering existing political societies and defusing longstanding political disagreements. Heinz Klug referred to this trend as representing a "global faith" in the power of constitutions.[2] Nation-states, some of which have invisible or underdeveloped systems of police enforcement, now view constitutions as powerful remedies against disorder and conflict; constitutions are seemingly a prerequisite for regimes looking to overcome deep divisions among the population. Jon Elster has written that constitutional reform in Eastern Europe in the late 1980s and early 1990s was spearheaded by concerns over ethnic conflict.[3] Cass Sunstein has echoed Elster's main premise, even going so far as to imply that the complex relationship outlined in post-Communist texts between positive and negative rights, and social obligations, denotes an attempt to reconcile historical differences in these heterogeneous states.[4] Efforts to transform political worlds in regimes such as South Africa and Iraq further suggest that constitution-making is on the rise, and that turning to constitutions as a means to provide regime stability represents a popular approach.

In a sense, this belief is not new. Throughout modern history many countries have looked to the constitutional text as a panacea for their political, cultural, and economic problems. The present difference, suggests Klug, is that the constitutional form is now seen as an institution that can all but erase those problems, when in reality their primary role is to help manage them. Constitutions are being asked to eradicate those ethnic, regional, cultural, linguistic, and religious differences that threaten to tear certain countries apart, and often they cannot achieve those lofty goals. When constitutions fail, they regularly do so because they are asked to accomplish more than they are capable of. Still, their inability to do everything should not detract from the fact that they can do some things quite well. It is crucial for any regime—even the most stable—to order its institutions in a self-conscious way, and the constitution is the chief platform for mandating that structured order. Moreover, a country that cannot articulate its first principles, or that cannot identify limits to the sovereign power, or that does not recognize the importance of enabling institutions to make policy in the name of the sovereign, is a constitutionalist country that will inevitably flounder. Constitutional aspiration, limitation, and empowerment are thus important features of any modern constitutionalist polity that aims for sustained growth and prosperity.

The increasing turn to constitutions since the mid-twentieth century further suggests that polities are beginning to see that the existence of a constitutional text escalates a nation's standing on the world's stage. The idea that a constitution is a country's international calling card is a product of the increasing importance many leaders place on governing charters. Founders (including the American variety) regularly believe in the practical wisdom of adopting a constitution text because it marks a territory, articulates a constitutive purpose, and, if all goes well, announces the polity's arrival in the community of nations. Again, the experience of Eastern European countries following the fall of the Berlin Wall tells the tale. In 1989, fresh off the events that severed Eastern European countries from Soviet control, these countries almost immediately turned to reforming their constitutional documents, in part as a means to demonstrate their independence and autonomy. The redrafting of constitutional texts in Eastern Europe amounted to an exercise in sovereign will; the message of self-determination from Poland, Hungary, Ukraine, and the other nations formerly within the Soviet sphere was broadcast to the entire world. Those countries had emerged.

Of course, not every constitutional transition follows a particular script, and not every country's founding narrative is instructive. Indeed, it would hardly be surprising to conclude that almost every constitutional founding is unique. At the same time, however, such an obvious conclusion does not mean that we cannot learn or that we cannot generalize from almost any recent constitutional transformation. Despite its utter uniqueness, the situation in war-torn Iraq, for example, presents a microcosm of the constitutional enterprise; it is an ongoing experiment in the exercise of constitutionalism and the difficulties of constitution-making. Under the watchful eye of the mostly American-led Coalition Provisional Authority, the Iraqi Governing Council signed into law an Interim Constitution for the nation of Iraq on March 8, 2004. That constitution, which was replaced by a permanent text in 2005, included a bill of rights, a provision for specific women's representation (Article 30), and an acknowledgement that Islam must remain an important "source" of legislative authority (Article 7). The permanent text maintains the principles laid out in the Interim Constitution. It too speaks of the centrality of Islam, the fact that religious rules trump secular law, the recognition of Arabic and Kurdish as the official languages of the regime, and the importance of democratic principles, the peaceful transition of power, and the rule of law.

Like so many new constitutions, the Iraqi text also articulates an extensive list of individual rights and freedoms. Beginning with an explanation of "civil and political rights," the constitution continues by identifying the long list of "economic, social, and cultural rights" enjoyed by the people. Here, the Iraqi constitution guarantees the right to work, the right to education, the right to a clean environment, the right to health insurance, the right to integrate into society if one is disabled, and the right to economic freedom, particularly for those children who have been "exploited" throughout the country's recent past. Even the right to "build hospitals, dispensaries or private clinics" is protected by Iraq's new constitutional charter. It is interesting that, following twenty-one separate articles outlining the basic rights and liberties of the Iraqi people, the text turns to a section titled "Freedoms," which includes an additional eleven articles enumerating the broader, more universal guarantees found in most Western constitutional instruments. The familiar rights to conscience, speech, assembly, movement, travel, and dignity are protected by the text.

That said, it is also clear that the circumstances that gave rise to the need for a new Iraqi constitution are, to put it mildly, extraordinary. A ruthless dictator, a frightened populace, and, eventually, a foreign invader, are not normally the ingredients of successful constitutional change. They are, however, part of a post–September 11th political landscape that makes constitutional authority—and specifically "fully operative," constitutionalist texts—all the more critical.[5] Even if not accomplished through actual imperial force, I suspect that many future constitutional foundings will be heavily influenced by the current state of global instability. Constitutions, after all, are typically born out of fear. The situation in Iraq suggests that questions of sovereignty will likely dominate future debates about constitutional governance. Iraq is not the only political regime that is currently witnessing a crisis in sovereign authority, and surely other unstable, polarized polities will surface. It will be interesting to witness whether more political leaders turn to constitutional reform as an immediate response to disorder.

Before concluding, one final question about the future of constitutions must be asked: Will constitutional charters remain within the exclusive domain of the nation-state? Another way of asking the same question is to wonder whether supranational or transnational compacts will continue to alter the global constitutional landscape or whether loose confederations like the European Union, with their governing constitutions, will become a relic of the recent past. Jeremy Rabkin is one who has contemplated this question. He posits that transnational agreements like the International Criminal Court, the Kyoto Protocols, and NATO are becoming more prevalent in the late twentieth and early twenty-first centuries and that they are stripping modern nations of their independent sovereignty. As these agreements begin to take on the responsibilities of the nation-state, governments become derelict in their duties to safeguard individual freedoms. People of the United States, he says, are forced to sacrifice some of the liberties they take for granted because their leaders in Washington are bargaining with those freedoms in an attempt to push a regional or international (as opposed to local or national) agenda. This is particularly troublesome, says Rabkin, because it seems to defy the very principles of independence and liberty on which the American Constitution was founded.[6]

Specific agreements aside, Rabkin's broader issue concerns constitutional government on a global scale. Consider the current relationship among polities in Eastern and Western Europe. On June 18, 2004, sitting at the organization's headquarters in Brussels, member states ratified a formal constitution for the European Union. The EU constitution condenses and organizes all the treaties of the member states, but it does a good deal more. It identifies offices and officers of the EU (including the president), the powers designated to the body itself, the procedures for ratification and amendment, and the rights and liberties retained by individuals residing in the confederation. Moreover, it acknowledges the independent sovereignty of each participating regime and the process by which nation-states can choose to leave the European Union. The constitution, in short, reinforces the principle that members join on a strictly voluntary basis and are under no contractual obligation to stay within the confederation.

The EU constitution obviously does not represent a typical constitutional form, and yet by all accounts it is a constitution. Its founding moment marked the birth of a new political order and a transformed European citizenry. Things were different once the constitution came into existence. Moreover, the document organizes and empowers the institutions of the transnational confederation, articulates the aspirations of the collective body, seeks to manage conflict through self-imposed institutional rules and regulations, and recognizes both national and sub-national identities. It is self-defined as a constitution, and it functions as a constitution. It must *be* a constitution.

Perhaps the success of the European Union as an economic, political, and social confederation will dictate the short-term future of transnational constitutionalism. Americans have, of course, dabbled in the business of transnational constitutionalism in the past, and the results have at times been less than stellar: the Articles of Confederation lasted only about a decade, and then they were replaced by a constitutional text that has endured for more than two centuries. At this early stage it appears that the EU has been reasonably successful in achieving some of its preliminary goals, but it has been less than half a decade since the experiment began. To what extent those successes are due to its constitutional text remains unclear. One thing is clear, however: the fact that member states join the European Union voluntarily and that they retain the unrestricted authority to opt out at any moment renders the constitutional ties that bind nations and individuals loosely to each other somewhat dubious. From a purely theoretical perspective, it seems reasonable to suppose that the original agreement between nation-states cannot be all that consequential if the subjects of the document are constitutionally empowered to ignore it. How authoritative can that constitution be when its principals are not entirely bound to it? When it comes to their own constitutional texts, few members of the world's population enjoy the luxury of opting out, and that fundamental lack of freedom may be the real key to a successful constitutional form. For this reason, constitutional futures may or may not include transnational texts. It is probably too early to tell.

In the end, what is far more important than speculating on the future of all constitutional forms is focusing on the ones that currently exist. Established constitutions must be rediscovered. That is, those constitutions that have endured through time—the U.S. Constitution, the German Basic Law, even the unwritten British constitution—should be returned from the margins and placed, once again, at the intersection of security and peace. In a world of uncertainty, it is even more essential that citizens and institutions stop and reflect on the fundamental principles of their constitutional text. What are a constitution's main functions, and how can they help us traverse this period of instability? To be sure, the primary burden will fall on those institutions charged with the responsibility of interpreting the constitutional documents, institutions such as legislatures, courts, and so on; but all should be at least aware of the relationship between terror and text. As Justice O'Connor wrote in her plurality opinion in *Hamdi v. Rumsfeld*, "striking the proper constitutional balance [between freedom and order] is of great importance to the Nation during this period of ongoing combat."[7] Similarly, it was John Jay, in his capacity as author of some of the earliest *Federalist Papers*, who insisted that a constitutional document could be a powerful antidote against the "dangers of foreign and domestic force."[8]

Constitutions matter. Perhaps more precisely, given the right conditions, constitutional texts matter tremendously. They design and empower political institutions. They articulate a polity's collective aspirations. Indeed, they even "insist that the sovereign itself—whether that be in a democratic regime or an aristocratic one—introduce limits, at the moment of founding, on its own political authority."[9] But perhaps even more important than those qualities, constitutions also furnish political communities with specific identities. They embrace particular principles in an attempt to "constitute" a citizenry, to order a populace around some collective goal. They are, in most regimes at least, the single most important public document, and for that reason alone they deserve our renewed attention.

Introduction

1. See Jacobsohn, *Apple of Gold*. See also Breslin, *Communitarian Constitution*.

2. See "Knowing It by Heart: Americans Consider the Constitution and Its Meaning," a survey conducted by Public Agenda for the National Constitution Center, 2002.

3. Recent federal legislation now mandates that those institutions of higher education that receive federal funds must commemorate the anniversary of the signing of the constitutional text in what the legislation calls "Constitution Day."

4. See Finn, *Constitutions in Crisis*.

5. See, among others, Sunstein, *Designing Democracy*; Schneier, *Crafting Constitutional Democracies*; and Murphy, *Constitutional Democracy*.

6. See Harris, *Interpretable Constitution*.

7. Raz, "On the Authority and Interpretation of Constitutions," 153.

8. For a concise description of the division between attitudinalists and scholars of judicial review, see Kersch, "Review of *The Democratic Constitution*."

9. Consider what Sotirios Barber, himself a noted constitutional theorist, says: "The postwar constitutional consensus shifted most of the legal academe to a court-centeredness that took the Constitution's authority and goodness more or less for granted and concentrated either on what the Court had to say and should say about constitutional meaning (academic law) or on the extralegal determinants of judicial behavior and decision (political science)" ("Notes on Constitutional Maintenance" 162).

10. See Whittington, *Constitutional Construction*; Tushnet, *The New Constitutional Order*; Waldron, "Precommitment and Disagreement"; Kramer, *The People Themselves*; Devins and Fisher, *The Democratic Constitution*.

11. Larry D. Kramer takes a slightly different approach in critiquing the judicial supremacy literature, arguing that such scholarship misunderstands the rich history in the United States of popular constitutionalism, the principle that the people, not the courts, are the supreme authority in interpreting the Constitution. See Kramer, *The People Themselves*.

12. Sanford Levinson recognizes the division between text and political institution. He writes: "To reject the ultimate authority of the Supreme Court is not in the least to reject

the binding authority of the Constitution, but only to argue that the Court is to be judged by the Constitution itself rather than the other way around" (*Constitutional Faith*, 43). George Thomas also defends a view of the Constitution that acknowledges this important distinction. His words resemble Levinson's: "If we take the Constitution seriously, we are bound by the Constitution and not the Court's interpretation of it, which are hardly the same thing" ("Recovering the Political Constitution," 239).

13. "Address by President Nelson Mandela to the Constitutional Assembly on the Occasion of the Adoption of the New Constitution," Cape Town, May 8, 1996.

14. It is telling that when one of the leading contemporary scholars of constitutional theory called for a constitutional convention to draft a new charter for the United States, his first concern was to convince us to abandon our veneration for the Constitution. See Levinson, *Our Undemocratic Constitution*.

15. *The Federalist*, no. 1.

16. To be sure, founders are concerned with all questions related to the constitutional form, but their more immediate and necessary role as creators is captured most accurately in questions related to transformation, aspiration, and design.

17. I will argue, implicitly, that constitutions are the primary force in performing these various functions, but I am not so naïve as to think that a polity s constitutional text is the *only* force behind many of these tasks. A country's aspirational claims, for example, cannot rest entirely within a single constitutional charter. Other documents and/or social movements also contribute to the formation of a polity's primary goals and objectives. Such was the case with the American Revolution and, perhaps even more tangibly, with its Declaration of Independence. But my argument is a bit different. My claim is that the nature of constitutions in general—the fact that they are, in most cases, the country's primary organizing document—compels them to perform most (or all) of the seven constitutional functions.

18. These functions follow a rough temporal sequence. I have placed "Constitutional Transformation"—the chapter devoted to a discussion of how constitutional foundings do violence to an old way of life and usher in a new political vision—first because the entire principle of constitutional functionality commences with the birth of a new nation. After that, it seems appropriate to comment on a constitution's aspirational qualities, especially since they are typically announced in the text's preamble. Constitutional design is next, followed by a discussion of conflict, recognition, empowerment, and, finally, constitutional limitation.

19. In a fascinating new book, Donald S. Lutz has contemplated the "general principles of constitutional design" that might lead to a successful political order. His overall conclusion is that in order for a constitution to be successful, it must reflect the particular ideals of the specific nation. In other words, success depends on recognizing national distinctions. See Lutz, *Principles of Constitutional Design*.

20. See Murphy, "Constitutions, Constitutionalism, and Democracy." See also Eisgruber, "Judicial Supremacy and Constitutional Distortion," and Perry, "What Is 'the Constitution'?"

21. See Finn, "The Civic Constitution: Some Preliminaries."

22. Ibid., 42.

23. See Jacobsohn, *Apple of Gold.* See also Jacobsohn, *Wheel of Law.*

24. See Amar, *America's Constitution: A Biography.* See also Amar, *The Bill of Rights: Creation and Reconstruction.*

25. Amar, "Rethinking Originalism."

Chapter One • Constitutional Order

1. Walker, "The Constitutional Good."

2. Sartori, "Constitutionalism: A Preliminary Discussion," 22 (emphasis in original).

3. Blaustein and Sigler, eds., *Constitutions That Made History,* xi.

4. See Breslin, *Communitarian Constitution,* 113–33.

5. Hegel, *Philosophy of Right,* 286–87.

6. Bolingbroke, "A Dissertation Upon Parties (1733–34)," quoted in McIlwain, *Constitutionalism,* 3.

7. Found in Wood, *The American Revolution: A History,* 65.

8. *Federalist* 1.

9. See Wood, *American Revolution,* 158–66

10. Ibid.

11. Found in Kaminsky and Leffler, eds., *Creating the Constitution,* 71.

12. This is not to suggest that constitutions are perfect; they are most often compromises, inspired not by what is possible but by what can be implemented. Nonetheless, they do represent an "advance" in the evolution of controlled political power.

13. Sunstein, "Constitutionalism and Secession," 637.

14. McIlwain, *Constitutionalism,* 21–22.

15. Franklin and Baun, eds., *Political Culture and Constitutionalism,* quoted in Jackson and Tushnet, *Comparative Constitutional Law,* 213.

16. Elster, "Constitutionalism in Eastern Europe," 465.

17. See Paine, *The Rights of Man,* 302–303.

18. Ibid. (emphasis his).

19. *Federalist* 84.

20. See Brown, *Constitutions in a Nonconstitutional World.*

21. Ibid., xiii.

22. Duchacek, "National Constitutions: A Functional Approach," 98.

23. See Okoth-Ogendo, "Constitutions Without Constitutionalism."

24. Ibid., 73.

25. See Boron, "Latin America."

26. Ibid., 344.

27. Montesquieu, *The Spirit of the Laws,* 1:xiv–xix.

28. See *Federalist* 51.

29. Brown, *Constitutions in a Nonconstitutional World.*

30. See Murphy, "Constitutions, Constitutionalism, and Democracy."

31. For an informative discussion of the variety of terms used to describe sham texts, see Finn, *Constitutions in Crisis,* 22–23.

32. It is important not to confuse constitutionalism with a fully operative constitu-

tional text. Some constitutionalist texts that purport to limit the authority of the sovereign are in fact ignored by those in power.

33. Nathan J. Brown has insisted that the Soviet constitutions were not shams because their fundamental goal was to "establish the dictatorship of the urban and rural workers, combined with the poorer peasantry, in order to secure the complete crushing of the bourgeoisie, the abolition of the exploitation of man by man, and the establishment of Socialism, under which neither class divisions nor state coercion arising therefrom will any longer exist" (*Constitutions*, 6).

34. Ibid., 7.

Chapter Two • *Constitutional Transformation*

1. Constitutional transformation can also occur without the abandonment of past texts and the adoption of new ones. In chapter 6, I talk about the important work of Bruce Ackerman in this area.

2. Consequently, we will return to the idea of constitutional foundings numerous times over the next three chapters.

3. To be sure, the founding moment is not always the "aha" moment; it is not always the case that a constitution is founded in a highly dramatic way. Constitutional change can take place over a period of time.

4. Wheare, *Modern Constitutions*, 8.

5. Friedrich, "The Political Theory of the New Democratic Constitutions," 215.

6. Russell, *Constitutional Odyssey*, 106.

7. Elster, "Forces and Mechanisms in the Constitution-Making Process," 370. Elster goes on to identify the eight "circumstances that induce constitution-making," all of which involve some serious crisis or perceived crisis.

8. Ibid., 394.

9. See Gordon, *Controlling the State*.

10. Webster's dictionary defines *alteration* as "the process of making something different." Thus, even if we are considering only minor changes to a polity's structure or identity, that change represents a destructive act. The old is gone, even if the institutions present in the old regime still remain.

11. R. W. Gordon, "Undoing Historical Injustice," 50.

12. Duchacek, "National Constitutions," 93.

13. School children in the United States are regularly reminded that the major constitutional framers were intimately familiar with the failures of past republics when they proposed a new constitutional order.

14. Cover, "Violence and the Word," 1601.

15. Secessionists were the victims of America's second constitutional transformation, the one that occurred as a result of the Civil War.

16. For an interesting discussion of the impact of amendments on the theory of (American) constitutionalism, see Sanford Levinson, ed., *Responding to Imperfection*, especially "How Many Times Has the United States Constitution Been Amended? (A) < 26; (B) 26; (C) 27; (D) >27: Accounting for Constitutional Change."

17. The Constitution of the Republic of South Africa, Chapter 1, Section 1(a).

18. "Address by President Nelson Mandela to the Constitutional Assembly on the Occasion of the Adoption of the New Constitution," Cape Town, May 8, 1996.

19. Ibid.

20. See Benjamin, "Critique of Violence."

21. Carl J. Friedrich, quoted in Duchacek, "National Constitutions," 95.

22. See Peled, "Ethnic Democracy and the Legal Construction of Citizenship."

23. See Tully, *Strange Multiplicity.*

24. Ebrahim, *The Soul of a Nation,* 4.

25. Amar, *Bill of Rights,* 27.

26. Murphy, "Civil Law," 129.

27. Ibid., 125.

28. See the *Czech Sociological Review,* Issue Number 6 (2005), an entire volume devoted to the topic of civic engagement in Eastern Europe.

29 Cover, "Nomos and Narrative," 109.

30. Ibid., 102.

31. *Bob Jones University v. United States,* 461 U.S. 574 (1983).

32. Cover, "Nomos and Narrative," 155.

33. Ibid., 155 (emphasis in original).

34. Ibid., 126.

35. Ibid., 172.

36. Ibid., 120–21.

37. See Duchacek, "National Constitutions."

38. See Jacobsohn, *Apple of Gold.*

39. See Breslin, *Communitarian Constitution,* esp. chap. 6.

40. Cover, "Violence and the Word," 1607.

Chapter Three • Constitutional Aspiration

1. Cover, "Violence and the Word," 1604.

2. See Levinson, *Constitutional Faith,* and Grey, "The Constitution as Scripture."

3. Whittington, *Constitutional Interpretation,* 64.

4. By its very nature, the "spirit" of a constitution, whether it be aspirational or not, is difficult to capture; it is a complicated, often subjective enterprise that requires one to defend a specific interpretation of the "ideals" or "principles" that one believes are embedded in the text. In that sense, therefore, any discussion about the spirit of a constitutional text inevitably becomes a political discussion about the meaning of the text. And yet I think some of that subjectivity can be transcended, especially if the focus is placed on the aspirational qualities of a constitutional document.

5. Amar, *The Bill of Rights: Creation and Reconstruction,* 27.

6. Jacobsohn, "Permeability," 1767.

7. See Jacobsohn. *The Supreme Court and the Decline of Constitutional Aspiration,* esp. chap. 6.

8. Jacobsohn, "Permeability," 1768.

9. Ibid.

10. On August 28, 1963, King spoke these words: "When the architects of our country wrote the magnificent words of the Constitution and the Declaration of Independence, they were signing a promissory note to which every American was to fall heir."

11. See Whittington, *Constitutional Interpretation*, 65–68.

12. Ibid., 66.

13. The Massachusetts Constitution of 1780 was the rare exception.

14. "A Native of Virginia, Observations Upon the Proposed Plan of Federal Government," in *Founders' Constitution*, ed. Kurland and Lerner (Indianapolis: Liberty Fund), 2:14.

15. Story, "Commentaries on the Constitution," in *Founders' Constitution*, 2:18.

16. For a more detailed explanation of the meaning of this concept, see Wayne D. Moore's excellent book, *Constitutional Rights and Powers of the People*.

17. Barber, *On What the Constitution Means*, 52.

18. See *Webster v. Reproductive Health Services*, 492 U.S. 490 (1989).

19. See Barber, *On What the Constitution Means*, chap. 2.

20. Found in Blaustein and Sigler, eds., *Constitutions That Made History*.

21. The Mozambican constitution can be defined as mostly constitutionalist and, especially after the end of the civil war of 1975–92, roughly fully operative.

22. *McCulloch v. Maryland* (1819), 17 U.S. 316, at 407.

23. See Klug, *Constituting Democracy*. See also Haynie's review of Klug's book in the *Law and Politics Book Review*.

24. The Democratic Republic of Congo has adopted several more constitutional texts since 1992, including an interim constitution in 2003 and a permanent one in 2006. The preamble of each of these successive constitutions closely resembles the 1992 text.

25. In certain parts of the world, national identity is used as shorthand for "ethnic identity," especially in those areas (like Eastern Europe) where national borders often reflect ethnic divisions. I use the term "national identity" throughout this discussion for consistency.

26. Elster, "Constitutionalism in Eastern Europe."

27. See Klug, *Constituting Democracy*.

28. Elster remarks that since 1989 there has been a "snowballing process in which events in one [Eastern European] country inspired and accelerated those in others." See Elster, "Constitutionalism in Eastern Europe," 448.

29. Comparing the Eastern European constitutions drafted in the early 1990s with those from the Soviet era reveals that many discarded constitutional texts also included assertions of sovereignty. The difference, of course, is that that the earlier constitutions were shams.

30. Duchacek, "National Constitutions: A Functional Approach."

31. It warrants mentioning that prior to the fall of the Berlin Wall, Eastern European countries regularly included positive rights in their constitutional texts as part of the Soviet Union's socialist agenda. Insofar as these constitutions were shams, they are obviously not considered here.

32. Justice Robert Jackson, *West Virginia State Board of Education v. Barnette*, 319 U.S. 624 (1943) at 638.

33. In the South African text, the provision discussing the enforcement of rights can be found in Chapter II, Article 38. The equivalent provision of the Canadian Charter of Rights and Freedoms is Article 24.

34. Hata, "Comment on Osuka, Nakamura," 35–37.

35. See *South Africa v. Grootboom*, 2000 (11) B.C.L.R. 1169 (CC). For an interesting discussion of the Grootboom case, see Sunstein, *Designing Democracy*, chap. 10.

36. See Whittington, *Constitutional Interpretation*, 66.

37. See Murphy, "Constitutions, Constitutionalism, and Democracy," 7.

38. Stephen Elkin refers to this multigenerational rationality in terms of a chain novel. Like future generations of constitutional citizens, "those who follow [the original entry into a chain novel] write the next chapters of the novel, building on what has come before. The authors of new chapters, in turn, are free to move the novel's characters in different directions, add new ones, and so forth. But to participate in the writing of this new novel [or in the interpretation of constitutional texts] requires that authors first pay attention to what has come before them in the text" (*Reconstructing the Commercial Republic*, 8).

Chapter Four • Constitutional Design

1. Murphy, "Constitutions, Constitutionalism, and Democracy," 8.

2. Murphy, "Civil Law, Common Law, and Constitutional Democracy," 118.

3. See Penn, "Preface to the Frame of Government," in Kurland and Lerner, eds., *Founders' Constitution*, 1:613–14.

4. See Baron de Montesquieu, *The Spirit of the Laws*.

5. Jefferson, "Letter to Samuel Kercheval, July 12, 1816," in *Thomas Jefferson: Selected Writings*, 90.

6. Murphy, Fleming, Barber, and Macedo, *American Constitutional Interpretation*, 118.

7. The Constitutional Court was asked to review the new text and it dealt a blow to the entire process by insisting, "We are unable to and therefore do not certify that all of the provisions of the Constitution of the Republic of South Africa 1996 comply with the Constitutional Principles contained in schedule 4 to the Constitution of the Republic of South Africa Act 200 of 1993." Accordingly, the Constitutional Assembly was mandated to return to the table to revise the text in accordance with the central principles stipulated in the interim constitution.

8. Ebrahim, *Soul of a Nation*, 170–71.

9. Ibid., 251.

10. See Waldmeir, *Anatomy of a Miracle*.

11. *You and the Constitution*, pamphlet produced and distributed by the South African Constitutional Assembly, 1996, 16 (emphasis in original).

12. See Sunstein, *Designing Democracy*, Introduction.

13. See "Knowing It by Heart: Americans Consider the Constitution and Its Meaning," a survey conducted by Public Agenda for the National Constitution Center, 2002.

14. Lutz, *Origins of American Constitutionalism*, 62.

15. See *Federalist* 84.

16. Ibid.

17. See Blaustein and Sigler, eds., *Constitutions That Made History*.

18. Bosnia, Ethiopia, Czech Republic, Vietnam, and Yugoslavia.

19. Gallagher, "Estonia," in *Legal Systems of the World*, 504.

20. Ibid.

21. I am not suggesting that earlier constitutions were not concerned with individualism, rights, and equality. They certainly were. I am merely suggesting that the explicit language aimed at these values has altered the composition of many constitutional forms.

Chapter Five • Constitutional Conflict

1. Edelman, "The Status of the Israeli Constitution," 6.

2. The most famous discussion of the need for constitutions to combat the impulses of humans to seek greater power can be found in *Federalist* 51.

3. Two of the most important books on constitutional theory published in the last decade have focused directly on these themes: Levinson, ed., *Responding to Imperfection*; and Barber and George, eds., *Constitutional Politics*.

4. See Glendon, *Rights Talk*.

5. See Zeisberg, "The Constitution of Conflict."

6. The principle of constitutional empowerment will be discussed in chapter 7.

7. Even if a regime has multiple documents that constitute the fundamental law (e.g., Israel), there is still but one constitution.

8. It is hard to fathom that any constitutional framer in the modern era would accept a definition of constitutionalism that did not include the recognition that the text itself represents a unique force, one that acts as an important mechanism to control the institutions of government, for to reject that definition would be to reject constitutionalism itself.

9. Remillard, "The Constitution Act, 1982: An Unfinished Compromise," 271.

10. Ibid.

11. See Article 33 of the Canadian Charter of Rights and Freedoms.

12. Many of those rules have an aspirational quality, but they are still rules.

13. See Alexander, "Introduction," in *Constitutionalism: Philosophical Foundations*.

14. For more on why it may be inadvisable, see the earlier discussion of the increasing length of recent constitutions in chapter 3, above.

15. Many commentators have spent the better part of their careers considering this exact question. The most interesting recent addition to the debate comes from Kramer's book, *The People Themselves: Popular Constitutionalism and Judicial Review*.

16. Kramer, *People Themselves*, 172.

17. Consider also the arguments made by Publius in *Federalist* 78–84 on this topic.

18. George Thomas has written about the American experiment that "constitutional conflict is a perennial, and uneven, feature of our constitutional framework" (*Madisonian Constitution*).

19. See Zeisberg, "Constitution of Conflict."

20. Ibid., 21 (emphasis in original).

21. See Alexander, "Introduction," 4.

22. Kay, "American Constitutionalism."

23. Glancing briefly at the Israeli illustration, it also seems clear that Raz may have noticed something important about constitutions when he insisted that each has a particularistic quality. Certainly, Israel's constitution can be called particularistic; Gary Jacobsohn (*Apple of Gold*) is just one of a number of scholars who sees the unique components of the Israeli constitutional polity.

24. Jacobsohn, *Apple of Gold*, 102.

25. See Breslin, *Communitarian Constitution*, 182–95.

26. Quoted in Jacobsohn, *Apple of Gold*, 101.

27. See McIlwain, *Constitutionalism: Ancient and Modern*; Alexander, ed., *Constitutionalism: Philosophical Foundations*; Henkin, "The United States Constitution as Social Compact"; Barber and George, eds., *Constitutional Politics*; Scott Gordon, *Controlling the State*; Holmes, "Precommitment and the Paradox of Democracy"; Greenberg et al., eds., *Constitutionalism and Democracy*.

28. Tribe, *American Constitutional Law*, 9.

29. See Levinson. *Constitutional Faith*, esp. chap. 3.

30. For a wonderful discussion about the continual ratification of the constitutional text, see Harris, *The Interpretable Constitution*.

31. Holmes, "Precommitment," 195.

32. Ibid., 197.

33. See Raz, "On the Authority and Interpretation of Constitutions."

34. See de Tocqueville, *Democracy in America*, vol. 1.

35. *Oxford English Dictionary* definition.

36. See Wood, *Creation of the American Republic*, esp. chap. 15.

37. Ibid., 614.

38. See Ackerman, *We the People: Transformations*.

39. The example of the Twenty-first Amendment overturning the Eighteenth Amendment of the United States Constitution is a good illustration.

40. A fascinating debate about the comparative benefits to a simple amending process emerged when Eastern European Constitutions were being drafted. See Holmes and Sunstein, "The Politics of Constitutional Revision in Eastern Europe."

41. Surely, Publius would be delighted with this idea, for it represents the essence of "deliberation and choice." See *Federalist* 1.

42. See Parkin, "CRIC Poll Shows Charter Part of Canadian Reality," at www.cric.ca/en_html/guide/charter/charter.html#cric.

43. *Patriation* is a uniquely Canadian term for making the constitution more reflective of the interests and personalities of all citizens.

44. See Russell, "Can the Canadians Be a Sovereign People?"

45. See Parkin, "CRIC Poll."

46. Ibid.

47. See Hogg, "Formal Amendment of the Constitution of Canada."

48. Russell, "Can the Canadians Be a Sovereign People?" 190.

49. Ibid., 255.

50. See *Federalist* 51.

51. *Federalist* 1.

Chapter Six • Constitutional Recognition

1. See Tully, *Strange Multiplicity.*

2. See Peled, "Ethnic Democracy and the Legal Construction of Citizenship."

3. See Cover, "Nomos and Narrative."

4. There are certain populations (African Americans, women, etc.) who were not part of the drafting and ratification process in the United States and for whom the original, unamended Constitution does not speak. The primary thesis of this chapter is that those (and many other) groups are not fully vested in the polity until they achieve a degree of constitutional recognition.

5. See Tully, *Strange Multiplicity.*

6. See Ackerman, *We the People,* vols. 1 and 2.

7. Thomas, *The Madisonian Constitution,* 13.

8. See Ackerman, "Higher Lawmaking."

9. Holmes and Sunstein, "The Politics of Constitutional Revision in Eastern Europe," 280.

10. Publius was concerned that, having "neither force nor will," the institution of the judiciary would be largely impotent in comparison to the legislative or executive branches. It was, after all, the nature of a judiciary to be "the least dangerous to the political rights of the Constitution." In response, the framers were forced to utilize more creative methods to strengthen the judiciary. See *Federalist* 78.

11. See McKenna, ed., *The Canadian and American Constitutions in Comparative Perspective*; Romney, *Getting It Wrong.*

12. Peter Russell has suggested that Canada has undergone no less than "five rounds of 'macro-constitutional politics.'" Each round, Russell argues, consists of a separate moment in Canadian history where the constitution has been either challenged in a fundamental way or changed dramatically. See Russell, "Can the Canadians be a Sovereign People?"

13. See Peacock, *Rethinking the Constitution.* See also McKenna, "Introduction: A Legacy of Questions"; Smith, "Canadian Confederation and the Influence of American Federalism"; and Waite, *Life and Times of Confederation.*

14. See Watts, "The American Constitution in Comparative Perspective." See also Wroth, "Notes for a Comparative Study."

15. See Wheare, *Federal Government*; Waite, ed., *Confederation Debates in the Province of Canada.*

16. Alan Cairns has described the original Canadian constitution "as a body of understandings which in turn define the basic institutions of government, the relationship between them, plus the relationships between governments in the federal system and between the citizens and those governments" ("The Living Canadian Constitution," 31).

17. See Skelton, *Life and Times of Sir Alexander Tilloch Galt.*

18. The Constitution Act, 1867, provides for two separate tools to maintain cultural diversity: (1) Section 133 guarantees the right of persons to use either English or French in the institutions of national government (including the federal courts) as well as the courts

of Quebec; and (2) Section 93 protects "established religions" with regard to funding for denominational schools.

19. See Tully, *Strange Multiplicity.*

20. See Russell, "Can the Canadians be a Sovereign People?"

21. See Weinrib, "Canada's Constitutional Revolution."

22. See Article VII, section 1 of the Canadian Charter of Rights and Freedoms.

23. See Article VI, section 2 (a) and (b) of the Canadian Charter of Rights and Freedoms.

24. See Article XV, section 1 of the Canadian Charter of Rights and Freedoms.

25. Cairns. "Citizens (Outsiders) and Governments (Insiders) in Constitution Making."

26. See Article XV, section 1 of the Canadian Charter of Rights and Freedoms (emphasis added).

27. See Article XVI, section 1 of the Canadian Charter of Rights and Freedoms.

28. See Article XXIII, section 1 (a) and (b) of the Canadian Charter of Rights and Freedoms.

29. The legislature in Quebec had earlier passed a number of laws relating to language, including statutes that regulated who could send their children to English schools and ones that mandated that all signs must be written in French. It was a significant achievement, however, and one that contributed greatly to the community's cultural survival, that in 1982 the rest of Canada acknowledged these priorities and safeguarded them in the national constitution.

30. See F. L. Morton, P. H. Russell, and T. Riddell, "The Canadian Charter of Rights and Freedoms; F. L. Morton, P. H. Russell, and M. J. Withey, "The Supreme Court's First One Hundred Charter of Rights Decisions."

31. Section 33 of the Charter of Rights and Freedoms reads: "Parliament or the legislature of a province may expressly declare in an Act of Parliament or of the legislature, as the case may be, that the Act or a provision thereof shall operate notwithstanding a provision included in section 2 or sections 7 to 15 of this Charter."

32. See Tushnet, "Policy Distortion and Democratic Debilitation."

33. See *Ford v. Quebec* (Attorney General) [1998] 2 S.C.R. 712 (Can.). The case involved a challenge to Bill 101, a law passed by Quebec's parliament mandating that all public signs and advertising be written in French. Ford, a shop owner, challenged the law (and thus the use of the notwithstanding clause) on the grounds that it violated the principle of free expression. The Canadian Supreme Court agreed.

34. Tushnet, *The NAACP's Legal Strategy Against Segregated Education, 1925–1950.*

35. In October 1995 a referendum on independence was defeated—50.6 percent against, 49.4 percent in favor.

36. Peter Russell argues that the failure of the Charter within Quebec precipitated the call for another constitutional moment where Canadian leaders—this time meeting at Meech Lake—attempted to hammer out an agreement that would forestall the possibility of secession. The Meech Lake accords attempted to accommodate further the French Quebecois by giving them a greater sense of self-determination through representation in

certain governmental offices, as well as the claim that Quebec will be "recognized as a distinct society within Canada." These accords, however, were not ratified by English Canada. See Russell, "Can the Canadians Be a Sovereign People?"

Chapter Seven • Constitutional Empowerment

1. *Federalist* 70.
2. See Klug, *Constituting Democracy.*
3. Holmes, "Precommitment and the Paradox of Democracy," 227.
4. Ibid.
5. See Fiske, *American Revolution,* esp. vol. 1, chap. 2.
6. Ibid., 81.
7. See Adams, *Revolutionary Writings of John Adams,* 118.
8. Ibid., 120.
9. James Otis, "Speech of February 24, 1761," quoted in Patrick, *Bill of Rights: A History in Documents,* 42.
10. *Revolutionary Writings of John Adams,* 118.
11. Ibid., 122.
12. Ibid., 132.
13. See Holmes. "Precommitment."
14. For a more detailed discussion, see Breslin, *Communitarian Constitution,* 175–81.
15. Whittington, *Constitutional Construction,* 8.
16. Ibid., 10.
17. Ibid., 18.
18. Kurland and Lerner, eds., *Founders' Constitution,* 1:301.
19. Stephen Elkin puts the point this way: "Liberty is a product of government" (*Reconstructing the Commercial Republic,* 246).
20. McMaster and Stone, *Pennsylvania and the Federal Constitution,* 143–44.
21. *McCulloch v. The State of Maryland,* 17 U.S. 316, at 413 (1819).
22. Storing, *Toward a More Perfect Union,* 119.
23. Hamilton, *Federalist* 63, quoted in Storing, *Toward a More Perfect Union,* 121.
24. It does not seem to matter if the rights derive from negative expressions of liberty (as in the U.S. Constitution) or positive expressions of liberty (as in many European and Third World constitutions).
25. Quoted in Storing, *Toward a More Perfect Union,* 124.
26. Ibid., 116.
27. Rousseau, *Social Contract,* 1:186.

Chapter Eight • Constitutional Limits

1. *Congressional Globe,* 11 April 1871, 574. Quoted in Finn, *Constitutions in Crisis,* 5.
2. Sunstein, "Constitutionalism, Prosperity, Democracy," 385.
3. Wood, *Creation of the American Republic,* 280–81.
4. Gordon, *Controlling the State,* 4.

5. "Constitutionalism," *Dictionary of the History of Ideas*, at http://etext.lib.virginia.edu.

6. The term originated in England in 1832, according to the *Oxford English Dictionary*.

7. Aristotle, *Politics*, quoted in Letwin, *On the History of the Idea of Law*, 30.

8. Ibid.

9. Dahmus, *History of the Middle Ages*, 121.

10. "Constitutionalism," *Dictionary of the History of Ideas*, 7.

11. Quoted from an interview with Maier in the PBS Series *Liberty! The American Revolution*, Episode Six.

12. Many of these contracts were inspired by the social contract theorists of the time, especially thinkers such as John Locke.

13. See Philbrick, *Mayflower: A Story of Courage, Community, and War*.

14. Quoted in Philbrick, *Mayflower*, 352.

15. See Lutz, *Origins of American Constitutionalism*, esp. chap. 8.

16. President Mandela's Address to the Constitutional Assembly, May 8, 1996.

17. Aristotle insisted that leaders should rule by law so as not to be influenced by personal passion.

18. See Griffin, *American Constitutionalism*.

19. Madison, "Vices of the Political System of the United States," in *James Madison: Writings*, 76–77.

20. *Federalist* 51.

21. *Federalist* 9.

22. *Federalist* 48.

23. This was the essence of the debate over the need for a Bill of Rights. Madison, Hamilton, and others thought it was unnecessary to include a list of freedoms within the constitutional text because a constitution is itself a bill of rights. See *Federalist* 84.

24. The Magna Carta (1215) and the British Declaration of Rights (1689) were the only contracts that effectively limited monarchical power.

25. See Schochet, "Introduction: Constitutionalism, Liberalism, and the Study of Politics."

26. Bolingbroke, "A Dissertation Upon Parties (1733–34)," quoted in McIlwain, *Constitutionalism*, 3.

27. Schochet adds to Bolingbroke's definition of constitutionalism by claiming, "Constitutional limitations included the accumulated traditions, folkways, and practices of a people as well as the overarching dictates of nature and/or divinity." See Schochet, "Introduction: Constitutionalism," 2.

28. See Lutz, *Origins of American Constitutionalism*.

29. See Breslin, *Communitarian Constitution*, chap. 4.

30. That is *not* to say that they should be immune from interpretation.

31. The characteristics of modern constitutionalism are developed more fully in Breslin, *Communitarian Constitution*, 120–33.

32. See Wood, *Creation of the American Republic*, chap. 7.

33. Paine, *Rights of Man*, 302–303 (emphasis in original).

34. Madison, "The Virginia Report."

35. The British Constitution is in every sense modern and constitutionalist. What helps to make it so are the agreements like Magna Carta and the British Declaration of Rights that set out fixed and stable rules.

36. Schochet, "Constitutionalism," 11.

37. Publius goes on to say, "This has always been deemed one of the strongest bonds by which human policy can connect the rulers and the people together. It creates between them the communion of interests and sympathy of sentiments, of which few governments have furnished examples; but without which every government degenerates into tyranny." See *Federalist* 57.

38. Elster, "Introduction," in *Constitutionalism and Democracy*, 2.

39. Pestritto and West, *American Founding and the Social Compact*, ix.

40. In fact, Locke believed that liberty would be maximized in a political society because individuals would be free to pursue passions and interests, knowing that their safety was more or less secure.

41. Lutz also reminds us that Locke himself refers to the "social compact." Only in the last century has the concept of social contract replaced the social compact. See Lutz, *Origins of American Constitutionalism.*

42. Ibid., 16–17.

43. Wood, *Creation of the American Republic*, chap. 7.

44. Ibid., 282–91.

45 Lutz, *Origins of American Constitutionalism*, 17.

46. I am using the term "amended" loosely here. A change in values could come from a variety of sources, including judicial interpretation, legislative action, or even cultural revolution.

47. Found in McIlwain, *Constitutionalism*, 2.

48. Lutz, *Origins of American Constitutionalism*, 111.

49. See Thomas, *Madisonian Constitution.*

50. Gladstone, quoted in Adair, "The Tenth Federalist Revisited," 55.

51. Amar, *America's Constitution*, 8.

52. See Breslin, *Communitarian Constitution*, chap. 4.

53. Wood, *American Republic*, 260.

54. Ibid.

55. *A v. Secretary of State for the Home Department* [2004] UKHL 56, [2005] 2 AC 68.

56. I am especially grateful for Douglas Edlin's insight into the Act of Settlement and British jurisprudence. For an excellent discussion of these and other weighty topics, see Edlin, ed., *Common Law Theory.*

Conclusion • Constitutional Futures

1. Address by President Nelson Mandela to the Constitutional Assembly on the Occasion of the Adoption of the New Constitution, May 8, 1996. Cape Town, South Africa.

2. See Klug, *Constituting Democracy.*

3. See Elster, "Constitutionalism in Eastern Europe," 447–82.

4. Sunstein, "Constitution-Making in Eastern Europe: An Interim Report." See also Horowitz, *A Democratic South Africa?*

5. See Murphy, "Constitutions, Constitutionalism, and Democracy."

6. See Rabkin, *Law Without Nations?*

7. *Hamdi v. Rumsfeld*, 124 S. Ct. 2633, at 2648 (2004) .

8. See Jay, *Federalist* 2–3.

9. Breslin, *Communitarian Constitution*, 132.

Ackerman, Bruce. "Higher Lawmaking." In *Responding to Imperfection: The Theory and Practice of Constitutional Amendment,* ed. Sanford Levinson, 63–87. Princeton: Princeton University Press, 1995.

———. *We the People,* Vol. 1: *Foundations.* Cambridge: Harvard University Press, 1991.

———. *We The People,* Vol. 2: *Transformations.* Cambridge: Belknap Press, 1998.

Adair, Douglass. "The Tenth Federalist Revisited." *William and Mary Quarterly* 8, no. 1 (1951): 55.

Adams, John. *The Revolutionary Writings of John Adams.* Indianapolis: Liberty Fund, 2000.

Alexander, Larry. "Introduction." In *Constitutionalism: Philosophical Foundations.* Cambridge: Cambridge University Press, 1998.

Amar, Akhil Reed. *America's Constitution: A Biography.* New York: Random House, 2005.

———. *The Bill of Rights: Creation and Reconstruction.* New Haven: Yale University Press, 1998.

———. "Rethinking Originalism: Original Intent for Liberals (and for Conservatives and Moderates, Too)." *Slate,* 21 September 2005.

A Native of Virginia. "Observations Upon the Proposed Plan of Federal Government." In *The Founders' Constitution,* vol. 2, ed. Philip B. Kurland and Ralph Lerner. Indianapolis: Liberty Fund, 1987.

Barber, Sotirios A., and Robert P. George, eds. *Constitutional Politics: Essays on Constitution Making, Maintenance, and Change.* Princeton: Princeton University Press, 2001.

———. "Notes on Constitutional Maintenance." In *Constitutional Politics: Essays on Constitution Making, Maintenance, and Change,* ed. Sotirios A. Barber and Robert P. George. Princeton: Princeton University Press, 2001.

———. *On What the Constitution Means.* Baltimore: Johns Hopkins University Press, 1984.

Baun, Michael J., and Daniel P. Franklin, eds. *Political Culture and Constitutionalism: A Comparative Approach.* In *Comparative Constitutional Law,* ed. Vicki C. Jackson and Mark Tushnet. New York: Foundation Press, 1999.

Benjamin, Walter. "Critique of Violence." In *Reflections: Essays, Aphorisms, Autobiographical Writings,* ed. Peter Demetz. New York: Schocken Books, 1978.

Blaustein, Albert P., and Jay A. Sigler, eds. *Constitutions That Made History*. New York: Paragon House, 1988.

Bolingbroke. "A Dissertation Upon Parties." In *Constitutionalism: Ancient and Modern*, ed. Charles H. McIlwain. Ithaca, NY: Cornell University Press, 1947.

Boron, Atilio A. "Latin America: Constitutionalism and the Political Traditions of Liberalism and Socialism." In *Constitutionalism and Democracy: Transitions in the Comparative World*, ed. Douglas Greenberg, Stanley N. Katz, Melanie Beth Oliviero, and Steven C .Wheatly. Oxford: Oxford University Press, 1993.

Breslin, Beau. *The Communitarian Constitution*. Baltimore: Johns Hopkins University Press, 2004.

Brown, Nathan J. *Constitutions in a Nonconstitutional World: Arab Basic Laws and the Prospects for Accountable Government*. Albany: SUNY Press, 2001.

Cairns, Alan C. "Citizens (Outsiders) and Governments (Insiders) in Constitution Making: The Case of Meech Lake." *Canadian Public Policy* 14, S.1 (1988): 121–45.

———. "The Living Canadian Constitution." In *Constitution, Government, and Society in Canada*, ed. Douglas E. Williams. Toronto: McClelland and Stewart, 1989.

Cover, Robert M. "The Supreme Court, 1982 Term-Forward: Nomos and Narrative." In *Narrative Violence and the Law: The Essays of Robert Cover*, ed. Martha Minow, Michael Ryan, and Austin Sarat. Ann Arbor: University of Michigan Press, 1995.

———. "Violence and the Word." *Yale Law Journal* 95, no. 8 (1986): 1601–29.

Dahmus, Joseph. *A History of the Middle Ages*. New York: Barnes and Noble Books, 1995.

Devins, Neal, and Louis Fisher. *The Democratic Constitution*. Oxford: Oxford University Press, 2004.

Duchacek, Ivo D. "National Constitutions: A Functional Approach." *Comparative Politics* 1, no. 1 (October 1968): 91–102.

Ebrahim, Hassan. *The Soul of a Nation: Constitution-Making in South Africa*. Cape Town: Oxford University Press, 1998.

Edelman, Martin. "The Status of the Israeli Constitution at the Present Time." *Shofar: An Interdisciplinary Journal of Jewish Studies* 21, no. 4 (2003): 1–18.

Edlin, Douglas, ed. *Common Law Theory*. Cambridge: Cambridge University Press, 2007.

Eisgruber, Christopher. "Judicial Supremacy and Constitutional Distortion." In *Constitutional Politics: Essays on Constitution Making, Maintenance, and Change*, ed. Sotirios A. Barber and Robert P. George. Princeton: Princeton University Press, 2001.

Elkin, Stephen L. *Reconstructing the Commercial Republic: Constitutional Design after Madison*. Chicago: University of Chicago Press, 2006.

Elster, Jon. "Constitutionalism in Eastern Europe: An Introduction." *University of Chicago Law Review* 58, no. 2 (Spring 1991): 447–82.

———. "Forces and Mechanisms in the Constitution-Making Process." *Duke Law Journal* 45, no. 2 (November 1995): 364–96.

———. "Introduction." In *Constitutionalism and Democracy*, ed. Jon Elster and Rune Slagstad. Cambridge: Cambridge University Press, 1988.

The Federalist. New York: Modern Library.

Fellman, David. "Constitutionalism." *Dictionary of the History of Ideas*. Available online at http://etext.lib.virginia.edu/cgi-local/DHI/dhi.cgi?id=dv1–61.

Finn, John E. *Constitutions in Crisis: Political Violence and the Rule of Law.* Oxford: Oxford University Press, 1991.

———. "The Civic Constitution: Some Preliminaries." In *Constitutional Politics: Essays on Constitution Making, Maintenance, and Change,* ed. Sotirios A. Barber and Robert P. George. Princeton: Princeton University Press, 2001.

Fiske, John. *The American Revolution.* Boston: Houghton Mifflin, 1891.

Friedrich, C. J. "The Political Theory of the New Democratic Constitutions." *Review of Politics* 12, no. 2 (April 1950): 215–24.

Gallagher, Michael. "Estonia." In *Legal Systems of the World: A Political, Social, and Cultural Encyclopedia,* ed. Herbert M. Kritzer. Santa Barbara: ABC-CLIO, 2002.

Glendon, Mary Ann. *Rights Talk: The Impoverishment of Political Discourse.* New York: Free Press, 1991.

Gordon, Robert W. "Undoing Historical Injustice." In *Justice and Injustice in Law and Legal Theory,* ed. Austin Sarat and Thomas R. Kearns. Ann Arbor: University of Michigan Press, 1998.

Gordon, Scott. *Controlling the State: Constitutionalism from Ancient Athens to Today.* Cambridge: Harvard University Press, 1999.

Greenberg, Douglas, Stanley N. Katz, Melanie Beth Oliviero, and Steven C. Wheatley, eds. *Constitutionalism and Democracy: Transitions in the Contemporary World.* New York: Oxford University Press, 1993.

Grey, Thomas. "The Constitution as Scripture." *Stanford Law Review* 37, no. 1 (November 1984): 1–25.

Griffin, Stephen. *American Constitutionalism: From Theory to Politics.* Princeton: Princeton University Press, 1996.

Harris, William F., II. *The Interpretable Constitution.* Baltimore: Johns Hopkins University Press, 1993.

Hata, Hiroyuki. "Comment on Osuka, Nakamura." *Law and Contemporary Problems* 53, no. 2 (Spring 1990): 35–37.

Haynie, Stacia L. "Constituting Democracy: Law, Globalism, and South Africa's Political Reconstruction." *Law and Politics Book Review* 11, no. 1 (January 2001): 35–37.

Hegel, Georg Wilhelm Friedrich. *Philosophy of Right.* Translated and annotated by T. M. Knox. Oxford: Oxford University Press, 1967.

Henkin, Louis. "The United States Constitution as Social Compact." *Proceedings of the American Philosophical Society* 131, no. 3 (September 1987): 261–69.

Hogg, Peter W. "Formal Amendment of the Constitution of Canada." *Law and Contemporary Problems* 55, no. 1 (Winter 1992), 253–60.

Holmes, Stephen. "Precommitment and the Paradox of Democracy." In *Constitutions and Democracy,* ed. Jon Elster and Rune Slagstad. Cambridge: Cambridge University Press, 1988.

Holmes, Stephen, and Cass R. Sunstein. "The Politics of Constitutional Revision in Eastern Europe." In *Responding to Imperfection: The Theory and Practice of Constitutional Amendment,* ed. Sanford Levinson, 275–306. Princeton: Princeton University Press, 1995.

Horowitz, Donald L. *A Democratic South Africa? Constitutional Engineering in a Divided Society.* Berkeley: University of California Press, 1991.

Jackson, Vicki C., and Mark Tushnet. *Comparative Constitutional Law*. New York: Foundation Press, 1999.

Jacobsohn, Gary J. *Apple of Gold: Constitutionalism in Israel and the United States*. Princeton: Princeton University Press, 1993.

———. "The Permeability of Constitutional Borders." *Texas Law Review* 82 (2004): 1763–1818.

———. *The Supreme Court and the Decline of Constitutional Aspiration*. Lanham, Md.: Rowman and Littlefield, 1986.

———. *The Wheel of Law: India's Secularism in Comparative Constitutional Context*. Princeton: Princeton University Press, 2005.

Jefferson, Thomas. "Letter to Samuel Kercheval, July 12, 1816." In *Thomas Jefferson: Selected Writings*, ed. Harvey Mansfield. Wheeling, IL: Harlan Davidson, 1979.

Kaminsky, John P., and Richard Leffler, eds. *Creating the Constitution*. Acton, Mass.: Copley Publishing Group, 1999.

Kay, Richard S. "American Constitutionalism." In *Constitutionalism: Philosophical Foundations*. Cambridge: Cambridge University Press, 1998.

Kersch, Ken I. "Review of Neal Devins' and Louis Fischer's *The Democratic Constitution*." *Law and Politics Book Review* 14, no. 12 (December 2004): 969–75.

Klug, Heinz. *Constituting Democracy: Law, Globalism, and South Africa's Political Reconstruction*. New York: Cambridge University Press, 2000.

Kramer, Larry D. *The People Themselves: Popular Constitutionalism and Judicial Review*. Oxford: Oxford University Press, 2004.

Kurland, Philip B., and Ralph Lerner, eds. *The Founders' Constitution*. 5 vols. Indianapolis: Liberty Fund, 1987.

Letwin, Shirley Robin. *On the History of the Idea of Law*. Cambridge: Cambridge University Press, 2005.

Levinson, Sanford. *Constitutional Faith*. Princeton: Princeton University Press, 1988.

———. "How Many Times has the United States Constitution Been Amended? (A) <26; (B) 26; (C) 27; (D) >27: Accounting for Constitutional Change." In *Responding to Imperfection: The Theory and Practice of Constitutional Amendment*, ed. Sanford Levinson. Princeton: Princeton University Press, 1995.

———. *Our Undemocratic Constitution: Where the Constitution Goes Wrong (And How We the People Can Correct It)*. New York: Oxford University Press, 2006.

———. *Responding to Imperfection: The Theory and Practice of Constitutional Amendment*. Princeton: Princeton University Press, 1995.

Lutz, Donald S. *The Origins of American Constitutionalism*. Baton Rouge: Louisiana State University Press, 1988.

———. *Principles of Constitutional Design*. New York: Cambridge University Press, 2006.

Madison, James. "The Virginia Report." In *The Madisonian Constitution*, by George Thomas. Baltimore: Johns Hopkins University Press, 2008.

———. "Vices of the Political System of the United States." In *James Madison: Writings*, ed. Jack N. Rakove. New York: Library of America, 1999.

Maier, Pauline. Interview. *Liberty! The American Revolution*. Episode 6. Produced by Catherine Allen. PBS. KTCA, St. Paul.

Mandela, Nelson. "Address by President Nelson Mandela to the Constitutional Assembly on the Occasion of the Adoption of a New Constitution." Cape Town: May 8, 1996.

McIlwain, Charles H. *Constitutionalism: Ancient and Modern.* Ithaca, NY: Cornell University Press, 1947.

McKenna, Marian C., ed. "Introduction: A Legacy of Questions." In *The Canadian and American Constitutions in Comparative Perspective,* ed. Marian C. McKenna. Calgary: University of Calgary Press, 1993.

———. *The Canadian and American Constitutions in Comparative Perspective.* Calgary: University of Calgary Press, 1993.

McMaster, John B., and Frederick Stone. *Pennsylvania and the Federal Constitution.* Lancaster, PA: Historical Society, 1888.

Baron de Montesquieu. *The Spirit of the Laws.* Translated by Thomas Nugent. New York: Collier Macmillan, 1949.

Moore, Wayne D. *Constitutional Rights and Powers of the People.* Princeton: Princeton University Press, 1996.

Morton, F. L., P. H. Russell, and T. Riddell. "The Canadian Charter of Rights and Freedoms: A Descriptive Analysis of the First Decade, 1982–1992." *NJCL* 5, no. 1 (1994).

Morton, F. L., P. H. Russell, and M. J. Withey. "The Supreme Court's First One Hundred Charter of Rights Decisions: A Statistical Analysis." *Osgoode Hall L.J.* 30, no. 1 (1992).

Murphy, Walter F. "Civil Law, Common Law, and Constitutional Democracy." *Louisiana Law Review* 52, no. 1 (1991): 91–136.

———. *Constitutional Democracy: Creating and Maintaining a Just Political Order.* Baltimore: Johns Hopkins University Press, 2006.

———. "Constitutions, Constitutionalism, and Democracy." In *Constitutionalism and Democracy: Transitions in the Contemporary World,* ed. Douglas Greenberg, Stanley N. Katz, Melanie Beth Oliviero, and Steven C. Wheatley. Oxford: Oxford University Press, 1993.

Murphy, Walter, James Fleming, Sotirios Barber, and Stephen Macedo. *American Constitutional Interpretation,* 3rd ed. New York: Foundation Press, 2003.

National Constitution Center. "Knowing It by Heart: Americans Consider the Constitution and its Meaning." Survey conducted by Public Agenda, 2002.

Okoth-Ogendo, H. W. O. "Constitutions Without Constitutionalism: Reflections on an African Political Paradox." In *Constitutionalism and Democracy: Transitions in the Comparative World,* ed. Douglas Greenberg, Stanley N. Katz, Melanie Beth Oliviero, and Steven C. Wheatly. Oxford: Oxford University Press, 1993.

Paine, Thomas. *The Rights of Man: The Complete Works of Thomas Paine.* London: 1793.

Parkin, Andrew. "CRIC Poll Shows Charter Part of Canadian Reality." Centre for Research and Information on Canada. Available online at www.cric.ca/en_html/guide/charter/charter.html#cric, accessed 13 June 2006.

Patrick, John J. *The Bill of Rights: A History in Documents.* New York: Oxford University Press, 2003.

Peacock, Anthony A. *Rethinking the Constitution: Perspectives on Canadian Constitutional Reform, Interpretation, and Theory.* Oxford: Oxford University Press, 1996.

Peled, Joav. "Ethnic Democracy and the Legal Construction of Citizenship: Arab Citizens of the Jewish State." *American Political Science Review* 86, no. 2 (1992): 432–42.

Penn, William. "Preface to the Frame of Government." In *The Founders' Constitution*, vol. 1, ed. Philip B. Kurland and Ralph Lerner. Indianapolis: Liberty Fund, 1987.

Perry, Michael J. "What Is 'The Constitution'? (and Other Fundamental Questions)." In *Constitutionalism: Philosophical Foundations*, ed. Larry Alexander. Cambridge: Cambridge University Press, 1998.

Pestritto, Ronald, and Thomas West. *The American Founding and the Social Compact.* Lanham, MD: Lexington Books, 2003.

Philbrick, Nathaniel. *Mayflower: A Story of Courage, Community, and War.* New York: Viking Press, 2006.

Rabkin, Jeremy. *Law Without Nations? Why Constitutional Government Requires Sovereign States.* Princeton: Princeton University Press, 2005.

Raz, Joseph. "On the Authority and Interpretation of Constitutions: Some Preliminaries." In *Constitutionalism: Philosophical Foundations*, ed. Larry Alexander. Cambridge: Cambridge University Press, 1998.

Remillard, Gil. "The Constitution Act, 1982: An Unfinished Compromise." *American Journal of Comparative Law* 32, no. 2 (Spring 1984): 269–81.

Romney, Paul. *Getting It Wrong: How Canadians Forgot Their Past and Imperiled Confederation.* Toronto: University of Toronto Press, 1999.

Rousseau, Jean Jacques. *The Social Contract.* Translated by Ernest Barker. Oxford: Oxford University Press, 1947.

Russell, Peter H. "Can the Canadians Be a Sovereign People?" In *The Canadian and American Constitutions in Comparative Perspective*, ed. Marian C. McKenna. Calgary: University of Calgary Press, 1993.

———. *Constitutional Odyssey: Can the Canadians Become a Sovereign People?* 2nd ed. Toronto: University of Toronto Press, 1993.

Sartori, Giovanni. "Constitutionalism: A Preliminary Discussion." *The American Political Science Review* 56, no. 4 (1962): 853–64.

Schneier, Edward. *Crafting Constitutional Democracies: The Politics of Institutional Design.* Lanham, MD: Rowman and Littlefield, 2006.

Schochet, Gordon J. "Introduction: Constitutionalism, Liberalism, and the Study of Politics." In *Nomos XX: Constitutionalism*, ed. John W. Chapman and J. Roland Pennock. New York: NYU Press, 1979.

Skelton, O. D. *The Life and Times of Sir Alexander Tilloch Galt.* Toronto: McClelland and Stewart, 1966.

Smith, Jennifer. "Canadian Constitution and the Influence of American Federalism." In *The Canadian and American Constitutions in Comparative Perspective*, ed. Marian C. McKenna. Calgary: University of Calgary Press, 1993.

Storing, Herbert J. *Toward a More Perfect Union: Writings of Herbert J. Storing*, ed. Joseph M. Bessette. Washington, DC: American Enterprise Institute Press, 1995.

Story, Joseph. "Commentaries on the Constitution." In *The Founders' Constitution*, vol. 2, ed. Philip B. Kurland and Ralph Lerner. Indianapolis: Liberty Fund, 1987.

South African Constitutional Assembly. "You and the Constitution." Pamphlet, 1996.

Sunstein, Cass. "Constitutionalism and Secession." *University of Chicago Law Review* 58, no. 2 (Spring 1991): 633–70.

———. "Constitutionalism, Prosperity, Democracy: Transition in Eastern Europe." *Constitutional Political Economy* 2, no. 3 (1991): 371–94.

———. "Constitution-Making in Eastern Europe: An Interim Report." Unpublished, October 1991.

———. *Designing Democracy: What Constitutions Do.* Oxford: Oxford University Press, 2001.

Thomas, George. "Recovering the Political Constitution: The Madisonian Vision." *Review of Politics* 66, no. 2 (Spring 2004): 233–56.

———. *The Madisonian Constitution.* Baltimore: Johns Hopkins University Press, 2008.

de Toqueville, Alexis. *Democracy in America*, vol. 1. New York: Vintage Books, 1954.

Tribe, Laurence H. *American Constitutional Law.* Mineola, NY: Foundation Press, 1978.

Tully, James. *Strange Multiplicity: Constitutionalism in an Age of Diversity.* Cambridge: Cambridge University Press, 1995.

Tushnet, Mark. *The New Constitutional Order.* Princeton: Princeton University Press, 2003.

———. "Policy Distortion and Democratic Debilitation: Comparative Illumination of the Countermajoritarian Difficulty," *Michigan Law Review* 94 (1995): 245–301.

———. *The NAACP's Legal Strategy Against Segregated Education, 1925–1950.* Chapel Hill: University of North Carolina Press, 2005.

Waite, P. B., ed. *The Confederation Debates in the Province of Canada, 1865.* Toronto: McClelland and Stewart, 1963.

———. *The Life and Times of Confederation, 1964–1867.* Toronto: University of Toronto Press, 1962.

Waldmeir, Patti. *Anatomy of a Miracle: The End of Apartheid and the Birth of the New South Africa.* New York: W.W. Norton, 1997.

Waldron, Jeremy. "Precommitment and Disagreement." In *Constitutionalism: Philosophical Foundations*, ed. Larry Alexander. Cambridge: Cambridge University Press, 1998.

Walker, Graham. "The Constitutional Good: Constitutionalism's Equivocal Moral Imperative." *Polity* 26, no. 1 (Fall 1993): 91–111.

Watts, Ronald. "The American Constitution in Comparative Perspective: A Comparison of Federalism in the United States and Canada." *Journal of American History* 74, no. 3 (December 1987): 769–91.

Weinrib, Lorraine Eisenstadt. "Canada's Constitutional Revolution: From Legislative to Constitutional State." *Israel Law Review* 33, no. 1 (Winter 1999): 13–50.

Wheare, Kenneth C. *Federal Government.* London: Oxford University Press, 1963.

———. *Modern Constitutions.* London: Oxford University Press, 1965.

Whittington, Keith. *Constitutional Construction: Divided Powers and Constitutional Meaning.* Cambridge: Harvard University Press, 1999.

———. *Constitutional Interpretation: Textual Meaning, Original Intent, and Judicial Review.* Lawrence: University Press of Kansas, 1999.

Wood, Gordon S. *The American Revolution: A History.* New York: The Modern Library, 2003.

———. *The Creation of the American Republic, 1776–1787.* Chapel Hill: University of North Carolina Press, 1969.

Wroth, L. Kinvin. "Notes for a Comparative Study of the Origins of Federalism in the United States and Canada." *Arizona Journal of International and Comparative Law* 15 (1998): 93–123.

Zeisberg, Mariah. "The Constitution of Conflict." Ph.D. dissertation. Princeton University, 2005.